From Occupation
to Cooperation

THE AMERICAN ASSEMBLY was established by Dwight D. Eisenhower at Columbia University in 1950. Each year it holds at least two nonpartisan meetings that give rise to authoritative books that illuminate issues of United States policy.

An affiliate of Columbia, with offices at Barnard College, the Assembly is a national, educational institution incorporated in the state of New York.

The Assembly seeks to provide information, stimulate discussion, and evoke independent conclusions on matters of vital public interest.

THE ATLANTIK-BRÜCKE (Atlantic Bridge), organized and incorporated as a private, independent, nonpartisan, and nonprofit association, was founded in Hamburg in 1952. Members and sponsors come from business, politics, the sciences, the media, and trade unions.

The Atlantik-Brücke seeks to strengthen both the understanding of Germany in the United States and Canada and of the United States and Canada in Germany. In particular, it conducts meetings between Germans and Americans in the economic, political, and cultural centers of both countries. The Atlantik-Brücke Study Group on the United States brings together important figures from public life in Germany for nonpartisan and confidential dialogue, covering such topics as foreign, security, economic, and domestic policy issues. Every other year the Atlantik-Brücke awards the Eric M. Warburg Prize to a public figure in Germany or the United States who has made an outstanding contribution to the German-American partnership.

CONTRIBUTORS

CHRISTOPH BERTRAM, *Die Zeit*

ROBERT D. BLACKWILL, Harvard University

ROBERT D. HORMATS, Goldman Sachs International

KARL KAISER, University of Bonn

CHARLES McC. MATHIAS, American Council on
Germany; Jones, Day, Reavis & Pogue

STEVEN MULLER, The 21st Century Foundation

PAUL H. NITZE, Johns Hopkins University

LOTHAR RUEHL, University of Cologne

GEBHARD SCHWEIGLER, Stiftung Wissenschaft und
Politik

NORBERT WALTER, Deutsche Bank Group

THE AMERICAN ASSEMBLY
Columbia University

THE ATLANTIK-BRÜCKE
Bonn, Germany

From Occupation to Cooperation

*The United States and United Germany
in a Changing World Order*

STEVEN MULLER
and
GEBHARD SCHWEIGLER
Editors

W · W · NORTON & COMPANY
New York   London

Contents

From Occupation
to Cooperation

Preface

G ermany's rapid unification inspired The American Assembly and the Atlantik-Brücke, Bonn, to join together in sponsoring an American Assembly program on how Germany and the United States should collaborate on regional and global problems in the medium term. Few events in recent years have been more significant in determining the future direction of Europe, and, indirectly, of the world, than the abrupt and effective end to the cold war, the fall of the Berlin Wall, and the important decisions made by both Eastern and Western Germany to unite.

To design and guide the program a steering committee was organized, chaired by program chairmen Paul A. Volcker of James D. Wolfensohn, Inc., formerly chairman of the Federal Reserve in the United States, and Walther Leisler Kiep, chairman of the Atlantik-Brücke. The members of the steering committee are listed in the appendix. They helped to identify the co-editors: Steven Muller, chairman, The 21st Century Foundation, and Gebhard Schweigler, senior research associate, Stiftung Wissenschaft und Politik.

Under the editorial guidance of the two editors, a distinguished group of authors prepared the chapters in this volume to serve as background reading for an American Assembly held on November 14–17, 1991, at Arden House in Harriman, New York. The participants at that program prepared a report of findings and recommendations that has been widely circulated in both countries, and is included as an appendix to this volume.

This publication is intended to lay the groundwork for scholarship in this area of policy analysis: the role of united Germany in Europe, and in its global relations with the United States. We believe that these papers have already helped leaders from both countries to think through the important implications of these dramatic events, and expect that many more people around the world will find that this book will help them in similar ways. We would like to express our special appreciation to the co-editors and the authors for their fine work.

We are also grateful to the following organizations for support of this program:

Funder · Robert Bosch Foundation

Contributing Funders · Draeger Foundation
EXXON
German Foreign Office
The German Marshall Fund of the United States
International Business Machines Corporation
Siemens Corporation

Contributors · American Express Company
Deutsche Bank AG
Diehl GmbH & Company
Korber Foundation
Volkswagen AG
James D. Wolfensohn, Inc.

Opinions expressed in this volume are those of the individual authors and not necessarily those of the funders, the Atlantik-Brücke, or The American Assembly.

Beate Lindemann
Executive Vice Chairman
    and Program Director
Atlantik-Brücke e.V.

Daniel A. Sharp
President
The American Assembly

1

Introduction

America and Germany:
A New Chapter Opens

STEVEN MULLER

For most of us, the full impact of the historic changes in Eastern Europe and the former Soviet Union is still hard to grasp. In some respects at least, these changes are analogous to an earthquake. There were the early seismic tremors of Gorbachev, *perestroika,* and *glasnost,* beginning in the mid-1980s. These were followed by the major ruptures that liberated Eastern Europe and in the process led to German unification. One aftershock disrupted

STEVEN MULLER is chairman of The 21st Century Foundation and president emeritus of The Johns Hopkins University. He served as the tenth president of The Johns Hopkins University from 1972 to 1990. Dr. Muller is vice chairman of the Board of Trustees of the American Institute for Contemporary German Studies; serves as a director on the boards of six American commercial corporations; and is the author of a textbook in comparative government and of a number of professional articles in this field. In recognition of his contributions to German-American relations, Dr. Muller was awarded the Commander's Cross of the Order of Merit by the president of the Federal Republic of Germany in 1980. Dr. Muller was born in Hamburg, Germany, and first came to the United States in 1940. He has been a naturalized citizen of the United States since 1949.

Yugoslavia; then followed the second major shock of the Soviet August revolution. The ground is still trembling, and more likely than not we are not yet at the end. The prospect ahead is for years—probably decades—of readjustment.

Amidst such prevailing dislocation and disruption, human beings inevitably seek to reorient themselves, to cope as rapidly as possible with change, and to discover new patterns of predictability and certainty as soon as possible. These human tendencies are natural, but they are also beset with futility, at least at the outset. The disruption of an earthquake is immediate. Recovery and restoration take much longer. Historic change of earthshaking dimensions demands a revolution in mental outlook that only slowly follows after the physical changes. At this time the world is full of questions. What does all this really mean? What different future lies ahead? What must be done at once to bring about the best responses in the longer term? What do events mean specifically for us—for me? The questions are obvious. Inevitably, the answers are not.

This volume attempts an appraisal of the new relationship between the United States and Germany that is emerging from vast change. It is, without apologies, short on definitive answers. Instead, the chapters assembled here address the most urgent and necessary task: to reassess the landscape so greatly altered by historic earthquake. Obstacles once insurmountable have disappeared. New avenues have opened. The earthquake has shifted bedrock, and previously familiar terrain is radically different. At this moment in history, it is not possible clearly to plot the course ahead. Instead, the only possible contribution with respect to the future is to redraw the map, as it were, and to lay out the new landscape on which the new course will then be charted, initially step by step.

Four aspects of this new landscape are examined in this volume. Eight distinguished observers—four Americans and four Germans—each address one of four themes: a vision of leadership for the United States, and one for Germany; the constraints on such leadership in each of the two countries; the strategic partnership between the two states, seen from the viewpoint of each; and the economic interplay between the two, again viewed from each side.

The analyses are thorough and timely, and they will serve the purpose of reorientation after the earthquake.

One of the few certainties at this time is that the unification of Germany marks the end of a chapter in German-American relations. A new chapter is beginning, and to an unavoidable extent, the new chapter will take over where its predecessor closed. It may be useful to step back for a moment and apply the full advantage of hindsight to the chapter that has now ended.

That chapter tells the amazing story of how two nations that were bitterly and destructively at war with each other between 1941 and 1945 became the closest allies. It tells a story of partnership forged by urgent needs and common goals; it ends with the achievement of those common goals and a great reduction in the urgency of mutual needs; and it does not directly address the future.

Two fundamental decisions in the period immediately after the end of the Second World War replaced German-American enmity with German-American partnership. On the German side, the leadership of Konrad Adenauer produced the German decision to cast its future unequivocally with the West. On the American side, the Marshall Plan for the reconstruction of Europe fully included defeated Germany, on an equal basis with other European states that only just before had been victims of German aggression. Both these decisions were noble in concept and purpose, but both were also brought about by the aggressive posture of the Soviet Union, which established Eastern Europe as part of the Soviet empire and included in it the Soviet Zone of Occupation in Germany that became the German Democratic Republic (GDR). It was this threat from the Soviet Union and the need to deter it that played the key role in shaping German-American relations from the late 1940s to the end of the 1980s.

The close alliance between the United States and Germany during this period was above all aimed at countering potential Soviet aggression. Its fundamental aim was the containment of Soviet power without resorting to the use of force, and to maintain this purpose unfailingly for as long as necessary. Hard early evidence of the firmness of this purpose was the Berlin Airlift, which supplied the small enclave of West Berlin by air, deep in Soviet held territory, when overland routes of supply were blocked. On the other side, the firmness of Soviet purpose was given evidence both by the use of armed force to suppress the Berlin uprising in 1953, and later by the erection of the Berlin Wall. On a larger scale, hundreds of thousands of American troops were deployed primarily on German soil to ward off Soviet military penetration into Western Europe; and under the aegis of the North Atlantic Treaty Organization (NATO) the American nuclear umbrella was extended over Western Europe in general and Germany in particular. Reciprocal nuclear protection was of course extended by the Soviet Union to Eastern Europe in general, and the German Democratic Republic in particular.

It was clear throughout that the United States–Soviet stand-off in the heart of Europe could end in one of only three ways: war, the collapse of the American commitment, or the collapse of the Soviet commitment. Those in the West always assumed that mutual deterrence would suffice to prevent war, that the American commitment would endure for as long as necessary, that the Soviet commitment would one day falter, and that that day would make possible both German unification and the liberation of Eastern Europe. However, little was done to promote these last two objectives, because the risk of war in the process was too great. Understandably, the West did not intervene when Soviet troops put down rebellions in Poland and Hungary in the 1950s and ended the Czech Spring in the 1960s. Throughout most of the 1980s, the freezing grip of the cold war on Europe was taken for granted for the indefinite future. Then the earthquake occurred.

Looking back on these developments, familiar as they surely are, one marvels nevertheless at the speed and totality that marked the evolution of German-American partnership. On the one hand, the American presence in the Federal Republic of Germany became a constant, and on the whole a welcome one. On the other hand, the postwar youth of the Federal Republic flooded the United States in enormous numbers, above all to seek education and training. As the nation most immediately exposed to Soviet aggression, Germans in the Federal Republic felt deeply beholden to the United States for their security, and in due course the prosperity that security enabled them to achieve. On the American side, the Germans were regarded as the most reliable and effective partners in the front lines of deployment against the Soviet threat. Americans did not even need to learn German, because English seemed almost to become a second language—the language of alliance—in the Federal Republic of Germany.

A foundation of friendship was laid, with every recognition that the need for that friendship was vital and enduring. The story of this chapter has now ended with German unification. And, more quickly and completely than any other of Germany's allies in NATO, the United States used the full extent of its power and influence to support the rapid and complete absorption of the former German Democratic Republic into the new and unified Federal Republic of Germany. It is therefore one of those stories with a happy ending. Two nations that were enemies became friends. Their friendship was rooted in mutual needs. So what will grow from such roots in the future, now that mutual needs are changing?

On the new maps drawn after the earthquake, united Germany appears once again in the very center of Europe, and in fact Central Europe itself is more clearly restored to visibility. But let there be no mistake: the division of Europe has by no means really ended. The enforced separation of East and West by the Iron Curtain has ceased, but, where the Iron Curtain was, an invisible line still marks the division between prosperity on the Western side and poverty on the other. Neither the two parts of Europe nor the two parts of Germany that have been brought back together are equals. The former German Democratic Republic proved totally unable to stand on its own and has therefore been wholly absorbed into the Federal Republic of Germany. Alone among its former Eastern European allies it has disappeared—by being incorporated into the West. There is symbolic meaning in the fact that German unification took the form of five new states joining the existing Federal Republic of Germany: the unified and enlarged Federal Republic remains just as much the most eastward part of Western Europe as before. Unified Germany has extended Western Europe into Europe's center, but it is there as part of the European Community and not as a newly assembled independent Central European state.

After two world wars in this century that both emanated from an autonomous and virtually isolated Germany in the center of Europe, Germany's only viable future lies in continued inclusion in the European Community. The Community will most likely over time include Central and East European members, just as it already is moving to include Northern and Southern European ones, but its core remains Western Europe. Germany is a leading member of the Community by virtue of size and productivity, but it also has been and will continue to be part of the Western core of the Community. The Federal Republic will very likely lead the way in the long-term expansion of the European Community eastward, but there is little likelihood of a Germany outside the Community, nor of Eastern European states newly realigned against the Community.

The crux of the future for Germany may very well revolve around the role of the United States vis-à-vis the European Community, and Germany's part in shaping the American role. Until now, the United States has been a de facto participant in European affairs ever since World War II, not of course as an actual member of the Community but if nothing else by virtue of its dominant role with respect to Western European security. Absent the Soviet threat, a reduction in concerns about security will reduce the American partnership with the European Community quite significantly. Any major diminution of American interaction with the Community, however, will complicate Germany's role in Europe as well. While French-German collaboration represents the indispensable key ingredient of the European Community and will continue to do so for the foreseeable future, such collaboration has not always come easily. Even if mainly as a counterweight to excessive pressure from France, Germany may well have great interest in maintaining vigorous partnership with the United States.

From the American side there would seem to be reciprocal long-term interest in partnership with Germany. Absent the Soviet threat and related security concerns, Germany per se may no longer be so interesting for the United States—just as the United States in the long run may be deemed less essential to Germany purely for security reasons. But the United States may well wish to cultivate Germany, not only as a—or, indeed, the—leading force in the European Community, but as an easier working partner than France and a more influential one than Great Britain. The newly opening next chapter in American-German relations might therefore cover a prolonged era of continued close partnership, based less on the exigencies of defense and security and more on the German need to keep America constructively involved in Europe, and the reciprocal American need for German leadership in American-European collaboration.

The possibility of partnership does however depend on the avoidance of major misunderstanding, and such avoidance will require continuing real effort both in Germany and the United States. In America, for instance, the resurgence of xenophobia in Europe in the wake of the cold war comes as an unwelcome and even inexplicable development. Americans understand the desire for national self-determination and may sympathize with it, but they have less understanding for violations of minority rights. There is virtually no expectation in the United States that European states should proclaim themselves as havens for immigrants, and there is ready acceptance of the need to put limits on immigration. On the other hand, mistreatment of foreigners—especially of other races—who are already resident in a country is unacceptable, and perhaps especially so in a nation with Germany's all-too-recent and not forgotten experience with racial extermination.

American misunderstanding and ill will may also arise in reaction to almost any and all effort to establish European initiatives independent of the United States, especially in the area of national security policy. German efforts, for example, to recognize the need for such initiatives and to do everything possible to see them cast in the best possible form may nonetheless result in American resentment of German involvement at all. Washington's reaction to the Franco-German announcement of a joint military corps, for instance, often expressed itself in comment that this was only to be expected of the French but represented potential betrayal by the Germans. Perceived as the leader within the European Community, then, Germany runs the risk that the rest of Europe will regard it as too closely tied to the United States, while in American eyes German cooperation will consistently seem insufficiently forthcoming.

Misunderstanding is equally likely to arise on the German side, as well. It is a fact that approximately one out of every five Germans who are now citizens of the Federal Republic was until recently a citizen of the German Democratic Republic. Aside from all the other problems related to this fact, it is also true that citizens of the GDR were prevented from contact with the Western world, heard only bad things about it, and were in particular exposed to persistently negative anti-American propaganda. The Germans in the five new states have a great deal to learn and adjust to with respect to their own new country and society. But beyond—and presumably only after—that, they are also confronted with the European Community and an American alliance that until recently had been presented to them only as the incarnation of everything hostile and threatening, and whose real nature is strange and new. The rest of the world appears to be assuming that the new citizens of the Federal Republic soon will essentially behave just like the familiar Germans of the Bonn regime, but there is at least a question as to how true such an assumption will turn out to be. Certainly one out of five votes is not, within a political democracy, a negligible proportion.

There is a further, and larger, question about the extent to which Germans over the long-run future will find close partnership with the United States comfortable and appealing. This is hardly a new question—Europeans in general are on the one hand attracted to the energy, openness, optimism, and even innocence of the United States, but on the other hand are repelled by a perceived American lack of discipline, gross manifestations of social inequality, and the corruptible nature of the social and political process. More fundamentally, however, there has been a bedrock of respect for American power—the crucial factor in victory in both world wars and more recently during the cold war as well. Now questions are raised at this more basic level about the reality of American power and how much it merits future respect. Considerations at this level are apt particularly to influence German attitudes toward the United States, because the lengthy period of German dependence on America during the cold war inevitably generated some resentment along with the obvious gratitude. The resentful side of such a love-hate relationship would welcome—

and might even wish for—an American loss of respect, even while the love side would deny and deplore it.

Only future developments will attest to the continued measure of American national strength and whether it will wax or wane, but two rather obvious factors can already be taken into consideration. The United States has for decades borne the principal burden of defense against the former Soviet threat, and the cost to the American economy has been enormous and debilitating. Huge and sustained American defense expenditures have not bankrupted the United States, as they did bankrupt the former Soviet Union, but they have taken their toll. It will take time for the United States' economy fully to recover from this drain. One should be careful, therefore, to try to distinguish between this kind of passing phenomenon, however serious, and chronic long-term economic decline.

In addition, the United States has been experiencing a social transformation of great proportions, and one that remains incomplete. In the wake of the Second World War, the American Far West, Southwest, and South have become much larger and more vigorous components of the United States economy. Women have fully become part of the labor force and have substantially—if not yet absolutely—achieved equal opportunity in the marketplace. The racial mix of the United States population is changing dramatically as annual immigration continues and in largest part emanates from Latin America, the Caribbean, and Asia. The character and quality of not only the economy but of the whole society have been transformed by automation of more and more of the production process and by the explosion of the so-called service and knowledge industries. The process of transformation along these lines has been anything but smooth and even, and at times has appeared to be chaotic to the point of dysfunction. Again, however, only careful discretion can attempt to distinguish between a passing phase that incorporates and will ultimately harness new energies, and the onset of an ever-increasing decline into lasting disorder and confusion.

Certainly there is no dearth of factors that potentially could well lead to misunderstandings that would bedevil German-American relations, regardless of whether they emanate from the American or German side or, more likely, from both. The chapters that follow are appropriately full of specifics as to the decisions and issues that may provoke both controversy and misunderstanding. All of the authors, however, also endorse the concept of continued German-American partnership.

Addressing a vision of American leadership, Paul Nitze speaks of a world of diversity—which should be supported, represents a welcome development in many respects, but also involves new dangers and challenges. He considers not only political, military, and economic challenges, but also environmental challenges now assuming ever-increasing priority. He argues for a strong and both indispensable and unavoidable world leadership role for the United States, but rejects an American role as either global police-man or champion of democracy, and points out that an American role as a model for others to emulate is contingent on a valid perception of the United States as a source of global solutions rather than problems.

Christoph Bertram points out that his discussion of a vision of German leadership is affected by prevailing German embarrass-ment with the abuses of both the terms vision and leadership dur-ing the Third Reich. Assessing post-Yalta Europe, he finds that the threat of Soviet aggression in fact greatly strengthened Western Europe and provided a safe haven for Germany, and that these Western European achievements must not be sacrificed by a re-turn to pre-Yalta Europe. He argues vigorously for the need to give top priority to the further integration and unification of the European Community, argues that a strong, cohesive European Community is the precondition for a strong, cohesive Atlantic alliance that remains equally necessary, and warns that an overly rapid effort to include Central and Eastern Europe would most likely transform the European Community into an inadequate and indecisive coalition.

Charles McC. Mathias appraises the limits of leadership for the United States. He first examines the demographic changes that are well on the way to an American population in which those of European descent will constitute a minority and then explains the degree to which domestic problems complicate an American con-sensus on foreign policy. He asserts that the potential of American power fully remains despite the need of the United States more effectively to put its own house in better order, and concludes that the United States lacks the will rather than the power to impose a global Pax Americana but will instead prove capable of meeting its unavoidable international responsibilities as long as it can continue to rely heavily on existing or newly reshaped alliances.

Discussing the limits on German leadership, Lothar Ruehl first points out Germany's pressing need to complete and digest the process of national unification and analyzes the many attendant difficulties. He then proceeds to point out that the burden of Germany's past also imposes constraints and examines the internal German debate concerning military involvement abroad. His observations conclude with a look at the competing external demands with which Germany is confronted, most notably the need to accommodate inescapable new responsibilities toward Central and Eastern Europe and the former Soviet Union alongside its European Community obligations, as well as Germany's task to provide for a continued American presence on the European continent.

Robert Blackwill's analysis of security relationships, as the crucial ingredient of the pattern of partnership between the United States and Germany, begins with a brief review of the evolution of these relationships in the most recent past, highlighting the observation that significant differences have marked and still characterize German and American attitudes toward Moscow. This is followed by an examination of the role of NATO, which concludes that NATO has a future role to play and must change dramatically to do so, but must not dilute its effectiveness by extending membership to the new democracies of Eastern Europe. Blackwill then propounds the continued presence of American troops in Europe, the difficulties attendant to American nuclear weapons in Germany, the imperative for rapid and real European defense cooperation in the context of European political union and without American opposition, and the need for Germany's ability and will to play a military role outside the NATO area.

In presenting a German view of the U.S.–German security relationship, Karl Kaiser first describes how Germany evolved from an utterly dependent client of the United States into the second

largest Atlantic democracy and a central ally, and then points out
that the relative strengths of Germany and the European Community have been increasing vis-à-vis the United States. He then
proceeds to an analysis of current aspects of European security,
ranging over the disappearance of the classical threats, the emergence of new nuclear problems, the threats of destabilization in
Eastern Europe and the former Soviet Union, and global challenge also involving the Third World. Looking directly at roles and
policies for both the United States and Germany, he then argues
against American isolationism and for continued American involvement in Europe, affirms Germany's need for a European
security structure, emphasizes the German inability to tolerate
disintegration, chaos, and violence among its neighbors to the
East, and favors a continuing role for NATO based on firm agreements among sovereign states.

Robert Hormats offers an American examination of the patterns of competition represented by United States–German economic relationships, beginning with a description of divergent
policies between the two nations with respect to monetary issues
and interest rates, trade relations, aid to the Soviet Union, and
Operation Desert Storm. He then puts forward a comprehensive
and detailed agenda for American-European economic relationships, based on the assumption that economic destinies will be less
intertwined than past defense ties were, and that there is great
potential for transatlantic friction. He explains that the fact that
trade policies reflect domestic policy makes differences between
the United States and the European Community difficult to reconcile, and examines the Uruguay Round and monetary policy in
this context. He concludes with an analysis of assistance to Eastern
Europe and the former Soviet Union as well as of global burden
sharing, and emphasizes the problems of present weakness in the
domestic American economy.

A German perspective on these economic interactions is set out
by Norbert Walter. He begins with a discussion of German-American economic partnership and rivalry, proceeding from a com-
mentary on the exceptional level of bilateral direct investment and
corporate links to an examination of the conflicts that suggest rivalry. Then follows a cautious but on the whole very positive as-

sessment of German unification, followed by a comprehensive assessment of Germany's future economic role in Europe. Walter's concluding points deal with Europe's role in the world economy, where he displays optimism concerning the European Community's enormous prospects for growth in the 1990s, and with the importance of overcoming protectionist trends. In this latter context, he argues that the United States represents an important partner for Germany in this endeavor, and that protectionism cannot be the answer to the Japanese challenge.

To believe that any new pattern of world order that can be created will bring about international peace and stability requires optimism. That same optimism is required for the belief that the United States and Germany will find new ways to continue the partnership that bound them together during the cold war. Their mutual need for their partnership to endure is present, but it does not of course guarantee success. There is no guarantee. What is clear is that a continued strong partnership between the United States and the Federal Republic would serve both countries and the world community well.

2

Visions of Leadership: The United States

PAUL H. NITZE

The global community is now embarked on a transition to a world quite different from the one we have known since 1945. The future course of this transition is uncertain, but some of the key characteristics of the new world are already evident. Most importantly, the collapse of the Soviet Union and the demise of the Soviet bloc indicate that world affairs will no longer be dominated by the confrontation of two different but roughly equal superpowers. The fall of the Berlin Wall, followed by the Russian Revolution of 1991, signaled the end of U.S.–Soviet bipolarity.

This radical change and the range of benefits it has generated, from freely elected governments to reforming economies to peacefully settled regional conflicts, provide reason for hope. But there are nevertheless myriad problems—political, military, economic,

PAUL H. NITZE, long-time and distinguished public servant, was most recently special advisor to President Reagan and Secretary of State Shultz on arms control. He is founder of and presently diplomat in residence of the Paul H. Nitze School of Advanced International Studies, Johns Hopkins University.

environmental—still facing us and new problems arising. They will test our skills and ingenuity, and will challenge the nations of the world as never before to rise above self-absorption and rivalry to cooperate for the common good. Experience indicates that such cooperation will flourish only if the world benefits from wise and effective leadership. Critical questions before us, therefore, are from where such leadership can come, and how it can be applied.

This chapter assesses the nature of the post-Wall world and its problems; addresses the role the single remaining superpower, the United States, should play in leading the effort to resolve these problems; discusses the key partnership with Germany; and concludes with some brief observations about the United States as a model for others.

The Nature of the Post-Wall World

In the near term, at least, the new world will be one of great uncertainty. Three dramas—revolution in the former Soviet Union, the transformation of countries throughout Eastern Europe, and continuing conflict in the Middle East—currently dominate world affairs, and in each case the likely eventual outcome is unclear.

Observing from the West the stunningly rapid and sweeping changes in the aftermath of the 1991 failed coup in the Soviet Union, it is difficult to estimate how the situation there will evolve before it becomes more stable. Although a second attempt by hardliners to reassert strong central control cannot be ruled out, it seems likely that the replacement of the union by a federation linking many, but not all, of the former republics as voluntary, sovereign members will be sustained. The nature of this federation, however, likely will remain fluid for an extended period as tension continues between the desire of the republics for maximum independence and their need to cooperate closely to deal effectively with economic problems and other concerns. Moreover, whatever political entity results is almost sure to be buffeted by the centrifugal forces unleashed by economic deprivation and nationalist hatreds.

Also uncertain are the prospects for success of the Eastern European countries in their efforts to shift to free market economies. The residue of decades of Communist leadership and command economies poses a number of difficult problems involving questions of ownership and property rights and how one goes about restructuring and privatizing state enterprises. Efforts to convert previously subsidized and monopolistic industries into firms that can compete and turn a profit in an open market will inevitably create disruption as weaker enterprises fail and their workers are laid off.

The difficulty of the conversion task has been demonstrated most vividly by the experience of the former East Germany. Starting with the strongest economy in Eastern Europe and bolstered by a huge influx of aid from West Germany, this region is nonetheless undergoing great economic difficulty, with unemployment rates soaring through the roof.

Finally, the future of the Middle East remains clouded. Once again, we have seen an effort to invigorate the peace process, between Israel and the Arab states on the one hand, and between Israel and the Palestinians on the other. In the aftermath of the Persian Gulf War, the problems of this region have seemed slightly less intractable than in the past, but one still cannot predict a successful resolution with any confidence. Added to this is the uncertain future of Iraq as well as the ferment created by the evolution of grass-roots political psychology in the Muslim world, which extends beyond the Middle East to large parts of North Africa, Russia, Azerbaijan, Pakistan, India, and east to Indonesia.

Despite all this uncertainty, a few characteristics of the new world are clear. Above all, it will be a world of diversity.

One of the most important lessons of the past few years is the near-impossibility of erasing cultural ties, ethnic identities, and social practices, especially in a world where communications, and thus ideas, cannot be suppressed. In country after country in Eastern Europe, and within the Soviet Union itself, beliefs and practices that had been long dormant under the yoke of oppression rose quickly to the surface once constraints were loosened. The decades-long efforts of Communist leaders to impose a common culture and society on their subjects and to eliminate ethnic heritages ended in failure.

Once again, we see emerging the Europe of the past, with its rich mix of nationalities and cultures. Not only are individual aspirations being realized, the constellation of the various cultures promises to enrich us all.

But unfortunately, we are also seeing a resurgence of some of the tensions between nationalities that diversity in Europe generated in the past. Such tensions can be a threat to peace over the years ahead.

Although the renewal of diversity has been most evident in Europe, we are witnessing a similar process on other continents as well, most notably in Africa. As in Europe, the realization of national aspirations elsewhere is also accompanied by tensions between ethnic groups.

In many cases, these tensions have led to renewed demands for self-determination. Groups such as the Kurds in Iraq and Turkey, the Croats and Slovenes in Yugoslavia, and numerous nationalities throughout the former Soviet Union have demanded either greater autonomy from central governments or complete freedom to govern themselves. Such movements have created a dilemma for those who wish to preserve the right of peoples to govern themselves without interfering excessively in internal matters of existing states and without producing the instability and conflict that can result from separatist efforts.

Thus the new diversity presents us with a mixed bag of effects. As democratic nations that honor freedom and the protection of the right to be different, the United States and its allies have supported this development. As peoples who can learn from the ways of others, we have welcomed it. As students of history, we understand that diversity cannot be long suppressed in any event. But as realists, we should recognize and try to deal with the dangers that accompany it and can threaten to destroy it.

The post-Wall world will also be one with a full range of challenges to its inhabitants. Diversity is not the only source of new problems. In addition, many problems of the past remain unresolved, and some are gaining increasing urgency.

Political Challenges. Politically, we must be concerned about revival of hostility toward the West from Russia or other former Soviet republics; about conflicts that continue or threaten to erupt in Southeast Asia, South Asia, Africa, and elsewhere; and about strains in relations with many of our friends and allies. The Communist ideology is now thoroughly discredited, and former Soviet republics are unlikely to be able to restore the international political influence the Soviet Union once wielded. On the other hand, the still-awesome military power retained by some of these republics, particularly Russia, provides them considerable potential for intimidation, and they retain significant capacity to make mischief in trouble spots worldwide.

Regional conflicts have diminished in number, partly as a result of the removal of cold war competition as an element of those conflicts. In some cases, settlements were fostered by U.S.–Soviet cooperation in brokering an agreement among the warring parties. In other cases, one side's victory owed much to the reduction in or withdrawal of superpower support for the other. Nevertheless, several conflicts continue, and tensions simmer between neighbors in many regions. Although these conflicts may be less frequent and numerous in the future, they may prove to be more dangerous as the arms proliferation detailed below heightens the intensity and destructiveness of war.

Among friends and allies, strains will inevitably arise as nations adjust to the new realities of the post-Wall world. In Europe, the Warsaw Pact threat no longer exists to serve as a glue holding together the Atlantic alliance. Differences that were put aside in favor of the greater good of allied unity may no longer be suppressed, and new differences will develop as new roles are assumed. Increased European economic and political unity, as well as the possible further integration of European security efforts, will pose a particular challenge to U.S.–European relations. Similar strains will be felt elsewhere, as the perception of a reduced military threat to the free world shifts the focus of relationships from security concerns to problems that the Western powers may not be as prepared to address. One recent example was the increased controversy over U.S. basing rights in the Philippines, where maintenance of U.S. bases was seen much more as an issue of economics and sovereignty than as a source of security.

Military Challenges. Militarily, we face a nuclear arsenal in the former Soviet Union that remains large and modern, the continuing proliferation of weapons of mass destruction, and excessive non-nuclear forces throughout the globe. There are today some 27,000 nuclear warheads in storage among the former Soviet republics.[1] The cuts in that arsenal mandated by the Strategic Arms Reduction (START) Treaty would still leave a large number of long-range missiles, submarines, and aircraft capable of delivering thermonuclear warheads on targets worldwide. Despite their economic difficulties, the Soviets continued to modernize these weapons at a rapid pace over recent years. Complicating the problem is the current instability in the former Soviet Union; no one can be sure into whose hands these weapons will eventually fall. Statements from civilian and military leaders in Moscow that the nuclear arsenal will remain under tight central control, and agreement to this condition by leaders of the republics, have been reassuring. But the security of this arsenal will continue to be a particular concern as long as the political situation is unsettled.

A growing number of other countries have either acquired or are on the verge of acquiring nuclear weapons. In addition to the five declared nuclear weapons states, four nations—Israel, India, Pakistan, and South Africa—are suspected to have built nuclear arsenals or to be able to do so quickly. Five others—Brazil, Argentina, North Korea, Iran, and Iraq—have ongoing research projects with nuclear weapons as the goal, but lack the materials or the facilities for actual production. Libya and Taiwan have in the past attempted to develop or purchase nuclear weapons, but were unsuccessful. Of these eleven nations, only Libya, Taiwan, Iran, and Iraq have signed the Nuclear Non-Proliferation Treaty and the accompanying International Atomic Energy Agency (IAEA) Safeguards Agreement, thereby placing their nuclear facilities under inspection by the IAEA. North Korea has also signed the treaty, but has not yet signed the safeguards agreement, leaving its existing plants free to operate without international inspection.[2] South Africa announced in June 1991 its readiness to sign the treaty and submit its nuclear facilities to IAEA inspection.

Chemical weapons are even more widespread than nuclear weapons, with the number of members of the chemical weapons club believed to be in the high teens and growing. A recent analysis prepared by the director of U.S. Naval Intelligence concluded that, in addition to the United States and the former Soviet Union, fourteen nations "probably possess" chemical armaments. They are Iraq, Iran, Syria, Israel, Libya, Egypt, China, India, Pakistan, Burma, Vietnam, Taiwan, North Korea, and South Korea. The report added that Saudi Arabia may also have chemical weapons and ten other nations are believed to be seeking such weapons.[3] Proliferation of these weapons is even more difficult to stop than that of nuclear weapons, since chemical weapons are inexpensive and relatively easy to develop and the chemicals needed to make them are among the most commonly used in the world. Iraq's use of chemical weapons in the Iran-Iraq war and against Kurdish villages has generated growing concern that other Third World nations will see these weapons as an important asset for their arsenals.

Exacerbating the problem created by the spread of weapons of mass destruction is the proliferation of potentially highly effective means of delivering those weapons—ballistic missiles. Iraqi use of Scud missiles in the Persian Gulf War, although militarily ineffective, provided a preview of the threat on the horizon. Today, about eighteen countries have ballistic missiles, and the number is likely to grow, since several countries have been willing to export these systems.[4] Countries are increasingly developing an indigenous production capability, which will make it tougher to stop proliferation through export controls. In the future, more modern, accurate, long-range missiles, coupled with more destructive warheads and in the hands of more nations, will present a far more serious threat to countries around the world.

Finally, other conventional arms pervade the globe in numbers far exceeding legitimate security needs. In 1988 worldwide military expenditures topped $1 trillion, and there has been no sign of a significant decline since.[5] Nations brimming with military arsenals cannot help but be a source of tension among their neighbors and beyond.

Economic Challenges. Economic problems plague both the developing and developed worlds. Runaway debt in many nations, developed and developing, threatens economic stability and reduces capital available for other purposes. In many cases, debt

payments from Third World nations pose severe threats to economies already made fragile by inflation and poverty. Debts incurred
by Communist leaders in Poland, Hungary, and Bulgaria have
saddled their current reformist leaders with payments that, if
made, would transfer 3 to 5 percent of those countries' gross national product to the West.[6] Latin American debt service since
1983 has transferred tens of billions of dollars each year to banks in
the industrialized North.[7] In both of these cases, these large
amounts of funds are leaving economies that are in dire need of
investments. Not only do these nations suffer from the reluctance
of lenders to extend additional credit, but the resultant shrinkage
of available capital and the reputation of the Third World as a
poor credit risk have reduced resources available even to countries
with good payment records.

Trade imbalances exacerbate the debt problem, and barriers to
trade are a source of tension among many trading partners. The
Uruguay Round of negotiations on the General Agreement on
Tariffs and Trade has been hampered by disagreements between
the United States and its European partners. Japanese-American
trade disputes have become severe enough to threaten relations
between the two nations. Fair trade practices remain an important
North-South issue as well. Unresolved concerns include demands
in the industrialized North for greater respect for intellectual property on the part of its Southern trading partners, who it feels profit
unfairly by ignoring patents and copyrights. The South, on the
other hand, insists that the North's agricultural subsidies be eliminated so as to open markets, now glutted with artificially cheap
farm products, to the commodities of the South.

Not only are large and growing disparities in wealth between
nations a problem, similar disparities exist within nations. With
the gap between rich and poor widening, and the numbers in
poverty increasing, many nations are sitting on a tinderbox of
seething resentment and despair that, if left unaddressed, could
explode in violence and social upheaval.

As nations in Eastern Europe, Africa, and elsewhere struggle to
cast off command economies and introduce market forces, they
will be forced to endure the near-term difficulties, noted earlier,
that seem inevitable as they seek the longer-term benefits and
opportunities of the free market.

Environmental Challenges. Among our environmental threats are global warming, ozone depletion, and the appalling reduction in the number of species inhabiting our planet. The build-up of carbon dioxide and other so-called greenhouse gases resulting from fossil fuel consumption and deforestation threatens to warm the atmosphere by 3 to 8 degrees Fahrenheit by the year 2030.[8] While this change may appear small, its effects will alter patterns of precipitation and local climates in unpredictable ways. These changes are likely to have drastic effects on agriculture, coastal erosion, water supplies, and the habitats of humans and other creatures.

The surprising discovery of the hole in the protective layer of ozone in the stratosphere indicated the unintended effects human activities can have on the earth. In this case, chlorofluorocarbons had been extensively tested for safety at the time of their introduction without any consideration for their effect on the upper atmosphere. The resulting ozone depletion has increased the ultraviolet radiation reaching the earth's surface, heightening the risk of human skin cancer and producing unpredictable effects on plant and animal life.[9]

Other unforeseen effects of supposedly safe activities probably remain to be discovered. Recent findings indicate that chemicals released into the environment with little apparent effect today may actually become "chemical time bombs," accumulating over time and suddenly creating serious problems as thresholds of safety are surpassed.[10]

It is already clear, however, that a range of human-made products and toxic by-products generated in the production process threatens our ecology. Agricultural pesticides, air pollutants, industrial wastes, and other results of modern economic activity have fouled the soil, air, and water in many areas of the globe. Even though recent efforts to reduce the environmental impacts of these activities through regulation and other mechanisms have had some beneficial effects, the damage already done is immense.

The extinction of species through loss of habitat and other conditions created by human activities threatens genetic diversity as well as the biological, economic, and human health benefits that such diversity provides. Destruction of rain forests accounts for much of this species loss, which is estimated to be occurring 1,000 to 10,000 times faster than the natural rate of extinction in these tropical environments.[11] Most of the species that are being lost have not even been discovered.

Other natural resources that are usually considered renewable, such as fisheries and forests, are also endangered. They are being depleted beyond the level of sustainability, and many face total destruction.

Much of the environmental stress causing these problems and others plaguing the global ecology is attributable to explosive growth in the human population. The consequences of this phenomenon, both the large shift of population distribution even further toward the developing world and the increased demand for resources, will have profound effects on any attempts to mitigate the environmental damage already done. A billion people will be added to the earth between 1989 and 1999, raising its human burden from 5 to 6 billion. This growth will occur over ten times faster than that from 1 to 2 billion.[12] By the end of the century, a full 80 percent of the world's people will live in the developing world, and most of the additional billion will live in poverty.[13] This tremendous growth will thus be concentrated in regions where governments and economies are least capable of relieving the strain on environmental resources that it will create.

In sum, the list of political, military, economic, and environmental challenges facing the post-Wall world is a long and daunting one. When one adds in other problems such as terrorism, drugs, and hunger, the magnitude of the task before us becomes quite evident.

Also apparent is that the problems of the post-Wall world will increasingly take on an international flavor, reflecting both their transnational character and our growing worldwide interdependence. From industries whose pollution travels far beyond national boundaries, to economic difficulties that work as a drag on the economies of trading partners, to conflicts that endanger critical resources and threaten to spill over borders, our neighbors' problems, and even the problems of those far away, will be more and more our own.

The international response to one such problem—the Iraqi invasion of Kuwait—represents perhaps the first defining event of the post-Wall world, for it is the first indication for leaders world-wide of the emerging mores of international behavior. Had Saddam Hussein's forces not been expelled from Kuwait, the lesson would have been that brutality and aggression pay, and potential tyrants would have been encouraged to imitate his approach in future international disputes. With Saddam's military defeat, a different message was sent. At least in this case, the message was that aggression against a sovereign neighbor would not be tolerated, intimidation and force were not acceptable means of resolving disputes among nations, and attempts to employ such means would be met by the concerted opposition of the world community.

If key members of the international community can resolve that the coalition effort to reverse Iraq's aggression will be a model for future responses to similar encroachments, and if they can make a demonstrable commitment to this view, future would-be aggressors should be discouraged and the prospects for a more civilized era should be greatly enhanced. If the same nations can also resolve to cooperate similarly in responding to other global problems, the prospects for a cleaner, safer, more equitable, and more satisfying world should be enhanced as well.

Such cooperation is unlikely to be fostered, however, without strong leadership. In the Persian Gulf crisis, the United States exercised such a role in assembling the coalition opposing Saddam Hussein and in facilitating that coalition's efforts. In dealing with future global problems, that role likely will fall again to the United States.

The Role of the United States

The Persian Gulf War confirmed what had become increasingly evident over the preceding two years: the United States is the sole remaining superpower in the world. No other nation could have organized and successfully led the anti-Iraq coalition. Similarly, no other nation or group of nations has a comparable capacity to contribute to solutions of other global problems.

A few examples illustrate the point. As noted earlier, whoever controls the nuclear arsenal of the former Soviet Union will retain, even after a START Treaty, a large and modern force of long-range nuclear weapons. Thus for the foreseeable future, they will continue to present a potential threat to the United States and to its friends and allies everywhere. To deal with this problem, the United States strives to maintain forces both to deter use of the Soviet weapons and to provide the necessary leverage to negotiate their reduction in a stabilizing manner. No other country is capable of relieving Washington of this burden now, and none is likely to be able to do so in the future, nor would it be desirable for any other country to deploy the nuclear arsenal needed to assume that role alone. Therefore, in the future as much as in the past, this should remain an American task.

On the European continent, the nationalist tensions cited earlier could erupt into civil or crossborder warfare. Peace throughout Europe and beyond could be threatened. To forestall such problems, efforts should be made to encourage and facilitate the peaceful resolution of these tensions. Should warfare erupt, efforts would be needed to contain and terminate the conflicts quickly.

In the absence of the United States, Germany would seem to have the greatest political and economic clout in Western Europe. But leadership in maintaining a European peace is not a role for which Germany is well suited. Suspicions of German intentions, whether justified or not, remain too high among the nations of Europe for Germany to be effective in the role of honest broker. France and, especially, Britain are hampered by economic difficulties. In addition, their political influence suffers from the traditional French inclination to act independently and from British differences with many of its European Community partners over the extent of European integration. Therefore the United States should remain in a position to contribute to the peacekeeping task should the European nations, including Germany, wish it to do so. This does not necessarily mean the continued presence of large numbers of American troops in Europe; Washington should keep only such forces there as are wanted and for only as long as they are wanted. A constructive U.S. role in European affairs can derive from much more than just the number of forces deployed; potential power can be symbolized by the presence of forces of limited size.

Similar examples of problems meriting a U.S. role exist in other regions of the world. In the Far East, the leading role could, perhaps, in time be assumed by Japan. But this would raise considerable concern among other Asian nations, especially those who have fallen under Japanese domination in the past. Further, it is doubtful whether the Japanese would find it feasible to consider the interests of others as being comparable to Japanese interests.

In the Middle East, the unique qualifications of the United States to play a central role were never more evident than during the events after the Iraqi invasion of Kuwait.

For certain problems that transcend regions, such as global economic and environmental concerns, the sheer size of the U.S. economy makes a central U.S. role unavoidable. With more than 20 percent of the world's gross national product, America will serve either as a catalyst or a brake for economic activity worldwide.[14] This, plus its willingness to exercise leadership in the World Bank and the International Monetary Fund, allows it significant influence over the direction and vision of international efforts for economic development and poverty reduction.

Similarly, the magnitude of U.S. industrial and agricultural activity means that the extent of American efforts to reduce humanmade pollution will either make a significant contribution to environmental restoration or will be a considerable barrier to it. For example, a recent study of relative national contributions to global warming rated the United States as the worst offender, accounting for 17 percent of the increase in greenhouse gas emissions during 1988.[15] Another example is the immense U.S. consumption of raw materials; one estimate found that between 1940 and 1976, the United states consumed more minerals than did all of humanity up to 1940.[16] Not only has the extraction and use of these materials caused significant environmental damage worldwide, this level of consumption generates high levels of waste. The United States is the world's top producer of garbage.[17]

In spite of, or perhaps because of, these large-scale contributions to environmental degradation, the United States has set the pace in establishing institutions and regulations to halt and reverse damage to the ecology. The U.S. regulatory approach to environmental protection was the model for many nations that have subsequently surpassed U.S. efforts, and Americans possess great expertise on clean-up techniques. This capability would permit the United States to be an important leader and innovator in the environmental area, especially in terms of training and institutional development.

All of this argues for a strong American role in the global arena. But there are constraints, both internal and international, on the ability of the United States to fulfill this function. Chapter 4 details the limits on U.S. leadership, so they are merely highlighted here.

Internally, the United States is constrained by limits on the amount of resources it can devote to its international leadership role. These limits derive from Washington's significant economic problems, particularly the huge U.S. budget and balance-of-payments deficits. As the world's greatest debtor, the United States cannot afford to spend heavily on a wide range of problems.

Another internal constraint is the traditional skepticism of the American public toward extensive involvement in international affairs, an attitude that can be traced back to George Washington's warning against entangling foreign alliances. There are those who argue today that, with the end of the cold war, the great threat to U.S. interests has collapsed, no comparable threat is evident, and the United States should therefore feel free to retreat from world affairs and tend to its own internal problems. More thoughtful observers realize that, more than ever, many of the problems on the global agenda will deeply affect U.S. interests and, thus, tending to its own problems requires an active U.S. role on the world stage. Nevertheless, American public opinion can be expected to be resistant to any U.S. role that might be perceived to place a disproportionate burden on the United States. In particular, the American public would be unlikely to support a U.S. role as a global policeman.

Internationally, the United States is constrained by the fact that many problems are insoluble absent continuing cooperation from other nations. For example, no amount of U.S. leadership on environmental problems could overcome the unwillingness of a few key nations to alter practices that currently endanger the global ecology. Similarly, widespread cooperation will be necessary to mount an effective response to the scourges of terrorism and drugs.

In addition, while U.S. prestige and influence reached a peak with the military victory in the Persian Gulf, they are unlikely to remain at such a high level. Over time, other nations can be expected to coalesce to cut the Americans down to size, a traditional reaction that occurs when one nation appears to be in a potentially dominant position.

An example of this reaction was provided within days of the cease-fire in Iraq by China, which sent a delegation to Moscow offering the Soviets some $800–900 million of assistance in the form of food. Some Chinese analysts have concluded that the old men still dominating the Chinese Communist party became frightened that the psychological pressure on them from the image of a strengthened United States would become intolerable. They therefore felt impelled to do what they could to help shore up the Soviet regime, the one group they could still talk with as fellow Communists. One can expect other nations to undertake similar, perhaps more successful, efforts to reduce what they perceive to be excessive influence by the United States.

In sum, the importance of the problems on the global agenda, their direct effect on significant U.S. interests, and Washington's unique qualifications to address them make a compelling case for a strong U.S. role in world affairs. On the other hand, there are definite constraints on what and how much the United States can do. It certainly cannot act alone.

Instead, the U.S. role in this new era should be to exercise leadership of international cooperative approaches to solving world problems. In this sense, U.S. leadership of the coalition effort in the Gulf War provides a model, as does its leading role in the World Bank and the International Monetary Fund. Similar efforts could be undertaken under the auspices of the United Nations or other supranational institutions, or through ad hoc global or regional arrangements. The key would be to bring America's unmatched set of attributes—its first-class military potential; its political, economic, and cultural strengths; and its demonstrated lack of territorial ambitions—to bear on cooperative efforts to deal with common concerns.

The Objectives of U.S. Leadership

In exercising this leadership, what sort of world should the United States seek to facilitate? In other words, what strategic objective should guide the U.S. approach to world affairs?

The lessons of the past era and the needs of the future argue for the fundamental goal of accommodating and protecting diversity within a general framework of world order.

The United States should seek to create a global climate in which a large array of political groupings can exist, each with its own, and perhaps eccentric, ways. It should seek to eliminate force and intimidation as acceptable means of resolving disputes between these groupings, and it should seek to foster cooperative efforts among these groupings to resolve common problems.

This emphasis on diversity provides certain guidelines for handling problems that are truly internal to individual nations. The overriding principle in such cases should be respect for sovereignty. There should be no effort to impose political, economic, or social preferences on others. Rather than being the "champion of democracy," the United States should encourage legitimate governments that do not threaten others. Certainly, there is no excuse for continuing the cold war practice of occasionally supporting an illegitimate government, or opposing a legitimate one, due to its role in the global competition with the Soviets.

This increased tolerance does not, however, preclude supporting national efforts to emulate Western successes. Where a legitimate national leadership is inclined to shift toward a more democratic form of government or a more market based economy, it should be encouraged, and this encouragement should extend to the provision of technical and other assistance to accomplish the transition.

It should also be emphasized that certain matters that tyrants have claimed to be internal affairs are not. The post-Wall world should continue to recognize basic human rights as matters transcending national sovereignty, and the international community should not shy away from efforts to protect those rights.

As noted earlier, the assertion by a number of nationality groups of the right of self-determination has created a particularly difficult

dilemma. Each of these situations is unique, and none of the territories in question is ethnically pure, so one cannot merely insist on
the right to self-determination in all cases. Any solution will inevitably leave minority groups that are governed by others, and any
change is likely to be highly disruptive. But, consistent with the
emphasis on diversity, the presumption of U.S. policy should be in
favor of the realization through peaceful means of aspirations for
self-determination where legitimate groups have clearly established the political and economic basis for autonomy.

For problems that transcend national boundaries, as more and
more will, supranational institutions should play an increasing
role. Organizations such as the United Nations and its components, NATO, the European Community, the Conference on Security and Cooperation in Europe, and the Organization for Economic Cooperation and Development should concurrently have
the task of providing stability and forward movement on important global and regional matters. Such institutions can deal with
these problems more efficiently and effectively than individual nations acting without central coordination.

This approach creates certain complications, however, that require careful consideration. It implies some loss of sovereignty for
individual nations and thus some constraint on diversity, so it is
important to balance the gains against the costs in each case.

The gains deriving from supranational authority most clearly
outweigh the costs in the environmental area. As noted earlier,
national efforts to reverse the growing damage to the world ecology can be easily undercut by the negligence of other countries.
There simply must be a coordinated, international effort if global
ecological problems are to be solved.

Similar considerations apply in the realm of economics. In an
increasingly integrated world economy, the need for international
coordination of fiscal, monetary, and exchange rate policies is
widely accepted. Consideration is also being given to greater international harmonization of banking regulations and other domestic
policies such as antitrust regulation, health and safety standards,
and the protection of intellectual property.

Where the gains of central coordination are most pronounced,
supranational institutions with greater authority to impose solu-

tions on potentially reluctant members can be used. Where national sovereignty is more important, institutions relying more on consensus would be preferable. But it should be kept in mind that the latter are at risk of being hamstrung by a single recalcitrant member.

A case in point is the United Nations. In the glow of the Persian Gulf victory, many commentators are projecting a greatly enhanced role for the organization, particularly the Security Council, in addressing problems of global security. But it was possible to construct the anti-Iraq coalition through the Security Council only because of the cooperation of the Soviet Union and China. It remains to be seen whether such U.S.–Chinese cooperation will continue and whether the U.S.–Soviet collaboration on regional matters and other issues of the past few years will be sustained by the entity that assumes the Soviet role on the Security Council. If not, the United Nations could face once again an era in which Security Council vetoes block significant action by the organization. In that case, the task of international peacekeeping would likely fall to one or more supranational organizations involving the United States and regional participants. In Europe, and perhaps elsewhere, NATO would seem to be the best candidate for such a role, and its recent decision to create a rapid reaction force to respond to European crises is a step in that direction. In the future, it may be desirable to expand this force's mission to include, as well, contingencies outside Europe, such as in the Persian Gulf.

The U.S. role in responding to transnational problems should be to seek to place them on the agendas of the appropriate supranational institutions, and then to take the lead within these organizations in the effort to get them resolved. This will require leadership by example, from restraining worldwide arms sales and transfers of potentially dangerous technologies, to avoiding barriers to free trade and emphasizing means of relieving debt and encouraging investment in developing nations, to altering industrial and agricultural practices that harm the environment. Just as much of Washington's leadership role in the Persian Gulf conflict resulted from its willingness to put its own troops on the front line in Saudi Arabia, its ability to exercise leadership on other problems will depend on its willingness to put its own economic house in order and then devote its available resources to solutions.

The U.S.–German Relationship

Even more than during the past forty years, Germany is likely to be a key partner in U.S. efforts to create a safer and more prosperous world. Many of the characteristics that give America strength—a robust, democratic polity; a thriving, free market; an energetic and creative people—are German strengths as well. We share similar visions of a world free from oppression, fear, and degradation. It is only natural, then, that we should rise above everyday strains and peaceful competition in trade and other activities to retain and enhance our partnership.

As we enter the post-Wall world, there are some in the United States who are concerned about a potential shift in German orientation. They fear that a unified Germany will be tempted to go beyond merely solidifying its relations with Central and Eastern Europe to the creation of an alliance with these countries, and particularly with remnants of the former Soviet Union (either republics or a federation), that could constitute a threat to the rest of Europe and the United States.

This seems unlikely on several counts. First, it is unlikely that Germany could have sufficient confidence in its relations with the most powerful remnants of the former Soviet Union. This is particularly so in light of Germany's lack of nuclear weapons and the improbability of its obtaining such weapons in the future. The German people and government do not want nuclear weapons, and other states do not want Germany to have them. If that continues to be the case, given the oft-demonstrated Soviet willingness to resort in the past to force and intimidation to get its way, any German alliance with whoever controls the former Soviet nuclear arsenal would be ultimately unbalanced to Germany's detriment.

More importantly, German values are rooted solidly in the West. It is improbable that Germany would turn its back on those who share those values in favor of an adventure elsewhere. It would, therefore, appear sensible for the United States to accommodate growing ties between Germany and Central and Eastern Europe.

The United States as a Model?

Finally, one might ask if the United States should aspire to be a model for other countries in the post-Wall world. Certainly, the type of world proposed in this chapter is not one where any nation should presume to impose its characteristics or preferences on others; except where supranational institutions come into play, it is quite the opposite. But if it is true to the guidelines outlined above, the United States could provide a model of a good citizen in the world community that other nations could emulate if they so chose.

One should not underestimate the conditions, however. They include restoration of the U.S. economy to health, a sustained and costly effort to resolve other American problems such as the high demand for illegal drugs, and the willingness outlined above to lead by example in tackling international problems. Until the United States can be perceived much less as a source of global problems and much more as a source of global solutions, the position of role model is likely to be elusive.

Conclusion

As we enter a new world and leave behind the fear and hostility engendered by the cold war, there is reason to hope that a happier and more rewarding existence is within our grasp. This chapter has emphasized the tremendous challenges that face us still, but also the tremendous resources we possess. Our wealth, knowledge, and human compassion provide us the means to meet the challenges of the post-Wall world. With enlightened U.S. leadership in an international community dedicated to cooperation for the common good, we can apply those resources to create the sort of world that, for our forefathers, was but a dream.

Notes

[1] Norris and Arkin (1991), p. 49.
[2] Spector (1990), p. 6.
[3] Michael Wines, "Navy Report Asserts Many Nations Seek or Have Poison Gas," *New York Times*, March 10, 1991, p. 15.

[4] "Briefing on the Strategic Defense Initiative," U.S. Department of Defense, February 1991.

[5] 1988 figure from U.S. Arms Control and Disarmament Agency, *World Military Expenditures and Arms Transfers 1988*, ACDA Publication 131, p. 1. The Stockholm International Peace Research Institute indicates that worldwide expenditures declined by 2 percent in 1989. SIPRI (1990), p. 143.

[6] Marer (1991), p. 5.

[7] Dornbusch and Marcus (1991), p. 11.

[8] Mathews (1989), p. 169.

[9] Mathews (1989), p. 171.

[10] Stigliani et al. (1991), p. 5.

[11] Wilson (1988), pp. 3–18.

[12] Mathews (1989), p. 163.

[13] Mathews (1989), p. 163.

[14] The Council on Competitiveness estimated in 1988 that the U.S. share of world product had held steady at 23 percent since the mid-1970s. Council on Competitiveness (1988), appendix II.

[15] Hammond, Rodenburg, and Moomaw (1991), p. 14, table 1.

[16] Kirby and Prokopovitsh (1976), p. 713.

[17] Brown et al. (1991), p. 45.

3

Visions of Leadership: Germany

CHRISTOPH BERTRAM

S ometimes there is more to a title than just the gist of what
follows, and so it is with "Visions of Leadership." Germans
today, probably regardless of generation and political conviction,
are deeply embarrassed by such terms as "vision" and "leadership," not least because of the twelve dreadful years in which their
Fuehrer claimed both leadership and a certain vision, only to lead
the country and all of Europe into catastrophe. And yet Germans
today must learn that in the future, they will have to exercise
leadership, and that this will require a sense of direction—a vision
of their country's place and role in the world.

Such a learning process has been under way for some time.
Indeed, even before the unification of Germany, its Western part,
the Federal Republic of Germany, played an increasingly important role in the collective structures of the Western alliance and the

CHRISTOPH BERTRAM is diplomatic correspondent for the German
weekly newspaper *Die Zeit*. He has been director of the International
Institute for Strategic Studies in London, and served on the planning staff
of the West German Ministry of Defense in Bonn. He is a guest fellow of
the Yomiuri Research Institute, Tokyo.

European Community (EC). Its very location in the heart of Europe and its economic strength also made West Germany, at a time of upheaval, revolution, and renewal in Eastern Europe and beyond, the first and foremost Western contact for the countries of that region and the Soviet Union.

But this position of influence is usually seen more clearly by Germany's neighbors than by the Germans themselves. After all, they lived through a period of more than forty years—spanning almost two generations—when their nation was divided, their states subjected to special prerogatives claimed by the victorious allies of the Second World War, and their country situated in the very spot where—if it were to happen at all—everyone expected a major East-West conflict to erupt. Not surprisingly, therefore, Germans became accustomed to seeing themselves mostly as objects, rather than subjects, of international affairs, as followers rather than leaders. Moreover, it was a convenient attitude to hold on to—even more so as it was being shared not with cynicism but with conviction: a (West) Germany that, despite its growing economic impact and emerging political veto power, could emphasize the restrictions on its power also stood a better chance of convincing itself and others that positions of leadership or responsibility were mostly for others to assume.

Now, of course, the restrictions imposed after World War II and the division of the country have been removed in the course of the sudden, exciting rush to national unification and the East European revolutions that have taken place since 1989. And yet the view in Germany that vision and leadership are still for others to exercise will not disappear rapidly. After all, nothing is as resilient to change as a mentality that has grown over decades. The immense effort required for the task of fully unifying the country in social, economic, and political terms, now that East and West Germany are formally united, will give further support to the arguments of those who believe that Germany should refrain from a more active international role. The German past and the German present are thus powerful justifications for German abstinence in the future, when foreign friends will call for German vision and leadership in the international arena. Yet these justifications will be insufficient for three reasons.

The first is that whatever Germany does will inevitably have international repercussions. The country is of pivotal importance to Western structures such as NATO and the European Community, and its economic weight is such that if it sneezes, others will get a cold. For Germany to abstain from an active international role thus cannot mean that it plays no role at all, but that it plays the potentially destructive role of abstention. There is simply no way in which Germany can avoid making waves on the international sea, whatever it does or does not do.

Secondly, to believe that German international passivity will remove the country from international controversy is the counsel of naiveté. German back-seat driving will all too easily be seen by suspicious neighbors as part of a plot or as mere camouflage, not as a demonstration of modesty. It is true that any active German involvement will also cause criticism and, at times, even resentment. But it will be difficult to prove that such criticism and resentment result more from the exercise, rather than the denial, of German leadership responsibilities.

Thirdly, and perhaps most important, there are few countries in the world today with a weight and influence similar to that of Germany. There are, in fact, only a few countries capable of helping to organize the resilience of the international community to the dangers of instability and crisis. At the same time, there are few countries that depend as much on international stability as Germany does. Hence Germany has no real choice: either it recognizes the responsibility that power bestows upon it and becomes involved in the job of promoting international stability, or it does not—and neither serves its own interests nor gains the respect and trust of its neighbors and partners.

This chapter will examine what German leadership may mean in the new conditions of the post–cold war world. It will look first at the changed circumstances that affect Germany's international involvement and then discuss what might be sensible German responses. Whether these will qualify as adequate visions of sufficient leadership is for others to decide.

Post-Yalta Europe

At a time when many of the assumptions that guided postwar Europe and cold war relations between East and West have crumbled, it would be futile to draw up a catalogue of all that will be different in the future. Surely there will be plenty of surprises, and any predictions made today are, even more than usually might be the case, informed speculations about the unknown, rather than analyses of likely trends. Hence it is preferable to look at those elements of the cold war world that have been removed or altered by its disappearance. Of these, three stand out in importance as far as Germany's international environment is concerned: the Europe of Yalta no longer exists; Germany's international visibility has increased considerably; and the organizations of Western collective action—NATO and the European Community—can no longer automatically be assumed to provide, for Germany, the same "safe haven" they did in the past.

The Europe of Yalta has come to an end. When Communist regimes all over Eastern Europe collapsed, the first Western reaction—and quite rightly so—was to rejoice that freedom had won over repression. However, what was little recognized then and is only slowly being realized now is that with the removal of the walls and the barbed wire that used to keep Western Europe immune from the ills of Eastern Europe, the Western part of the Continent can now no longer go its way alone. The rich Europe (which has historically been that of the West) is no longer cut off from the poor Europe (which historically has been that of the East).

In retrospect, the Europe of Yalta—the shorthand term for the Europe divided between East and West in 1945—has turned out to have been a most astonishing aberration of history, in that the militarily victorious but economically weak Soviet Union insisted at Yalta on taking the burden of Eastern Europe away from the economically powerful West. It thus not only embroiled itself in the increasingly awkward task of maintaining internal security over traditionally proud and Western oriented societies, it also had to subsidize their economies in order to assure them of a living standard higher than was available for its own citizens. The Soviet rule over Eastern Europe was, in a sense, perverse colonialism: the poor, underdeveloped colony became the mother country that, instead of exploiting its new dominions economically, actually had to pay for them.

The other, no less astonishing aspect of the forty years of Yalta has been that, as a consequence of Europe's division, the European West was able to develop into a close-knit, economically prosperous community, unencumbered by the poor cousins in the East. If the Soviet strategic objective was to weaken the West, it achieved the very opposite result.

Had Europe not been divided in 1945, the Western part of the Continent would not have been able to concentrate its efforts on itself to the same extent as it actually did. Franco-German interdependence, the very objective of the Schuman Plan of 1950 and the nucleus of European integration in the Common Market, might well have been impossible had France faced not a divided Germany, but one that would have been large, potentially powerful, and oriented neither to the East nor to the West. Germany would have been tempted, as it had been over the previous century, to pursue once again that romantic and ill-fated *Sonderweg* (unique path) of separating itself from the ideals of Western democracy and liberalism. The economic devastation in Eastern Europe after World War II would have pulled down, like a millstone, the economic recovery in the West that became the catalyst and condition for political and economic integration. In the old, pre-Yalta Europe, a community of West European states willing to pool markets and to merge individual sovereignties had been unthinkable; it became possible only because of the division of Europe agreed to at Yalta.

Now this division has come to an end. Already the impact of Eastern Europe on Western Europe has emerged as the dominant policy issue in the West. East European governments are demanding economic assistance, they urge Western security backing, they are pushing to become members in Western institutions, and they want to sell their products on Western markets. Immigration from Eastern Europe has already increased considerably, and there are exaggerated if widespread worries that, should political and economic reforms in the new democracies of Eastern Europe fail, the number of people trying to escape, as their forefathers did in pre-

Yalta Europe, from the poverty of the East to the prosperity of the West, could turn into a flood threatening to overwhelm Western societies.

The most obvious case of Eastern Europe entangling West European politics is, of course, that of German unification. While this case is in many ways unique, there are aspects that nevertheless apply not just to East Germany but to Eastern Europe as a whole. The immense task of transforming a centralized planning economy into a market one while maintaining political stability; the human hardship facing those who have to learn to live in a competitive society; the mortgage of degradation piled up by the old regimes, which will have to be paid off for a long time to come; the task of introducing the rule of law into what was a discretionary political system—all of these problems have to be solved throughout Eastern Europe.

Yet East Germany is in a very different position from the countries further east. It has been incorporated into democratic, well-ordered, and wealthy West Germany, and consequently receives a degree of financial, administrative, and moral assistance that vastly exceeds anything to which other East European countries can aspire. Given all the differences, the length of time it will take for German unification to be completed is an indication of the problems the rest of the former Communist empire will experience. The return to pre-Yalta Europe means that this difficult period will not just affect Eastern Europe alone, but Europe as a whole.

Nor will the impact of Eastern on Western Europe be merely economic. The European view of the world will be influenced by the new additions; perhaps they will even shape the mainstream of future European political thinking. This should not come as a surprise. In contrast to Western Europe, where material well-being and liberty have removed most deeply controversial themes from public debate, East Europeans have so far gained only liberty and are still striving for material well-being. They are not very interested in the wider world, but instead are preoccupied mostly with themselves; they bring to the East-West debate an urgency of their plight that has already put its stamp on public discussions in Europe as a whole. The fact that German politics are dominated today by the issues of unification reflects, no doubt, a special case. But there are other, no less telling examples of the influence of East European preoccupations and perceptions on political life in all of Europe, such as the understanding shown for East European security concerns vis-à-vis the old Soviet Union, or the widespread view that the European Community should now "open up" to whatever East European country wishes to join.

The point here is not that any one of these aspects is without merit. Rather it is the readiness of Western opinion makers to accept them without much questioning—as if, for instance, there were a real threat to East European security from the East, or as if enlarging the European Community by bringing in economically immature new members would not fundamentally alter the course of European political and economic integration. Not only in the realm of economics, but also in that of public moods, views, and visions could pre-Yalta Europe reassert itself, and in the process even undermine the unique structures of Western integration that the Europe of Yalta has made possible.

Germany's New Status

The second major change affecting Germany, deriving directly from the previous one, is its new status. This is the result of several factors. First, Germany is no longer divided and no longer limited in its sovereignty. Second, Germany plays a central role in the process of East European recovery, due to its location and its economic strength; indeed, over half of all Western assistance to Eastern Europe (even excluding the former German Democratic Republic) has so far come from German sources. Third, German centrality in post-Yalta Europe has made the country more prominent on the international scene as a whole. It also contributed to increased expectations by others concerning German initiatives and, yes, leadership. Finally, it furthered Germany's blocking power.

The context in which this has received most public attention so far is the old "out-of-area" issue, i.e., the question of German participation in efforts to reduce crises and conflicts beyond the NATO area. This was probably understandable in the wake of the

Gulf crisis, where German public abstinence (as opposed to covert massive logistical support) raised many eyebrows in the West. Yet it would be highly misleading to take the Gulf case as a precedent and to regard contingencies outside of Europe as the main testing ground for the international credibility of the new Germany.

The true story of the Gulf crisis confirms, rather than disputes, the importance of Germany for any Western effort at military intervention outside the Western Hemisphere. Had it not been for air bases located in Germany, from which troops were flown to the Gulf, and for the availability of massive German ammunition supplies, Operation Desert Storm would scarcely have succeeded. Although future intervention in Third World crises is unlikely to demand a similarly massive deployment of forces to the theater, logistic dependence on German installations, on troops stationed in Germany, and on supplies provided by Germany will continue to prevail—and so will the need for German willingness to provide such support.

The Gulf analogy is misleading in another, more fundamental, respect as well, namely as it pertains to the widely shared assumption that what happened in and around Kuwait in 1990 was a precedent to future Third World conflicts. For one, each of these conflicts will be special; few, if any, are conceivable in which over half a million men and women must be dispatched abroad, or in which international action is facilitated both by the risk to oil supplies and by the flagrancy of behavior shown by Iraq.

No less important: the popular view that, with strategic bipolarity and the cold war behind us, Third World instability will inevitably proliferate and call for Western intervention, military force included, is no more than an assumption, not a fact. It is by no means certain that the end of strategic rivalry between the Soviet Union and the West will lead to a proliferation of Third World conflicts or an increased need for Western intervention. After all, one of the dangers inherent in the cold war was precisely that of sucking the major powers and their allies into conflicts beyond the immediate arena of East-West competition. Instead of enhancing the risks of proliferation of Third World crises, the new era may well produce better, more efficient methods of crisis resolution. Moreover, the industrialized countries of the North may

generally prefer to respond to turmoil in the South not with intervention but with indifference and noninvolvement. This will, indeed, often be the wiser strategy. Europe's preoccupation with the
task of integrating its Eastern part will give additional justification
to such a preference.

And yet however limited Third World crises may turn out to be,
however rarely they may demand some kind of military intervention, Germany's new status will also be assessed by its behavior in
such contingencies. However much Germans may deplore this, it
is the consequence of a most happy development, namely the
rapid waning of the old threat in Europe and its replacement by
unpredictable, unplannable, and quite possibly secondary crises
around and beyond the European periphery. If the Western security alliance wants to survive, it cannot turn a blind eye to what is
left of real security challenges. If Germany wants to stand aside
when those challenges occur, its credibility as an ally is bound to
suffer. Similarly, if not NATO but perhaps the United Nations or,
at some future stage, the Conference on Security and Cooperation
in Europe (CSCE) were to call on its member states to provide
military units for collective crisis management, and Germany were
to refuse, this would in itself weaken the very chances of collective
action and thus undermine those organizations' ability to operate.
Here, too, Germany's new international status carries with it new
responsibilities.

This does not apply, of course, to Third World contingencies
alone. The visibility of Germany pushes the country into a new
role on practically all international issues. It would be possible, and
may indeed often be desirable, for Germany to refuse active involvement. The problem is that such refusal will, because of the
country's weight, very often amount to blocking collective international efforts altogether. Power, after all, is an objective fact. It
does not disappear for not being exercised in one way or the other.

It is true that the old West Germany already was an influential
factor of international life. But with unification and the changes
that made it possible—the decline of East-West rivalry, the disappearance of the Soviet Union as a Central European power, the
ascendancy of economic over military strength as the most effective instrument of international influence short of a direct military

challenge—Germany has become a major player in the orchestra of nations and has to contribute to the success of the concert.

The European Community

The third change in Germany's international environment concerns those Western organizations that first helped the Federal Republic to acquire international respectability and then became the chief framework for its foreign policy: the Western alliance and the European Community. In post-Yalta Europe, both face a difficult, even painful reorientation of their original purposes. The question for Germany (and indeed for Europe) is whether both will be able to continue to provide the collective framework in which Germany can exert its influence and in which the exercise of its power remains, at the same time, acceptable to its neighbors and allies.

Of the two, the European Community is by far the more ambitious. Its familiar name—the Common Market—hides a far-reaching political vision: that of a new form of union among its member states that will exercise jointly many of the powers that currently are the preserve of national governments. The Germans, having just experienced their own excesses of nationalism, became, after the war, the most enthusiastic supporters of the United States of Europe. Indeed, before the European revolution of 1989, the European Community seemed set on a course of becoming one large market without national barriers (the common internal market as of 1993), one monetary and economic zone (Monetary and Economic Union), and a body progressively merging foreign, security, and even defense policies (Political Union). Although there were often rather theological debates among leading politicians in the twelve member states about the "finality" of the merger, with some—like Margaret Thatcher—emphasizing the sovereignty to be retained by each member state and others stressing the sovereignty to be transferred to European institutions, the march toward a tighter integration of the Community's twelve members seemed well on its way. Western Europe, unentangled by the problems of Eastern Europe, was completing its own house.

But then the revolutions of 1989 brought to an end the Europe

of Yalta. The chief structure for integrating Germany permanently into the West had to adjust to circumstances for which it
seemed ill-prepared. The most important question today is
whether the European Community can make this adjustment
without, at the same time, losing its political cohesion and its vision
of a common future.

The initial reaction of most EC governments when the wall
dividing Europe crumbled (particularly of the most "federalist"
minded, i.e., France and Germany) was to call for an acceleration
of the processes of West European unification, both in the economic and monetary as well as in the political areas. Monetary
policy was to be "communized" beginning in 1993, the European
Council of heads of state and government was to lay down guidelines for a common foreign and security policy to be implemented
by majority vote, and some operational defense cooperation was
similarly envisaged.

In the meantime, all this has been watered down. A new Community treaty, formulated in December 1991, will, as far as external policies are concerned, be rich in words and poor in substance.
This, of course, has been the European practice all along: to lay
down the principles and to leave their implementation for later.
But in this case, something has happened that makes that a dangerous precedent. There is a growing sense in Western Europe
today that the Community will have to depart from its familiar
procedures in order to respond adequately to the exceptional challenge of the wider Europe, which now includes not only the former
European Free Trade Association (EFTA) countries but also those
of Eastern Europe.

Now it is true that the European Community is, of all Western
institutions, the one best equipped to provide hope and stability for
the struggling democracies of Eastern Europe. In this respect, the
Community has acquired a truly strategic role. Since all of these
countries aspire to closer links with the West, and since for all of
them the prospect of economic recovery is the central condition
for the success of their political reforms, the Common Market is
their natural focus. Governments in the East that can claim to
have obtained a special relationship with the Community are in
much better shape to demand those sacrifices from their citizens

that the passage to a market economy necessarily implies.

Thus the Community must not only open itself to the industrialized states of Western Europe, but it must also seek to establish formal relationships with Poland, Czechoslovakia, Hungary, the Baltic states, and others—the list gets longer with every newly independent country emerging from the collapse of those artificial unions that the Soviet Union or Yugoslavia always were. However, these countries do not want to be second-rate members; they want to enjoy full and formal membership in all Community institutions. An increasing number of Western politicians is inclined to promise them just that, as if the state of integration already achieved within the Community were no more than a disposable asset, a bank account from which one can draw whenever one wants to make a major new purchase.

In Community parlance, this poses the dilemma between "deepening" and "widening," i.e., between a policy of pushing economic and political integration among the twelve before opening the Community up to new members, or a policy of admitting new members even at the risk of ending up with a much diluted, more vaguely defined Common Market that would be a trading bloc without either the will or the institutions to act cohesively in the international arena. While politicians claim, of course, that there is no contradiction between these two objectives, the Community has nevertheless arrived at a crossroad. If present trends are any guide, it could well choose the low road of widening membership rather than the high road of deepening integration.

This would be a major reorientation, and one that could profoundly affect the German role in Europe and beyond. Were Western Europe progressively to speak with one voice, the question about German leadership would concern the German role within this Community only. But political union will not happen without a serious commitment. There is a growing risk today of renationalization, fueled on the one hand by the fears felt in many parts of Western Europe about the demands of the internal market starting in 1993, and on the other hand by the new respectability that nationalism has acquired as a result of the East European revolutions of 1989, when it was the most powerful force to overcome Communist regimes. The danger is real that the Community could sacrifice the embryo of political identity for the chance of a Europe-wide network of trade and economic relations. Such a loosely constructed framework would no longer be the kind of Community into which Germany could easily blend and in which it can invest its major influence.

The Atlantic Alliance

The other framework for German international involvement has been the North Atlantic alliance and its primary organization, NATO. It was created to produce, under American leadership, a collective Western response to Soviet power plays and expansionism after the Second World War. Over four decades, NATO became the most successful alliance in modern history. Not only did Western cohesion hold during all those years of East-West tension and detente, in the end the power that had made the whole effort necessary withdrew from the competition and lapsed into a protracted period of disintegration. Thus NATO earned the highest marks possible. As a result, however, it now finds itself deprived of the rationale that gave it purpose.

Of course, old NATO hands would protest and claim that security risks—to be addressed jointly—remain for the West, whether they result from the large remaining arsenal of nuclear weapons on the territory of the former Soviet Union, from the dangers of ethnic troubles in the East and Southeast of Europe escalating into interstate conflict, or from unsettled regions of the Third World. In addition, NATO supporters point to the fact that not one of the sixteen member states has made use of its right to give notice to leave, and that not only its own members, but leading figures in Eastern European politics, too, regard the continuation of NATO as highly desirable.

And yet these protestations of continued relevance cannot camouflage the deep crisis in which the Western alliance finds itself as the result of its own success. It was established to counter an aggressive superpower—that power no longer exists. It was built on the assumption that the threat to the West was calculable and appropriate countermeasures plannable, hence the NATO organization, including the integration of staffs and forces—but the threats of today and tomorrow are, by definition, unpredictable. It remained strong on the basis of a shared priority concern for military security—now that concern no longer dominates. And it offered to the United States, because of its position as a military superpower, the natural role of alliance leader—now with military considerations being pushed into the background, that leadership role is no longer as natural as it once was.

So while NATO's continuing usefulness and the political support it still receives from members and nonmembers alike cannot be denied, the spirit of the enterprise is no longer there. Even if its military organization should survive in greatly reduced size, NATO will become much more peripheral to the chief policy concerns in both Europe and North America—convenient yes, but no longer essential. The difficult question facing the Atlantic alliance is whether it can articulate other collective interests, in addition to the military ones, that demand a common European-American approach. If it cannot, its success will lead to its retirement.

For Germany, the alliance has had, and continues to have, a special function, namely that of making German power controllable and hence acceptable to allies and political adversaries alike. German international acceptance in the 1950s would have been much more difficult without NATO, and Germany's emergence as a major factor in European politics would have caused severe strains. When Mikhail Gorbachev, after some initial hesitation, agreed in July 1990 to united Germany's membership in the Atlantic alliance, he, too, was probably motivated by the consideration that this would help reduce, rather than increase, whatever German dangers he and his country still feared. Britain, France, or Italy outside of NATO would scarcely raise international concerns; Germany without the NATO connection, by contrast, clearly would.

This concern, moreover, is shared not only by non-Germans, but by many Germans as well. German membership in the Western alliance and in the European Community served as the best demonstration that the dangerous German illusions of a *Sonderweg* have finally disappeared. After all, when West Germany joined the alliance and its military organization in 1955, there were many who would have preferred neutrality for their country. But Konrad Adenauer, the Federal Republic's first chancellor, quite rightly decided to give priority to his country's anchorage in Western institutions. Today we know what many did not believe then, namely that this was precisely the road to eventual unification. If the organizational brackets of Germany's "Westernization" should fall into disrepair, a sense of uncertainty over the future of Germany would grow both within and outside the country.

So the conditions of Germany's international involvement are changing, often dramatically. The Europe of Yalta is gone, the visibility of Germany on the international scene has increased, and yet the structures that offered German power a collective purpose are becoming looser. To ask what German leadership should achieve and German visions define is to ask what the priorities of Germany should be in this very different world of the 1990s.

The Priority of European Unification

German political leaders like to argue that the foremost German contribution to international stability is to complete the process of unification, i.e., the integration of East Germany into the Federal Republic of Germany. Although this argument is, in many regards, a self-serving one, it nevertheless cannot be dismissed entirely, for the simple reason that a Germany constantly preoccupied with problems of national unity is unlikely to play any major international role.

The trouble is, of course, that in politics, as in life, it never rains, it pours. In other, more protected circumstances, the German preference for putting its national house in order before accepting additional international responsibilities might have stood a chance. Under the conditions of post-Yalta Europe, however, other issues will not wait, in particular not the decision on the future shape of Europe—which is, in the first instance, the shape of the European Community. In fact, should the European Community degenerate into nothing more than a large free trade area, it would neither provide the collective framework in which Germany's power becomes palatable for its neighbors, nor would it be capable of generating serious support for the countries of Central and Eastern Europe. It would also not develop into a true partner for the United States. Hence what happens to the European Community is a strategic decision of the first order. It is here that German leadership and vision have to prove themselves.

Without a coherent, politically effective, and progressively integrated European Community, Germany could well become a burden rather than a support for European stability. This danger arises not only, and not even primarily, from the fears that Germany's past still keeps awake in the memories of its neighbors. It is also, and more decisively, the consequence of Germany's size and weight in European affairs. Powerful, overbearing countries are rarely capable of generating trust among their smaller neighbors, however much these may appeal to the stronger country for help and support. If, once again, Germany's neighbors should want to coalesce against it, in order to balance its power, Europe could be pushed into the old cycle of shifting balances and instabilities it has experienced before. The looser the European Community, the more strongly German power will stand out. There will be a new German problem, just when the old one has been laid to rest.

Similarly, if the Community becomes no more than a free trade area from the Atlantic to the Urals by accepting many of the newly democratic states of Eastern Europe into full membership, its ability to assist these countries on the difficult march to economic prosperity and political stability will be severely circumscribed. EC membership would, it is true, satisfy their yearning for equal status and full political participation. But it would fall well short of any effective help toward their immediate economic difficulties. Membership in the Common Market could be the kiss of death for those fledgling economies; indeed, what they need most is long-term protection against the onslaught of Western industrial competition on the one side and access to Western markets for their products on the other. Even if the twelve governments of the Community—all of which have to agree to admit new members—were to allow Poland, Hungary, or even Lithuania into their midst (and this is highly unlikely in the near future), it would amount to a relationship that would be healthy neither for any of those countries nor for the Community as a whole. In economic terms, these countries would remain second-rate members for a very long time, while in political terms they could slow down and even block the process toward closer political integration.

The full admission of East European countries would threaten to turn the Community into an indecisive coalition, unwilling and unable to mount the kind of generous assistance programs that would be required for Eastern Europe, as well as too unwieldy to move down the road to political integration. While there is no guarantee that the twelve EC members will display the generosity needed, there is at least a greater chance for collective action when those that need assistance address the Community from without, rather than when they are members themselves and have to compete with others in the framework of established Community procedures.

Finally, a strong, cohesive European Community is the precondition for a strong, cohesive Atlantic alliance. That may come as a surprise to those in the United States and Europe who have been, and still are, highly suspicious of a European Community that, in addition to economic, fiscal, and trade issues, also wants to develop common foreign, security, and defense policies. The beginning of 1991 once again brought forth this traditional Atlanticist concern as Washington shot a verbal broadside across the bow of the slow-moving European ship when, in response to modest Franco-German ideas concerning joint European defense efforts, it warned of terrible dangers this could cause NATO. But however familiar the inertia of large organizations, however natural such a clinging to the status quo may be, however both may even have been justified in the Europe of Yalta, they are today a demonstration not of vision, but of shortsightedness.

For one thing, as has been pointed out earlier, the Atlantic alliance, under new international circumstances, cannot remain what it has been. It must broaden its mission beyond that of military security. That requirement, however, means that the European Community, in all areas in which integration has already occurred, is America's natural opposite number in Europe. This applies not only to trade (where the Community, not its individual member states, is in charge of negotiations), but also to such strategic tasks as that of assisting East European democracies and Soviet republics. The Bush administration, as a series of major speeches by the president and his secretary of state during 1989 and 1990 amply demonstrated, has fully recognized this role of the European Community.

The idea that defense—the next step, so to say—should be excluded from European integration is not only illogical, it also runs against the interests of both the Community and the Atlantic alliance. A European Community in which most other aspects of national policies, but not defense, are being merged will never be credible as a political union. It would be capable neither of providing a European framework for Germany, nor a European partner for the United States. However understandable the American desire to maintain NATO (and American influence within it) as it is, and however justified American concerns that European NATO members should not exclude the United States from decision-making processes that affect its role and responsibilities in Europe, both of these concerns are, in essence, not primary and strategic but secondary and tactical. They should not blind American leaders to the fact that without a functioning, vibrant European Community, the North American link to Europe would become progressively tenuous.

Thus the German vision must be to integrate a United Germany firmly into a uniting Europe, the Europe of the Community. The future will show whether this vision can become reality. But one thing is certain: it will not come true if Germany fails to put its full weight behind the integration effort. German leadership will, therefore, have to prove itself first and foremost in the construction of a united Europe. The Federal Republic will have to push, to compromise, to build coalitions, to offer material incentives. It will have to respect the institutions and procedures of the Community, while making good use of them at the same time. In this Germany will be the more successful, the less its European faith is in doubt.

Whether Germany will practice this kind of leadership is, of course, another matter. The preoccupation with national unification drains energy from efforts at supranational unification. The economic strains that result from the task of rebuilding East German industry and commerce could weaken both Germany's readiness to use its economic power for the furtherance of European integration and Germany's political clout among its partners and allies. Concerns over Eastern Europe, coupled with dismay over intra-Community squabbling, could take the conviction out of Germany's European commitment. Helmut Kohl may well be the last instinctively pro-Community chancellor; his successors will be less unquestioning in their support. Yet leadership means precisely not to swim with the tide if it goes in the wrong direction, but against it. The leadership test for Germany in the 1990s will be found here. And there still is a good chance that the test will be met.

Of course, this falls well short of that "partnership in leadership" to which President Bush invited Germany (and West Germany at that) in 1989. That notion conveys the image of a tandem of two powerful countries that get things moving in the right direction, of two chief executive officers in a joint company. Instead, this chapter suggests a united Germany in a united Europe, and Europe as the natural partner of America. This is not a proposal to escape responsibility, quite the opposite.

For what better alternative is there for the United States? A powerful Germany, unconstrained by any European framework, might please the realpolitiker in Washington. But its very existence would imply a failure of U.S. postwar European policies. Moreover, the United States has learned, over the past four decades, to cope with lesser powers without hurting their feelings too much or reducing its own ability to get its way; that is an achievement that will continue to be helpful in dealing with Europe. America's European position will depend, even more than before, on Europeans wanting America to be there.

Above all, it would be extremely shortsighted for the United States to appeal to U.S.–German bilateralism at the expense of Germany's European role. If Germany were to respond accordingly, this would put the cohesion already achieved within the Community at risk. Were Germany to decline the offer, this would be interpreted, without much justification, as an anti-American move. France under Charles de Gaulle and many of his successors made the fundamental mistake of asking Germany to choose between Paris and Washington, a choice the Germans wisely refused to make. But if the United States were now to ask Germany to choose between Europe and America, Germany would in all probability not pick America.

Cooperation without such ultimata is, however, likely to be much easier for the United States of the 1990s than that of the 1980s. There has been much criticism of President Bush's notion of a "new world order"; many ridiculed it as an idea devoid of substance. Perhaps they should reconsider. For behind that notion lies the proposal that the United States, far from wanting to be the world's solitary policeman, is no longer prepared to "pay any price" and "bear any burden" to ensure international stability. It will pay a price, but as its contribution to a collective effort. America, so the president's message goes, is willing to take part, even take on the major part, in international order keeping. But it is no longer willing to do this alone. Thus the "new world order" actually depends on America finding suitable "partners in leadership." If this analysis is correct, and it seems supported by the growing pressure on Washington to turn its attention to internal American issues, then America's future foreign policy will be focused on coalition efforts, not on unilateral action. America, in other words, will be better prepared for the kind of partner into which the European Community can develop—and it may not have much choice.

Those who think that a Germany acting in and through a united Europe will be let off the hook of international responsibility should think again. It would be much easier for Germany to rely on its own weight and influence rather than blend its resources and interests with those of the European Community. But it will make an enormous difference to American interests whether Germany plays a role separate from the Community or stays in the European chorus line.

Moreover, Germany will assume international responsibility for the major strategic challenges facing the West in the 1990s more effectively within than outside the European Community. This obviously applies, for reasons outlined above, to the task of solidifying political and economic reforms in Eastern Europe. It applies no less to the future relationship with Russia and the remains of the Soviet Union. On one level, of course, this can only be addressed by the United States itself, namely, insofar as the weapons of central nuclear deterrence are concerned. But in all other respects, dealing with the Eurasian power conglomerate that was once the Soviet Union will be a collective Western task, whether it concerns conventional arms control, proliferation, or economic and other assistance in nation building for the major republics.

In these areas, the era of German- (or, for that matter, American-) Russian bilateralism is clearly over. The one more or less bilateral Soviet-German issue left after unification is the departure of Soviet forces from German territory, scheduled to be completed by 1994. For the rest, the German government has repeatedly stressed that its own resources do not allow any additional unilateral assistance. The post-Soviet problem is not how to relate to any one country, but how to relate to the collective structures of the West—and hence there can be no lone Western riders. Germany may push here and there, as it has done in the past, for a more forthcoming Western response to the Soviet Union. But this has to be a Western, not a German, response if it is to make any sense at all.

The collective framework will also be the one most effective in dealing with the issue of German military intervention beyond the NATO area. For reasons discussed above, it is difficult to imagine that this will be, for any Western country, the major part of its defense activities. But even in the likely lesser contingencies, Germany will grow into a participatory role much more easily if the call is not for Germans but for Europeans to go to the front. The Yugoslav crisis of 1991 confirmed this. The debates over a German contribution to a possible "buffer force" were much less dominated by the familiar (and largely unfounded) constitutional arguments than by the real question, namely, whether such a force would make much sense under the circumstances.

Collective procedures thus will increasingly define the substance of policy, both for Germany and its partners. Nobody can be sure of future contingencies. Hence precise strategies will be less important than agreed procedures on how to arrive at a common response. What is needed now in the Atlantic alliance is to develop those common political procedures in addition to those that already exist in the military and arms control field—and to develop them jointly with the European Community.

Germany in Europe—this is the answer to the question about Germany's vision and leadership. It is, in a way, an old-fashioned answer in that it endorses the vision of Jean Monnet, Robert Schuman, Konrad Adenauer, and, hopefully, Helmut Kohl. It is, at the same time, an imperfect answer. Nobody can be certain today that the European Community will indeed progress to the stage envisaged here. Yet there is no more constructive way in which Germany can contribute to international stability in post-Yalta Europe than through the completion of the European Political Union. Everything else will only be second best.

4

Limits of Leadership: The United States

CHARLES McC. MATHIAS

I n this final decade of the twentieth century, the United States appears to stand alone as a superpower. After four decades during which both the USSR and the United States of America possessed the ability to wreak massive destruction anywhere on the globe, there is now reason to question whether the formidable array of weapons that remains in Soviet territory could be effectively deployed on a global basis. To the extent that one may also question the capacity of the Soviet arsenal to be deployed as a deterrent to American force, except for United States military

CHARLES McC. MATHIAS served as United States senator from Maryland from 1969 to 1987. He was previously a member of the Maryland House of Delegates and the U.S. House of Representatives. In 1985 he was unanimously elected president of the North Atlantic Assembly, which is composed of members of legislative bodies of the NATO countries. He has received the Order of Merit of the Federal Republic of Germany. He is Commander of the Legion of Honor (France), and a Knight Commander of the Order of the British Empire. Senator Mathias is a partner in the international law firm of Jones, Day, Reavis & Pogue. He is chair of the American Council on Germany.

action directed against the Soviet republics themselves, one may perceive the degree to which American power alone stands out worldwide. It is no surprise, therefore, that there is deep interest in America's role in the world, and some concern about whether the new world order will in fact be a Pax Americana imposed by American power.

This chapter argues that the constraints on American power remain substantial despite the absence of a rival superpower. The principal argument here is that the limits on American power are primarily internal rather than external. Some of these internal constraints derive from the nature of the American political process and are therefore somewhat familiar, even if not necessarily well understood. Others, however, are newly the result of substantial changes within American society—changes whose total impact has only recently become visible after successive years of gradual evolution. The United States of the 1990s is vastly different from that of the 1940s, and in a crucial manner the dimensions of that difference will define and limit the role of American power around the globe.

Demographic Change

Perhaps the largest and most meaningful change in the United States is the continuing change in American demographics. The United States has been a nation of immigrants from its beginnings, and it is no surprise that immigration into the United States continues and is likely to continue for the indefinite future. However, in the post–World War II period the majority of those who voluntarily entered the United States year after year were not of European origin but rather came primarily from Latin America and the Caribbean, or from Southeast Asia. In addition, a substantial component of immigration into the United States during the most recent decades has been illegal and is, therefore, difficult to count precisely. The present and future results of continuing immigration swelled by an illegal component beyond such restrictions as apply to the lawful immigration process can already be perceived as dramatic and will become markedly more dramatic in the near future. At mid-century, the American population was still preponderantly of European origin, with a relatively stable African-American component of approximately 12 percent and significantly smaller fractions of the population of Asian or Latin American origin. United States government projections based on the decennial census of the American population now indicate that at the turn of the twenty-first century only three of every five Americans will be of European descent, and the most explosive growth within the population of the United States is among citizens of Latin American origin, resulting from a combination of immigration and subsequent human reproduction.

The long-range forecast is that by the middle of the twenty-first century a majority of American citizens—approximately three out of five—will be of non-European descent. The proportion of the African-American population will increase only slightly, to approximately 14 percent. The population of Americans of Asian descent will have more than tripled between the mid-twentieth to the mid-twenty-first centuries, from slightly less than 3 percent to some 11 or 12 percent. The proportion of Americans of Latin American descent is expected to reach nearly 30 percent.

Obviously such major change in the domestic demography of the United States is subject to an enormous range of interpretation and comment, and no attempt will be made here to address this subject in depth. However, at least two aspects of a demographic evolution of a scale that suggests a revolution do have an inevitable impact on the role of the United States in the world. Because the American democracy requires a workable consensus with respect to foreign policy, substantial changes in the composition of the American population increase the difficulty of forming such a consensus. Also, it has been generally assumed, both in the United States and abroad, that the American population of European descent retained some combination of interest in and memory of Europe. To the extent that such may have had some validity in the past, it is less applicable in view of the demographic changes taking place in the United States.

There has been speculation in recent years that somehow the American national interest might be in the process of tilting toward the Pacific and away from the Atlantic relationships. While it is true that the continued population explosion in the western

American states and the emergence of major new trading partners along the Pacific Rim—most notably, but no longer exclusively, Japan—have resulted in major new transpacific American interests, this seems more like a correction of a balance between transatlantic and transpacific interests than a definitive Pacific tilt.

A more likely gloss that can be applied to these fundamental demographic changes would invoke the likelihood that they will result in some lessening of popular interest in the United States in a variety of international matters. It is already proving difficult to digest the full extent of demographic change in the United States. Until recently, for example, it was universally taken for granted that the American version of the English language was the sole official language of the United States. Today, however, that seems a more questionable assumption. In a variety of ways, Spanish has begun to emerge as a second language in the United States. Ballots for local elections are already bilingual in a number of American communities, and a vigorous and controversial discussion is under way in a number of states as to whether public schools should continue to offer instruction exclusively in English or whether instruction in Spanish should be made available to children whose knowledge of English is so scant as to constitute a major impediment to their ability to learn in English. It is also a fact that ethnic slurs and jokes, which remained a staple of discourse in earlier decades, are now being eradicated from public utterance as part of an understandable—if overdue—effort to maintain a public climate of civility within the increasingly diverse American population.

Crisis in the Cities

A forecast that the population of the United States is likely to be more inclined toward preoccupation with America's internal affairs does not hinge solely on the phenomenon of change in ethnic demography. It depends at least as much on one or two other socioeconomic developments. The first of these has to do with the emergence of the large American city as an enormous problem area. On the one hand, there has been a continuing flow of the American population from rural areas into the metropolitan concentrations. At the same time, the more affluent population has abandoned the urban core and established rapidly growing new communities on the outer metropolitan periphery. It is a mistake to characterize these new communities as suburbs, although most of them are of suburban origin. These new communities are in fact emerging as cities in their own right and increasingly lack the extent of dependence on the core city that is characteristic of suburban areas. Office and shopping space is increasing in these new cities on the metropolitan fringe substantially faster than within the city itself. Even cultural institutions such as symphonies and museums are becoming part of these new communities, which compose a metropolitan area and use metropolitan public services, such as water, sewage, and transportation, but have less and less dependence on the core city that still lends its name to the metropolitan area.

There is an obvious and potentially destructive component to this metropolitan evolution. In fact, economic vigor continues to drain from the core of the metropolitan area to the new communities on its edges. The bulk of the population on those edges is of European descent. The inner city increasingly has become or is becoming the home of Americans not of European descent. To a notable extent, poverty and concomitant crime are becoming the hallmarks of the American inner city. A vicious socioeconomic circle has become operative. As economic vigor in the inner city declines, the tax base shrinks. Public services shrink along with the tax base. Older housing stock now populated primarily by those with severely limited economic means continues to decay and turns into slum. Funding for the support of public education becomes increasingly scarce, and a growing number of those who drop out of the educational process in early youth become part of a growing population of unemployed. A hostile observer might go so far as to ask whether the present state of American metropolitan life can be characterized as apartheid in reverse, with the inner city serving as a ghetto for a majority of economically poor who are not of European descent while the more affluent of European descent have created new communities for themselves on the metropolitan fringe.

Such hostile comments may go too far, but there are worrisome portents in the current discussion about the privatization of metropolitan public services. To the extent that the primary dependence on the inner city on the part of the new communities on the metropolitan edge is represented by shared public services, it has been possible to sever even that linkage through a process of privatization that would allow those who could afford it to pay for public services, while abandoning the quality of publicly financed services for those who cannot afford the cost of privatization.

These developments in the socioeconomic evolution of the American metropolis are related to a major shift in the practice of American federalism that was accomplished in the 1980s. At that time, a major effort was undertaken by the American federal government to reduce, or at least contain, the growing federal deficit without reducing expenditures for national defense or raising taxes. A principal instrument toward this purpose was a major devolution of social responsibilities to the state and local levels of American government. By the 1990s, this process had been largely completed, and as an inevitable consequence, almost all states and localities in the United States face deficit problems, and the delivery of social services has necessarily been curtailed. Fiscal pain at a local level generally is harder to bear than at the national level. Understandably, therefore, slow but inexorable pressure is beginning to build for new forms of relief at the federal level to help restore local social services.

In the short run, this translates into an evident desire to take advantage of the waning of Soviet power by reductions in national defense expenditures on a scale that would free tax revenues for social programs without requiring a significant increase in federal taxation. In the long run, however, the same pressure, if it continues or grows, is likely to result in a prevalent public consensus that addressing a whole host of severe social problems at a local level must take precedence over international matters, at least and particularly with respect to expenditures. Even today, all discussion of major new programs of assistance to Eastern Europe and the former Soviet Union is immediately accompanied by a chorus of comment referring to the primacy of domestic needs that demand greater domestic expenditures in the multibillion dollar range.

Costs of the Cold War

There can be no doubt but that the United States paid a substantial price for what can properly be described as its victory in the cold war. To some extent, the superpower rivalry between the United States and the USSR created a mirror image between the two rivals. Nowhere was this more visible than in the degree to which both superpowers taxed their internal resources in order to support their military establishments. It is generally assumed that it was in fact the strain of striving for continuous parity with the United States that broke the back of the Soviet economy and brought on *perestroika*. The enormous burdens carried by the United States to support its military establishment fell far short of destroying the American economy, but it was the principal factor in the escalation of the American national debt from roughly $1 trillion at the beginning of the 1980s to $3 trillion by the beginning of the 1990s.

There is a paradox in the fact that at the moment when capitalism seems to have won a final victory and the United States is a virtual symbol of capitalism, there is a shortage of capital in the United States and, indeed, in the industrial world. The condition seems to be the result of unprecedented demands for capital in the immediate future (e.g., German unification, Persian Gulf War, environmental initiatives, and the savings and loan/failed bank bailouts in the United States) and of policies that have not adequately encouraged the formation of capital. The paradox is illustrated by the status of the United States, the world's preeminent capitalist country, as a net importer of capital rather than a net exporter of capital.

Whenever a nation must depend on foreign sources for a vital commodity, it surrenders some measurable fraction of its sovereignty, or at least a measure of its freedom of action. This is no less true of capital than of food or energy, and dependence on external supplies of any one of them becomes a limiting factor in the development and execution of foreign policy. Foreign central banks in a recent year provided funds to cover approximately 85 percent of the United States budget deficit. This is a serious enough reliance on outside assistance to affect official views on foreign policy in significant ways. If the access to foreign capital is obstructed either by deliberate action, which is not currently likely, or by extraneous events, such as the economic demands of German unification, some sober solutions will have to be sought.

The reversal of the policies that created this situation seems a remote possibility. The 1981 reduction of government revenues by a massive tax cut became an icon for the Bush administration as it was for President Reagan. The other course, to reduce expenditures enough to make the difference, is not feasible. Therefore the resulting weakness in foreign policy options will continue.

As one begins to consider the possible ingredients of a new domestic consensus with respect to the foreign policy of the United States, one cannot fail to recognize an initial expectation on the part of the American people that there will be an economic reward for the successful conclusion of the long struggle to maintain the cold war. It will seem obvious that the disintegration of the single rival power should produce the benefit of substantially reduced expenditures for national defense. Whatever Americans expect of the post–cold war world, they want and expect it to be cheaper. Americans proved willing for decades to carry the full burden of national defense as long as they felt a constant and real threat from abroad to the security of the United States. Unless a threat of similar magnitude arises, Americans have every reason to wish to give first priority to domestic expenditures and to reduce the burdens of national defense as much as possible.

Difficulties of a
Foreign Policy Consensus

The greatest problem that confronts American leadership with respect to future foreign policy is to achieve a new national foreign policy consensus in the absence of a powerful external threat. It is generally true throughout human society—not just in the United States alone—that it is easier to rally popular sentiment against a threat than in support of something positive. Increasingly, however, the workings of a democratic American political process appear to put a premium on this negative aspect of public motivation. The fundamental reason behind this observation seems to lie at least in some part in the extraordinary diversity of the American population.

The current practice of American politics encourages the formation of pressure groups, whose presence, of course, is universally recognized by observers of the political scene in the United States. The power of these pressure groups is primarily fiscal. They are legally entitled to spend money in support of political candidates, and in the American democratic process that support not only begins with candidacy but continues in order to maintain incumbency. In the United States, paid political advertising is the norm in political campaigning. That advertising primarily involves the medium of television, in which airtime as well as the production of advertising material is becoming increasingly expensive. In most states, candidacies for statewide office now require multimillion dollar budgets, and even local candidacies for the House of Representatives or for mayoral office in most cities may demand expenditures of at least a million dollars.

Pressure groups exercise their influence by contributing to particular political campaigns, and the most effective pressure groups in practice have proven to be those that concentrate their efforts on a single issue. Each pressure group generates its funds from contributions, given by individuals, organizations, or both. The amassing of funds by a single issue pressure group is facilitated not only because a single issue is relatively easy to explain and understand, but because progress in support of that issue is relatively easy to measure. Over time, an interesting inversion is becoming more commonplace. This inversion involves the fact that while almost all pressure groups are named and publicly explained in positive terms in support of a positive goal, their actual activities tend more and more to be defensive, i.e., negative. To a significant extent, the majority of pressure groups in American politics measures their success more by preventing legislation or other action that would set back their cause than by the achievement of positive legislation or administrative action that would positively promote their cause.

These observations on the American political process are not intended as a mere digression into a civics lesson. They have a direct bearing on the conduct of American national policy on the larger scale, and therefore have quite immediate relevance to the nature and conduct of American foreign policy. The mythology of American politics generally still clings to the hypothesis that policy is made on the basis of agreement by a majority and that candidates are elected on the same basis. Increasingly, however, the reality of American politics is that policy is arrived at on the basis of offending the fewest, and that candidates also tend to be elected by a shrinking electorate, relative to total population. The political scene in the United States is now studded with aggregations that are relatively few in number, but are quite well organized and funded to promote and defend an ever growing variety of special interests.

This vastly complicates the achievement of any kind of political majority. The larger the issue, the harder consensus is to find. Large issues are, therefore, more likely to be compromised, less to attract more support but more to avoid alienating identifiable and very specific groups of voters. This process is reinforced by the fact that voter participation in the American electoral process is generally not marked by large turnouts.

Thus the winning of elections at all levels of American politics is not based on an effort to attract large numbers of potentially un-committed voters who are motivated to vote from a sense of civic duty. Rather, elections are won either by attracting voters to participate in the election, and/or by remaining attractive to voters who are persuaded to vote by pressure group activity devoted to a series of single causes. The "silent majority" in American elections consists of the citizens who do not vote at all and not of those who are motivated to go to the polls.

Ever more refined techniques for polling public sentiment greatly assist the process of pressure group politics. Contemporary campaigning no longer thinks of or deals with voters en masse. It deals not only with voters clearly identified with individual pressure groups, but also voters electronically grouped together by age, sex, ethnic derivation, income status, geographic location within neighborhoods, and the like. On this basis, new truisms have become widely known and accepted. It is dangerous, for example, to alienate senior citizens of middle-income status, because they tend to participate in elections in large numbers. On the other hand, it is relatively safe to alienate low-income urban citizens of non-European extraction because their electoral participation tends to be minimal.

In this context, it can generally be observed that international matters only play a significant role in the American electoral process when the American people perceive themselves to be directly threatened, as was eventually the case in World Wars I and II and during the cold war. The population of the United States has a deserved reputation for a relative lack of awareness of international affairs when compared with most other highly developed societies. However, pressure group activity devoted to an international cause, as exists in the American electoral process, tends to be disproportionately effective because it will frequently lack competition. Committed special interests such as support of Northern Ireland, Israel, Greek rights in Cyprus, racial justice in South Africa, or other overseas causes often operate in the absence of pressure groups explicitly opposed to their goals.

In the light of these observations, one can begin to grasp the enormous difficulty of forming a new American consensus with respect to the future American role in the world. In the volatile democratic society of the United States it is, in fact, easier to describe the nature of such a consensus in the abstract than to give it specific content. Therefore, a new consensus with respect to foreign policy should rest on relatively few fundamental propositions that both make sense and are simple to understand and explain. It should have practical goals, at least in the sense of being able to reach relatively clear results in a relatively short time. At the same time, it should not be too clear on any point that would significantly offend a whole variety of special interest groups, and it should also allow for some continuity because it will need to be invoked for longer than simply one election.

Two illustrations of how these considerations apply may be useful. It was possible for the Bush administration to obtain a consensus to oppose Iraq's seizure of Kuwait. There was widespread public understanding that unchecked naked aggression represented a threat to any prospect of a world of peace and, therefore, to the United States' national interest; that aggressive action potentially capable of threatening current American dependence on

Middle East oil represented an even more serious threat; and that unopposed Iraqi aggression also represented a vital threat to Israel. However, the relief and acclaim that subsequently greeted the unexpectedly rapid and total triumph over the Iraqi military forces should not obscure the anguished and deeply controversial debate that accompanied the decision to undertake massive military intervention during the months between the initial aggression and the ultimate outbreak of hostilities. Furthermore, there was no consensus as to how to deal with Iraq after victory, which had an obvious influence on the lack of clear policy in the wake of the military triumph.

A different example is offered by current American foreign policy with respect to the People's Republic of China. In general, a consensus with respect to China should present no particular difficulty because by and large, public American attitudes toward China tend to be marked primarily by indifference. However, the televised and direct images of naked repression in Tiananmen Square left an indelible mark on popular American consciousness that will take considerably more time to eradicate, and that has created a prevailing negative consensus within the American public toward the Chinese government. This negative attitude is further reinforced by the fact that the official policies of population control in the People's Republic of China are deeply offensive to the well-organized right-to-life pressure group in the United States, which primarily operates in the domestic context alone, but could easily be mobilized against any pro-Chinese foreign policy if effectively stimulated.

On the broadest scale, a fundamental consensus has governed American attitudes toward the rest of the world from the inception of the republic right through to the present. It was true at the beginning and remains true that Americans seek to live in a world sufficiently peaceful so as not to threaten or interfere with the pursuit of happiness and prosperity within the United States, and sufficiently open to free commerce so as to enable Americans to buy and sell abroad on a fair and reciprocal basis. Such a broad statement may at first reading seem to be virtually devoid of content, but this is not the case. The concept that the United States does not seek domination over the world, nor any part thereof, remains valid today. There is also no territory beyond the borders of the United States that America covets. There have been additions to American territory in the past, but some came by purchase and, with the exception of the American-Mexican War of 1846–48, even those that came through acts of war did not constitute the goal of the war, nor has there been a determined effort to retain them. The power of the United States is sufficiently great for America to attempt to play an imperial role, but there is very little in the American past or present that makes it likely that the United States would ever embark on such an effort, or that a public American consensus would ever support a policy designed to do so.

Objectives of American Power

Some observers of the collapse of the Soviet Union and of the problems so clearly evident on the American domestic scene believe that there is evidence that the United States is a power in decline whose worldwide influence is therefore on the wane. In large part this would seem to be a misjudgment. It is true that Americans have traditionally lacked the will to impose their authority on others by the use of force. However, it is equally true that the United States has unfailingly responded effectively to an obvious threat directed against it. Some will argue that power wanes unless it is exercised. The counter argument is that the latent power to respond to challenges is sufficient both to deter such challenges and to defeat them when they arise.

There should be little doubt as to the continuing latent power of the United States. There have been periods in the past when Americans were much preoccupied with digesting continuing and dramatic demographic changes produced by immigration. In fact, it can be argued that the severe problems of the core cities in the United States today had something of a precursor in the latter part of the nineteenth century when continuing waves of immigration from Eastern and Southern Europe also produced slum conditions in the major inner cities. Whatever problems immigration brings, it brings new strength and energy as well. The vitality and energy of the American population remain as impressive as ever, and this is likely to be true as long as the immigration process continues, even though recent immigration is so predominantly of non-European origin. If, in fact, more of America's resources can be applied to address domestic problems, it should be expected that the energies and talents of the American population will be more than sufficient to maintain the power of the United States at the highest level for the indefinite future.

Therefore the future role of the United States in the world will be determined less by power potential than by the will to use power. Thus the fundamental challenge to the formation of a new foreign policy consensus in the United States is to create a rationale for the use of American power. The lack of will to establish a worldwide American empire also argues against a consensus for the role of the United States as world policeman. There is too little difference between an American empire and a world order enforced by the United States alone. However, this is not to say that the American people do not seek and would not support a world order designed to promote international peace and free trade. Rather, this is an objective of United States foreign policy. The American path toward this objective is likely to be the same as that followed after World Wars I and II—namely, the use of an international organization in which the United States is prepared to play a leading role. It is possible to envision a world order based on the fullest possible use of the United Nations, or a world order based on a different pattern of alliances in which again the United States would be a leading actor. It is not possible to envision a world order based on American hegemony because there is no likelihood of an American consensus to support such a role.

The two aspects of a fundamental American consensus with respect to the rest of the world that have been identified are sufficient stability and peace to avoid a direct threat to the United States, and free commerce. At this stage of the evolution of the United States, a third and possibly a fourth ingredient appear to have emerged, or to be emerging. The third ingredient is a commitment to human rights that speaks not only to the American tradition of the past, but to the pressing domestic needs of an ethnically diverse population. Americans have come to regard the violation of human rights as a potential threat to the continuing well-being of their own future as the ethnic diversity of the population increases. This conviction is constantly reinforced by those new immigrants to the United States who are motivated to leave their former domiciles because their human rights were being violated.

There is no evidence that the American people have much interest in using their resources and the power of the United States to propagate democratic forms of government in lands abroad. There is, however, growing evidence that the American people are prepared to use both resources and power to prevent the violation of human rights elsewhere in the world because these violations deny the very basis of the American existence. Therefore the opportunity does seem to exist for the explicit inclusion of a worldwide commitment to human rights within a future American foreign policy consensus. This would represent a somewhat more positive and assertive potential than merely the preservation of peaceful stability and free commerce.

The potential fourth, and only emerging, ingredient of a consensus relates to the preservation of the global environment. Americans clearly share a concern regarding developments that would adversely affect human life on the planet Earth. As far as the general public is concerned, too little is known or certain about a number of such potential threats or developments. There would seem to be little doubt, however, that the American people would be prepared actively to oppose actions clearly known and acknowledged to cause serious environmental damage. Problems relating to climate change, depletion of the ozone layer, possible eradication of species, and toxic effects of industrial or agricultural production have come to the forefront of public attention only very recently. This, coupled with the fact that there is still so much ignorance, should not preclude anticipation that concerns about these matters are likely to grow, and equally likely to emerge as a significant new factor in international affairs.

The United States from its beginnings has positioned itself as a nation apart from all others, both as the home of a free society increasingly committed to the absolute attainable human freedom, and as the last and best refuge for the oppressed of the world. Because America remains a nation of immigrants, it seems very likely that this self-image will continue in its seasoned form, both as a prevailing mythology and a goal to be pursued. Therefore, a worldwide role for the United States as guarantor of human freedom may prove attractive to the American population. However, freedom, by definition, cannot be imposed. Others can strive to achieve it, but no one can bestow it on them.

It has also proven difficult, if not impossible, to achieve freedom for others by the use of force. Certainly this is one of the bitter lessons learned by America's venture in Vietnam. The trauma of Vietnam, America's single greatest failure in international affairs during the twentieth century, has made it difficult for Americans to draw conclusions from the experience. More recently, however, the inability of the astonishing success of the use of force against Iraq to produce freedom for the Iraqi people may make the lesson easier to absorb. It is, therefore, unlikely that an American role as the guarantor of human rights would serve simply to mask an American role as world policeman. What is more likely is that the United States will use economic and financial power, rather than military force, to promote human rights on an international scale.

A Look Ahead

There may now be a period during which the United States and the American people can reassess their worldwide responsibilities without the threat of external aggression and within the context of higher priority for domestic ills. However this is far from certain. One may continue to hope that a world released from the enduring threat of superpower nuclear confrontation will not erupt into a series of local conflicts. Unfortunately it is much too soon to know whether such hope will be realized or disappointed. The revolution of August 1991 ended the form in which the Soviet Union had existed for most of the twentieth century, but the restructuring of the Soviet republics into some durable new patterns will likely take years to achieve. Under the best of circumstances, that restructuring will occur without armed conflict, but that too is hope rather than certainty. Therefore, the only likely forecast for the international scene is a period of extreme uncertainty and relatively high risk.

Although a return to more stable and durable new patterns of international order may be a number of years away, the United States has already begun a restructuring of its military establishment away from possible conflict with a rival superpower to a greater ability for rapid and potentially large-scale intervention in more limited conflicts on a global basis. The continuing analysis of "lessons learned" during the conflict in the Persian Gulf is certain to influence the course of that restructuring, as will the dramatic new developments with respect to the reduction of nuclear weapons in the United States and the Soviet Union.

The United States will also continue to rely heavily on existing alliances and make every effort to reshape these alliances in response to the new circumstances. There has already been, for example, a decision not even to consider the termination of the NATO alliance, but rather to recast NATO so that it will continue to play a significant role. The United States will also reconsider the possible role of the United Nations in the still highly guarded expectation that a leading American role will not inevitably be handicapped by those who cast the votes of the Soviet Union or the People's Republic of China in the Security Council. Major evidence of such reconsideration can already be found in the willingness of the United States to cooperate in the current deliberations toward restructuring the United Nations administrative organization.

The American effort to rely as much as possible on alliances, and perhaps on the United Nations as well, is a necessary component of the American need and desire to avoid unnecessary entanglements whenever possible. The best example of the determination is offered by the case of Yugoslavia. The United States and, therefore, NATO have refrained from the effort to intervene in this Balkan tragedy, and the United States looks to its European allies to deal with the problem instead. On the other hand, the United States has not been able to avoid profound entanglement in the Middle East, but there also an enormous effort was made to involve allies and to avoid a unilateral American role as much as possible.

The principal purpose of such short-term strategies is, of course, to work toward the possibility of greater stability and more durable arrangements in the long run. The overriding objective is to avoid conflict if at all possible, and to prepare and preserve the most attractive long-term options. The USSR may have ceased to be an effective superpower, but it still casts a huge shadow over world affairs. It is inconceivable that long-term strategies toward a more stable world order can evolve until more definite calculations and expectations can be applied to the future form of the Soviet republics.

With respect both to Europe and to the former Soviet Union, the only effective course for the United States is to refrain from undertaking a lead role and to rely on its allies instead. It cannot and will not be the United States that decides how the nations of Eastern Europe will best relate to their West European neighbors in the long run; neither can the United States play a determining role in reshaping the former Soviet Union. These considerations apply not only to the use of military force, but to a great degree to the use of economic power and influence as well. If it is unlikely to expect United States military intervention on the European or Russian scene—and it is—then it is equally unlikely to expect that either the European or Soviet future will be influenced by massive economic intervention from the United States. It is both reasonable and predictable that the United States may participate on a large scale in humanitarian aid to counter famine or natural disasters, but it is neither reasonable nor likely to expect that ruined economies can or will be rebuilt with extensive American assistance drawn from public funds.

The whole burden of this chapter has been to point to the domestic constraints on American leadership that make it possible to be so definitive on this subject. The consideration of domestic needs and the clear recognition of the relative wealth of its allies inhibit American leadership from huge new public expenditures for overseas purposes, even if that leadership were tempted to embark on such a course. The wealth of the United States can and probably will be extensively applicable to the economic revival of Eastern Europe and the former Soviet Union as well, but only if it is made available in the form of private investment by American industry, and therefore on a commercial basis.

There may therefore be a difficult—even potentially tragic—interval between the desperate need for such investment and the willingness to commit it. Free markets work, but they only work by their own rules. The profit motive of a capitalist economy is not a fiction. American business will need no persuasion once it can be demonstrated that investments in Eastern Europe or the former Soviet Union will earn an appropriate and certain return. But no persuasion will suffice to induce American business to make such investments as long as prospects for profit remain highly uncertain. The American people, and therefore the United States, will resist the notion, not of sacrifice to relieve emergencies, but of putting their own well-being at risk on a long-term basis to rebuild economies ruined by the mismanagement and lunatic ideologies of others.

It is a given that the United States will look to unified Germany as a—probably as the—principal ally in its future relations with respect to Europe and the former Soviet Union. In part, this American expectation is a natural, unavoidable response to Germany's economic strength and location in the heart of Central Europe. In large part, however, this American expectation is a product of the German-American alliance that emerged during the cold war. Americans still tend to believe that today's Germany is what it is and where it is primarily because of the United States. From the Marshall Plan and the beginnings of NATO onward, from the Berlin Airlift to the stationing for decades of American troops primarily on German soil, the United States has made it possible for the Federal Republic of Germany to exist, to survive, to prosper, and ultimately to achieve national unification.

The question is not whether deep bonds have been forged, it is how strong these bonds will prove to be in this new era of extraordinary stress. A German-American alliance is inevitable. Its strength and effectiveness, however, will be put to the test not just once, but over and over again. Happily, the German people—at least in the old Federal Republic—have come to know the United States as well or better than most of America's allies.

One may hope, therefore, that their expectations of the United States will be realistic. Like all of America's allies, if they expect too much of the United States, they will be disappointed. And, if they expect too little, they will be surprised. The United States is now cast as the key player on the international scene. It will play that role, but in its own way. American power will be omnipresent. Its exercise will be constrained. And its use is likely to be cautious.

5

Limits of Leadership: Germany

LOTHAR RUEHL

Introduction

W hen President Bush, in his speech in Mainz after the Brussels North Atlantic Summit Conference in May 1989, called on the United States and West Germany to become "partners in leadership," Chancellor Kohl and West German public opinion understood the offer as an exhortation for active German participation in the management of East-West relations in Europe. The main areas of Western policy toward the Soviet Union and the Warsaw Pact were the negotiations on conventional forces in Europe, just begun in March 1989 in Vienna, the continuing process of the Conference on Security and Cooperation in Europe (CSCE), the implementation of the 1988 Treaty of Washington on Intermediate-Range Nuclear Forces, the application of the Stockholm agreements on military "Confidence Building Measures"

LOTHAR RUEHL is a member of the economic and social sciences faculty at the University of Cologne, international correspondent for *Die Welt*, and secretary general of the Forum für Deutschland. From 1982–89 he was under secretary of defense in the Bonn government.

and disarmament in Europe for increased security, and finally a solution to the problem of short-range nuclear weapons in Europe, especially ground based missile systems.

These issues show that President Bush's offer was part of an alliance policy for a common approach to all European security problems as they were then known, that is, for an American-German partnership in shaping alliance proposals to the USSR and the Warsaw Pact. This intra-alliance background gave the offer to become "partners in leadership" its real meaning: it was oriented toward shaping Western arms control and security policies in order to overcome differences within NATO and to further the progress of negotiations and of the general dialogue with Moscow and its allies on European security. West Germany was thus singled out as one of the major allies of the United States in Europe and as the *critical* partner for all alliance efforts and initiatives in the field of European security. It was called upon to accept new international responsibilities and to define new burden-sharing arrangements within the alliance.

The democratic revolutions in Eastern Europe and the breakdown of Soviet power drastically changed the basic conditions and thus the perspectives of a German-American "partnership in leadership." Now it had to focus on the management of the rapid decline and disintegration of the Soviet empire, although all the specific tasks remained under fundamentally changed conditions. The success of Western policies during the upheavals of 1989–90, when opportunities were seized for optimal outcomes, was crowned with the unification of Germany in its postwar borders as a sovereign state and still a member of the North Atlantic alliance.

This is the main feature of the new situation of Europe. Previously it had been assumed that German unification would either mean a neutral Germany or the end of all alliances. The disintegration of the Warsaw Pact left the North Atlantic alliance, with NATO as its military-political structure and with allied forces in Europe under a joint command, as the only military alliance in Europe and thus as the foundation of European security. This new reality implied the end of all policies based on the continued existence of Soviet hegemonial power and its threat to Western Europe. Accordingly, it meant the end of any presumably "symmetrical" solution to security and arms control problems. Finally, it brought to an end any balance-of-power and spheres-of-interest politics, as far as the Soviet Union and its influence in Europe are concerned.

This optimal outcome of the crisis and eventual collapse of European communism and the Soviet empire had been anticipated neither in West nor in East Germany. Even until the early weeks of the year of German reunification, 1990, dominant political thinking in both parts of Germany clung to the belief that national unity could only be achieved by virtue of patience, over a period of time stretching for more than a decade into the twenty-first century. This had been the perspective opened up by Chancellor Kohl's "Ten Points" program of November 28, 1989, which in reality laid down the political conditions for an organized cooperation between the Federal Republic of Germany (FRG) and the German Democratic Republic (GDR), designed to lead eventually to "confederate structures" with the ultimate objective of establishing a German "confederation."

When Chancellor Kohl took this initiative to accelerate the process of change in relations between the two German states, he did not project national unification on the horizon of an indeterminate future. Whatever his personal views on the matter, he kept a prudent reserve regarding future opportunities, for which, however, he remained prepared. Only two months after the beginning of the East German revolution, he went much farther down the open road to national unity than any other German politician or Western statesman. With the notable exception of Willy Brandt, who, when he was chancellor in the early 1970s, had brought about a fundamental change in West German attitudes toward the USSR and the Socialist countries of Eastern Europe and who now was among the first to recognize the revolutionary character of the popular uprising against the East German regime and thus the historic opportunity for national unification, Chancellor Kohl was almost alone in daring to promote this cause. The opposition Social Democratic party followed the course first charted in the late 1960s and early 1970s, which had long since become the policy line of all of Brandt's successors: to seek peaceful coexistence, more on democratic Western than on Communist Eastern terms, with a perspective of "peaceful change" between "the two German states," formally based on an equal footing and each firmly set into the international framework of its alliance. This was the official policy of all major political parties. It was supported by the vast majority of the electorate of the Federal Republic of Germany.

The shocking experience of open opposition to the Communist regime was at first interpreted according to the conventional wisdom of this time-honored policy. The general assumption was that the ruling party would institute reforms, change its leadership, offer political and economic concessions to the people, return to the pure sources of the Socialist ideal, and negotiate some real political coalition with democratic parties. Under such favorable circumstances the GDR could be restabilized, particularly if West Germany agreed to offer help. New and better relations would be the result, while more far-reaching developments could be left for another day.

The general elections of March 1990 in the GDR, which resulted in a massive vote of confidence in parties supporting the cause of national unity, effectively ended the rule of socialism and enabled the newly formed government to proceed with unification. Still, even the new East German government expected unification to be achieved only under conditions that would satisfy the Soviet Union and the other "allies" of the Warsaw Pact. This approach had its merits, as it contributed to an effective international management of eventual unification, but it did so less by design and more through the workings of some "invisible hand." It also had the disadvantage of clouding the issues and of nourishing the illusion that the GDR could continue to exist as a separate and sovereign state in an economic and monetary union with the FRG (and thus within the European Community). In the end, the economic collapse and the increasingly evident weakness of the Soviet Union did not provide the GDR the time necessary to adjust, even if such reforms had been possible.

This policy objective of holding on to the GDR as a formal entity, if only better to be able to bargain it out of existence by negotiating satisfactory arrangements for a confederation or even a federalist union with West Germany, had several serious and potentially disastrous consequences. For instance, it protected the essential structures of the Socialist economy and hence the instruments of bureaucratic state control, which had already proven incapable of managing the economy. Thus the deeply rooted hierarchies of party control prevailed for at least one year after the collapse of the regime. These well-established interests continued to obstruct change, to protect themselves, and to promote their own institutional and personal benefits by transferring public assets to their own private ownership or by converting large quantities of the GDR's near worthless currency into valuable Deutsche marks.

In the process of this policy, large portions of the East German population became increasingly discouraged. They were afraid that a return to some kind of socialism was in the offing and that the GDR with all its oppressive bureaucratic structures would not disappear after all. This led to fears that the establishment of a market economy might be retarded and, in any case, be overburdened with unproductive state-run enterprises, and that, in the end, it would take too long for East Germany to adopt the Western ways of proven success. The result was a combination of passivity and emigration to the West, which aggravated the acute economic crisis in the East, thinned out the net of public services to the point of rupture, and contributed to tear up what remained of the social fabric after the end of socialism in the GDR. For the same reasons, much needed capital investments did not materialize, although there were other compelling reasons as well, such as the uncertainty of property ownership, catastrophic ecological conditions, and the lack of adequate infrastructures.

The East German government's tenuous approach to unification also added to the general state of confusion not only about the future internal order of united Germany, but also about its international status—whether it would be neutral or allied, the center of a geopolitical configuration revived from the past called "Central Europe," or part of Western Europe, governed by the principles of Western-style democracy or by a new blend of "democratic socialism." The declaratory policy of the East German government about a surviving East German "identity" (which is probably a psychological reality at least for part of the population), about an "erect approach" to unity, about "social achievements" to be preserved in a "new Germany" contributed to a mostly artificial debate about the constitutional order.

This debate, now closed for the main issues, lingered on during 1990 and spread unease about economic prospects as well. It contributed to shape West German reactions to the demands arising in the East, which were all aimed at a sharing of Western resources. Calls for a massive transfer of capital, for certain compensations and adjustments, and for special rights in some cases led to a confrontation of social and economic interests, which would seem to be only natural, but which tended to harden reticent West German business attitudes regarding employment policies, social insurance, public health schemes, environmental regulation, and the conditions for acquiring industrial and commercial properties.

By and large, the year 1990, which saw the achievement of German national unification through the extension of the Federal Republic onto the territory of the GDR after the latter's access to the FRG on the basis of the Unification Treaty, ended extremely well for Germany. Many negative developments were cancelled out by successive events and by the beginning processes of internal integration. Unification did not come about as the result of negotiations between two equal partners. It could not have, since the GDR—this artificial creation of Soviet power politics—was unable to meet the test of competition under conditions of freedom. The people did not want any *Ersatz*. This meant that no amount of economic assistance could help support even a reformed and truly democratic "German Democratic Republic." Unification had become an absolute must, the categorical imperative of German politics. In Leipzig, Dresden, and other large East German cities, the demonstrators' chants changed from "we are the people" to "we are *one* people"; their demands for speedy reunification eliminated all alternatives. Policy makers were afraid, in turn, that the "window of opportunity" for unification would remain open for only a brief period of time. Political considerations thus very quickly came to override economic concerns.

In consequence, unification was not a merger between two parts of a divided country, but, in fact, a takeover. Chancellor Kohl's forecast that nobody in the ex-GDR would be worse off after unification than before must not be taken literally. It was mostly a gesture of reassurance at the critical moment of choice before a jump into the unknown as well as a promise of political convenience in the course of an election campaign. Above all, it was a political necessity. The balance of gains and losses cannot yet be established. Efforts, however, have to be made by all, and more than might have been expected in 1989. The new necessities were at first not sufficiently understood, and the public debate on the real issues of unification took place mostly on the surface. Here lies the most important leadership challenge in German politics after unification, and the response by the political figures will tell whether they are indeed leaders.

Priorities of Unification

There are several political, social-psychological, economic, as well as administrative and legal priorities for German national policy after the reunification of Germany. These problems must be recognized, and they must eventually be brought to a solution. The first is easier than the second, but there is general agreement in Germany on these priorities:

- economic recovery of East Germany through reconstruction and modernization of its industrial base;
- agricultural modernization;
- building of a modern infrastructure for transport and communications, urban renewal, and housing;
- creation of an efficient public sector ranging from hospitals and sanitation to clean water supplies;
- creation of a liberal and democratic system of public education with schools and universities on a level comparable to West Germany;
- ecological transformation of industrial and agricultural production, transportation systems, and construction, leading to systematic efforts at environmental protection;
- new energy supply systems for clean energy according to West German standards (this implies the shutdown of all nuclear power plants based on Soviet designs and the build-up of a new electric power industry);

• creation of an internationally competitive labor force at a high
  level of employment;
• build-up of functioning local and regional administrations and
  the extension of the West German system of justice to the East.

In general, these problems will only be solved if a number of
conditions can be met. Thus public as well as private investments
in East Germany will yield expected returns over the long run only
if they contribute to an increase in productivity, in the quality of
goods produced, and, therefore, in the competitiveness of the
economy as a whole. Of decisive importance will be the nature of
the labor force in East Germany and its employment levels. About
50 percent of 1991 unemployment in East Germany was due to
the inefficient economic structures of the former GDR and of its
system of overadministering the country for the sake of authoritarian political control. This portion of the now jobless cannot be
easily absorbed by new economic activities under market conditions or by Western-style public administrations and social organizations.

The other 50 percent of East German unemployment results
from the collapse of Eastern European markets following the end
of the Council for Mutual Economic Assistance (COMECON)
and the introduction of the Deutsche mark. This source of unemployment may well be eliminated until the mid-1990s. In one year
alone—from October 1990 to October 1991—about 1 million
new jobs have been created in the East, mostly by small businesses
in the service sector, operating primarily in the construction business and the automobile industry. In all these branches, the expansion of production—and thus of employment—will likely pick up
momentum. In general, East Germany will be unable to maintain
its preunification level of industrialization, which contributed 65
percent of its national product (compared to 45 percent in West
Germany). It must reduce not only its level of industrialization, but
also its agricultural production in favor of enlarging its service
sector, if it is to become a fully modernized and competitive part of
Germany.

Economic progress in East Germany will be determined largely
by a speedy solution to the problem of defining and ascertaining

ownership rights. As long as the question of who legally owns a piece of real estate or an industrial plant cannot be reliably answered, a massive legal as well as psychological burden will hinder the economic and social development of East Germany. This mortgage may even prove to weigh more heavily on postunification Germany than is now generally assumed, since the legal basis for deciding competing ownership claims is by no means unequivocal and may thus result not only in lengthy processes of litigation, but also in considerable political conflicts.

Aside from legal problems, the main difficulties are to be found in short-term conflicts of interest and in long-term contradictions between priorities. One set of major contradictions relates to the opposing necessities of creating employment on the one hand, and of raising pay scales on the other. A second set of competing requirements pertains to the necessities of environmental protection on the one side, and of protecting the competitive edge of the German economy on the other side. Finally, social integration and economic development in the former GDR are not yet in harmony and may well pose problems of discrepancy. Such problems cannot be simply solved by a transfer of resources from West to East. Social integration of the East Germans on the level of West Germany will only succeed if East German productivity levels reach West German standards, at which point social services could be provided without costly support from the Western portions of Germany.

Psychologically this is all the more difficult since West German authorities from politics, the churches, and academia tended to answer the partisan allegations that the West German society was only interested in its own profit by raising false hopes concerning internal burden-sharing arrangements, without themselves agreeing what this might mean. This became clear prior to the first all-German general elections in December 1990, when the party in opposition raised the divisive issue of tax increases and the ruling coalition parties denied any such needs or plans. Rarely has a government, recently victorious in an election, lost so much political credibility in such a short time as did Chancellor Kohl when, shortly thereafter, taxes did indeed have to be increased considerably. It is irrelevant for unification purposes whether this government and its parties will regain the confidence thus lost. The problem runs much deeper and is more general than the struggle for political power between competing parties. The false public debate in the context of a heated election campaign misled the Germans, if only briefly, about the necessity for a change of social habits. This affected the East Germans in particular, who still clung to the idea that the state could and should assure them a "decent" life and dispense "social justice" for "equality," while in reality no amount of West German money could buy them, all at once, social security, employment, a high standard of living, and individual freedom at the West German level.

The political rhetoric about nonintervention into allegedly internal affairs of the East Germans, the warning against a supposedly unjust takeover, and the claim that somehow the Communist GDR had created social achievements worthy of preservation in a free and democratic society confounded the real issues of German unification and social integration. This phraseology drew a cloak of illusion over the simple reality that the international—but especially the European—economic environment of Germany remains an important factor limiting any process of setting national priorities in favor of the East Germans.

The rush of international, and in particular West European, goods into East Germany after the conclusion of the economic and monetary union in July 1990 amply illustrates this point, for now the East German customers, in possession of real money and free to choose, rejected their own goods in favor of products coming in from outside. East Germany simply succumbed to the economic power of competently—and competitively—managed Western firms. The insolvency not only of the remaining GDR, but of its East European trading partners within COMECON, led to the breakdown of trade with Eastern Europe and robbed the East German economy—once ranked tenth in the world and still estimated in late 1989 at about 50 percent of the West German economy in terms of industrial productivity—of its markets in the East and thus of all chances to prevail in an economic union with West Germany (and the European Community).

Estimates of the economic costs of German unification depend on the criteria of what is deemed to be necessary. In 1990 the transfer of resources amounted to roughly DM 100 billion, in 1991, to about 150 billion; projected costs for 1992 were 175 billion. These sums included financial transfers of all kinds. Until the end of the decade, this level will likely not change significantly. But sooner or later, all of that money, thrown, as it were, at East Germany in order to meet dire needs, will produce modernization, new employment, economic growth, resurgent competitiveness, and, in the end, new wealth. Much speculation will take place and laws will be evaded; by all standards, injustices will occur. Illegal fortunes will be amassed through criminal activities, and not all the new self-made people will be honest, nor will all the deals be proper, even when they are not illegal. The same will happen in politics, as is already apparent in some careers. A touch of the "Wild West"—or perhaps the "Wild East"—is likely to prevail, and international organized crime will enjoy a particularly free field in the ex-GDR, given the persisting inadequacy of public administration and the inexperience of local politicians. But all this will finally level out and produce a public order similar to that now prevailing in West Germany; the population will not be much worse off for it. Toward the turn of the century, the ex-GDR will be more or less integrated in economic and social terms.

The psychological dimension of German unification is important, but its current state is difficult to establish. The shock of events still persists, and first reactions may not indicate final orientations. More enterprising individuals adapt themselves more quickly and often better than those who wait for guidance and help. A lack of initiative is widespread in East Germany, but how could it be otherwise after more than half a century of totalitarian dictatorship and complete dependence on one-party rule? Its labor force, after decades of working under conditions of Socialist planning, is hardly accustomed to regular work and to the high quality standards required in modern production facilities. Now those who retain their jobs must learn to work regularly, efficiently, and at a much faster pace. Experiences with those who came to work in West Germany after the fall of the Wall in 1989 reveal that even skilled workers need up to a year in order to adapt to Western conditions and to perform according to Western standards. In the East, this may require more time and more of a psychological effort, since the working environment is still largely the same, with old bosses often in control, paying lip service to the principles of democracy and a market economy. But even opportunism can help to change things in the right direction; many negative developments have been corrected thanks to the opportunism of those who were responsible for them in the first place.

A favorite theme of public debate refers to these psychological difficulties: a "wall in the heads" allegedly newly arisen after the real Wall had come down. It appears to be an elusive phenomenon, mostly observed in the ivory towers of academia and in the fenced-in gardens of other intellectuals prominent in the worlds of media, the churches, and indeed politics. The exhortation to tear down this mental wall is full of good intentions, but not always well-founded. The difficulty lies in the definition: where is this wall in the heads that seems to be on so many observers' minds? What does it mean in practical terms and how can it be removed? Such questions are rarely answered; and where they are, the answers seem generally useless. All too often, the answer consists of one word: "sharing." But what is to be shared, if sharing does not simply mean more money to the East?

The risks of such an essentially unpolitical debate without recourse to economic realities are gradually emerging. Germany is in danger of becoming a society where one part subsidizes the uneconomical work and the uncompetitive products of another part (a problem already evident in West Germany with its highly subsidized coal miners and farmers). While this may be an appropriate solution in individual cases of dire need, it is detrimental as a general policy. Much money is being spent on measures to retrain workers for jobs that cannot be guaranteed. The precious time of transition to real change and new opportunities is being wasted in many cases just for temporary relief. This protracted escapism eventually will have to be paid for with jobs, with money, with dashed hopes, and with broken hearts. Funds thus squandered will not be available a second time to pay for more useful measures of adaptation. Confidence in the market system and in democracy stands to suffer.

There are a number of major obstacles that have to be overcome if the risks inherent in the unification process are to be kept at a minimum. For instance, the new technologies required to build up competitive production lines, to improve transportation systems, or to provide modern communication systems do not offer massive employment opportunities. But new employment is urgently needed in order to absorb the structural unemployment that is part of the economic heritage left by the defunct GDR. Workers have to be retrained for new qualifications, and jobs can only be offered in smaller numbers at higher wages. The social conflict between high levels of employment and high levels of pay will remain for some time to come, as will the economic conflict between full employment and the use of new labor-saving technologies for competitive production.

The employment picture is muddled by growing generational conflicts. In West Germany, their impact has been dulled by habit and social welfare programs; in East Germany, however, these conflicts are likely to increase sharply. Here most workers and employees above forty-five years of age will have to face the prospect of being laid off permanently. Policy makers are confronted with the difficult choice of giving work either to the young or of keeping a large number of older personnel. For political as well as for economic reasons, the choice can only be in favor of the young. Society has no acceptable alternative. The social security network is tightly woven, flexible, and quite robust. Thus it should be able to provide the necessary means of support, as long as it can draw on the benefits of high labor productivity and sufficient social security contributions and general tax returns. A system based more on economic than on social welfare considerations is an obvious precondition for a well-functioning social security system. This is one of the main lessons to be learned from the West German experience. Therefore, the political, ideological, and purely emotional tendencies toward a "social" mitigation of the difficult employment situation through an uneconomic manipulation of the labor market should be resolutely resisted. Trade unions as well as employers must respect the fundamental law of productivity and economic growth, without which the means for an effective social security system cannot be provided.

Another difficult problem is the proper balance between environmental concerns and economic necessities. The general devastation of the environment in the ex-GDR and, more specifically, the serious ecological damage to urban communities, housing, and industries make it necessary to invest several hundred billion Deutsche marks in the restoration and future protection of the environment alone, even before other kinds of investments can take place. General German sensitivities concerning the environment create the temptation to accord this sector special privileges and to assign it top priority. Powerful pressure groups insist on the priority of environmental concerns, while a bureaucracy with strong regulatory traditions is ready to go into action. The combination of both has already reduced the margin for productive investment in West Germany; the same may happen on an even larger scale in East Germany, especially since "Wild West" methods allowing early investors to proceed without due regard for ecological and social consequences may well provoke a backlash of much more restrictive policies. Environmental and economic policies will have to be brought into harmony. This will put considerable strains on policy making and limit the government's room for political maneuver.

Finally, a fully functioning system of public administration at all levels has to be built up in very short time—a daunting task indeed, given the lack of qualified personnel. Of particular importance in this regard are an adequate system of tax collection and an effective system for the administration of justice (based on West German laws). *Rechtssicherheit* and *Rechtsstaatlichkeit,* meaning a reliable legal system with a full range of formal guarantees, must be developed for citizens to enjoy their newly won rights and for investments to be safe. The hasty and often improvised operations of 1989–91 must soon give way to a system of administration that not only functions reasonably well, but that also merits the trust and support of the citizens it is designed to serve.

All in all, the initial period of unification will have to be considered a period of great opportunities as well as of great temptations, faults, and errors. So far, achievements outweigh the negative aspects of unification. Nevertheless, Germany will have to shoulder heavy burdens for years to come in order to master the task of national reunification in economic and social terms. The costs of environmental restoration will be high, as will be the costs for better housing and improved infrastructures. Some of those who

cannot find employment in industry or commerce might be offered work in these areas at reduced wages (supplemented, perhaps, by other forms of public support), but that depends on the
consent of the trade unions, which will not be easily obtained, and
on concomitant reforms of Germany's welfare system.

Economic, social, and psychological factors work in combination. Solutions must address all relevant issues. Thus "market
forces" alone cannot be allowed to decide everything by themselves; otherwise the political framework and the social fabric, in
which all markets are set and all economic activities take place, are
in danger of being damaged. One of the critical factors on all three
accounts is the influx of poor immigrants, many from far-away
countries, and the related abuse of the constitutionally guaranteed
right of asylum. Here, too, the public debate and political attitudes
are marked by fallacies, and a spirit of illusion has spread through
the ranks of the educated elites over the last decade.

Germany does not have the luxury of choice in the question of
becoming a "multicultural society." However, exactly what this
may mean in the future with a native population of about 75
million people in one of the most densely populated countries of
Europe and about 350,000 immigrants per year (in 1991) remains
unclear. Of these immigrants, roughly 120,000 claimed to be of
German origin in their East European home countries and were
thus given automatic German citizenship. The other 230,000 immigrants (ten times more than in 1982) sought asylum for reasons
of political persecution. Many of these asylum seekers come from
Asia and Africa; they bring with them age-old habits and precon-
ceptions concerning freedom, duties toward society, solidarity
with others who are not members of their own clan or family,
religious tolerance, and social discipline that are at odds with prevailing European ideals and concepts. Most immigrants, understandably enough, simply seek the material and social advantages
of life in a highly developed, well-organized, and wealthy country.

In general, Germany's problem with immigrants is no different
from the problems faced by other countries in Western Europe or
North America. One specific difference, however, pertains to the
legal situation in Germany, where the Constitution guarantees the
right to political asylum to just about anyone asking for it, but a

coherent and rational immigration policy is otherwise lacking. In fact, though, Germany has long been an immigration country; it even finds itself the target of a profitable refugee infiltration business, made possible by the systematic abuse of the Basic Law's asylum guarantee as interpreted by the courts. Some 95 percent of all asylum seekers are not recognized as legitimate political refugees. Nevertheless, once rejected, most of them are allowed, on humanitarian grounds, to stay anyway.

This legal impasse has so far prevented Germany from developing an adequate immigration policy. According to prevailing interpretations of the Basic Law's guarantee, each individual asylum seeker must be granted a hearing in court. Overwhelmed courts result in delayed procedures, which lead to prolonged stays of the refugees. This, in turn, creates a sort of moral claim to be allowed to stay even after asylum claims have been duly denied. This obvious failure to administer justice fairly and speedily, and thereby to protect the interests of the people against illegal immigration, has aroused popular protest and created widespread frustration with political parties and local authorities. Such frustration has encouraged right-wing extremists to engage in brutal violence against foreigners in general, and asylum seekers in particular.

Police suppression and moral condemnation of such violence are necessary, but unfortunately do not solve the problem. Eruptions of hatred and assaults on homes for refugees in East and West Germany have shown that popular reactions tend to get out of control once people feel left alone with their concerns and are afraid of drastic impairments of their living conditions as a result of the influx of immigrants. Thus it should not have come as a surprise that this phenomenon first erupted on a larger scale in East Germany, where freedom, mobility, and foreign influences are still new. But it did not remain restricted to East Germany; even in West Germany, where living conditions are much better and openness to outsiders enjoys a long tradition, rightist radicalism raised its ugly head. Leftist radicalism, apparently, had paved the way for some of these excesses.

How real is the danger that Germany might be turning back to radical nationalism and rightist extremism? There should not be much ground for worries. Such excesses are not entirely new. Election results such as in Bremen in 1991, where less than 10 percent of the voters opted for the rightist German People's Union, are comparable to similar election outcomes in the mid-1960s, which did not lead to any stable right-wing vote. Parties of the extreme right have, on occasion, gained between 5 and 10 percent of the vote in regional and local elections, but such gains could never be translated into political power or maintained over a longer period, let alone consolidated at the national level. Even though the right-wing potential might be somewhat larger today due especially to developments in East Germany, right-wing parties are unlikely to gain a new political foothold in Germany. A continuing flow of immigrants could, however, pose an additional risk of more widely spread dissent and alienation. Still, recent electoral successes of rightist forces are, for a large part, more an expression of protest than a commitment to rightist and nationalist politics.

There is no evidence that the moderate political climate that prevailed in the preunification Federal Republic with its political culture of liberalism and social democracy will change as the result of unification. The overwhelming votes of confidence in democratic politics and in the political, economic, and social systems of the Federal Republic by large majorities of voters in the former GDR bear witness to this basic political stability; so do election results in West Germany since 1989. The democratic parties have the political means to steer clear of danger and to satisfy the legitimate concerns of the electorate in both East and West without departing from humanitarian, liberal, and moderate policies.

Constraints

The main constraints on Germany will derive from the myriad tasks of full and effective unification, which will limit German resources and concentrate political efforts on domestic concerns. Yet there are other, more traditional constraints as well. One, for instance, is the burden of Germany's past. It has weighed down German policies through its effects on the collective conscience in general, but particularly through the working assumptions of Germany's political class—i.e., what it considers appropriate and practicable.

However, assumptions based on German perceptions of external apprehensions are of dubious value, as they have quite often been proven wrong. The Western allies of the Federal Republic were, by and large, much more optimistic and sanguine about the future of Germany, its role in the world, and the German qualification for contributing to international security even with military forces outside the NATO treaty area than German policy makers assumed. This was particularly the case with respect to German military support for international peacekeeping efforts. More recently, an active German part in the defense of common Western interests, for instance the protection of international waterways or even of Western allies outside Europe, was considered highly welcome. As experiences in the late stages of the Iran-Iraq war (1987–88) and the Gulf War of 1991 revealed, the presumed constraints imposed by Germany's historical legacy and the apprehensions of its allies and partners were quite overstated.

There is one particular aspect critical to Germany's international standing: Germany's potential role in the transfer of technologies suitable for manufacturing weapons of mass destruction. False reports in 1982 about alleged German support for an "Argentine atomic bomb" (an absurd hoax provoking near hysteria on the part of antinuclear groups) had already laid bare that particular nerve, as did revelations about possible German participation in the construction of a chemical weapons plant in Libya (the "Auschwitz in the sands" near Rabtah). When Saddam Hussein threatened Israel with the destruction of its cities and actually launched Scud missiles against Israel (though without chemical warheads), all could measure how thin the ice is on which Germany stands in the world. Even though other countries had also played a role in providing Iraq with the means of manufacturing weapons of potential mass destruction, the onus for such misdeeds was on the Germans. German policy makers were once again forced to recognize how stringent and comprehensive German export controls need to be. After years of vacillation and equivocation—and much lost time—they finally responded to this challenge, but they may have reacted too severely, as German firms now face unusually restrictive export controls. Still, because of the legacy of German history and some uncontrolled activities on the part of a few rogue firms, Germany had no choice but to clamp down hard.

But this critical issue must be kept separate from legitimate military exports to non-NATO countries that have genuine security needs and are subject to international standards and controls. If, for instance, conventional submarines may be delivered to Israel, why should they not also be sold to Egypt or Saudi Arabia? This question points to the extremely difficult balancing problems faced by German foreign policy in the Middle East. It is obvious that such a balancing act between Israel and moderate pro-Western Arab countries is extremely risky in political terms, since Germany exercises little control over potential clients in the Middle East and has few ways of influencing conflicts or moderating crises. This is one area where Germany cannot become involved without assuming disproportionate risks to its own interests; German leadership is thus nearly impossible. Germany can support its allies only indirectly and contribute to common policies in the framework of European political cooperation.

Should Germany have come to the active support of the international coalition against Iraq after the latter's plunder of Kuwait and thus to the defense of commonly accepted values and interests? The public debate in Germany on this issue showed that many Germans still have not learned the moral lessons of Hitler's aggression, namely to differentiate between right and wrong in international life. The predominant attitude in Germany was antiwar, meaning against *any* war, although Saddam Hussein, by attacking Kuwait, had started the war (as Hitler had in 1939) and had violated a member country of the U.N. The German debate also revealed an old tendency to argue the case not on its own merits, but in terms of general ideas and abstract principles, behind which one could conveniently hide. At the same time, reasons were advanced (mostly by the self-styled peace movement) why the ruler of Kuwait ought not be defended against aggression or be restored to power, as if the violation of Kuwait affected only the ruler and his dynasty and not the people of Kuwait.

The unescapable logic of the German debate was that the numerous advocates of peace at any price were not willing to admit the legitimacy of defense against aggression and refused to distinguish between attacker and attacked. They even argued that the aggression may have been "provoked." This argument was also advanced in regard to Turkey, when it joined the international coalition on behalf of the U.N. These examples show the impact of the historical legacy on German attitudes. Fortunately, these recent experiences offered some important lessons, which may well contribute to a change in attitudes.

Those in Germany who refuse to consider the possibility of military involvement abroad (at least outside Europe and the NATO treaty area) usually seek refuge behind history and the Federal Republic's Constitution. The constitutional issue, however, is less complicated than it is made out to be in political rhetoric. The Basic Law does not impose stringent constraints against international military contributions by Germany outside the NATO area. Participation in a system of mutual collective security, including limitations on national sovereignty and the transfer of sovereign rights to international organizations (without restrictions or qualifications concerning armed forces), is clearly permitted. The Basic Law only forbids preparations for, and the actual conduct of, a "war of aggression" as a criminal offense.

According to the Basic Law, the purpose of armed forces is— without any further qualifications—"for defense." Defense is generally understood to take place in the alliance context and hence for the NATO treaty area, but the Basic Law itself does not specify such limits. Had the NATO area been attacked before 1990, allied forces (including German troops) were free, according to the NATO treaty, to extend their defensive efforts beyond NATO borders onto the territory of the aggressor. This question is primarily one of international law and has little to do with the German Constitution.

This was the prevailing legal opinion of both the Ministry of Defense and of the Foreign Office (with the concurrence of the Ministry of Justice) until 1982. It was applied in 1967, when the United States asked for German warships to participate in an international naval force of allied countries to patrol the Gulf of Aqaba in order to deny Egypt the option of blockading the Israeli port of Eilat. But a new theory was introduced in 1982, which has since become the official interpretation of the Basic Law and the NATO treaty. However, this interpretation—that German military activities are restricted to the defense of the NATO treaty area—was never subjected to a ruling by the Federal Constitutional Court. Germany's political establishment, apparently always searching for ways to entrench itself behind the paper wall of the Basic Law, imposed this new interpretation without explaining why and how the Constitution does not allow what it does not even mention.

In reality, the alleged constitutional constraints forbidding the Federal Republic to participate with military forces in the defense of international law and security as either a member of the United Nations, as a member of an international coalition, or even in a bilateral alliance for mutual defense, are artificial. In contrast to prevailing expert legal opinion, the political establishment expresses a myth in its interpretation of the Basic Law. With the help of public opinion, it has tried to give this myth credibility not only as a valid constitutional philosophy, but also as a constitutional practice of long standing. This may be so, as long as the real meaning of the Basic Law cannot be secured through legal processes against erroneous interpretations. But it is clear that this self-imposed constraint constitutes, in fact, a self-induced political impotence on the part of Germany. It prevents the German government from acting in accordance with national interests (it even inhibits a proper definition of the national interest in a given situation) and from choosing its options in accordance with international law, treaty obligations, and policy decisions taken in cooperation with its allies and partners.

It may not have been in Germany's national interest to participate militarily in the international coalition's efforts during the Gulf War of 1991. But Germany denied itself this option. Instead, it spent considerable sums of money supporting other countries, it participated in voting U.N. resolutions, it offered logistical support to the allies in the international coalition, and finally it even sent a mine-sweeping flotilla to the Persian Gulf after the war had ended. Whatever the value of these contributions may have been in political terms, this was not an exercise of partnership in leadership. Denying oneself the options to act with appropriate means of last resort in a case of acute danger to uphold peace or to restore international law and security may be a political constraint, but it certainly limits the ability to exercise control in a given situation and to show political leadership. The quality of leadership is determined by this self-imposed lack of options.

In the case of the Yugoslav crisis since 1989, the German government has adopted policies that amount to direct involvement through political intervention into the presumably internal affairs of a CSCE member country. Its approach to this crisis has been based on political, not legalistic, considerations. The political constraints on Germany (as well as on Austria, Italy, and Hungary) with respect to Yugoslavia are obvious. In this case, recent history and common sense argue for military abstention. German policy, therefore, had to avoid involvement with military forces. The false accusations against Germany and Austria concerning an alleged conspiracy with Slovenia and Croatia against Yugoslavia's continued existence, and the generally hostile attitude of Serbian public opinion, show how difficult it is for Germany to exercise any moderating influence on Belgrade. The German government finally pronounced itself in favor of the right of national self-determination for Slovenia and Croatia and thus gave political support to their independence efforts, but it did so only after Moscow had recognized the independence of the three Baltic states—thus paying tribute to the international complications of this issue.

Once it had become obvious that no amount of outside pressure could keep Yugoslavia united and that Serbia was intent on gaining as much territory as possible at almost any price, Western Europe was forced to take sides politically and give up its policy of apparent even-handedness. One could argue that both the German and the Dutch led West European policies were wrong or, in any case, without much effect, that neither could succeed under the dramatic circumstances, and that, in the end, the only realistic course would have been a determined intervention with all available means, from an economic blockade of Yugoslavia to a military occupation of the areas under contention. But such an argument is based on doubtful assumptions concerning the likely success of any such effort. Certainly the exclusion of any German military participation in an international peacekeeping force remains in the best interest of all parties to the conflict (unless one side were to seek the annihilation of the other). The Yugoslav crisis dramatically revealed the faultlines in European security policies and thus also the limitations of useful political leadership on the part of Germany in European affairs.

External Competing Demands

Ever since the admission of West Germany to NATO and the Western European Union in 1955, the foreign policies pursued by various governments in Bonn have been based on the assumption that objectives in the West—that is, West European political union with economic integration—and in the East—i.e., national unification without a separation from the West—were not in contradiction. The larger European context was only considered in general terms, and the question of what kind of Europe would come into existence with the reunification of Germany was left open. This pragmatic approach was historically validated by the events of 1989 and 1990. Chancellor Kohl kept pursuing both goals at the same time, and even when reunification became a matter of top priority, the European goal was never abandoned or downgraded. The collapse of the Soviet empire and the disintegration of the Warsaw Pact left the Western alliance as the only organized multinational political and military force in Europe. This fundamental change, more than the end of the East-West confrontation by itself, opened up the historic opportunity of uniting Germany within its postwar borders as a sovereign nation-state *and* as a member of the North Atlantic alliance.

This outcome of the cold war in Europe, which ended the struggle for Europe after forty-five years, contributed to a situation in which Germany finds itself without debilitating constraints as a European power among others of similar importance. The agreement to this outcome, given by President Gorbachev in July 1990, places Germany in the role of a major player on the Continent, consolidates German–West European ties, and creates a vested German interest in close relations with Russia and whatever will remain of the Soviet Union in Eastern Europe.

Germany will once again have to look East, as well as West. It must and will be a reliable partner in security and cooperation for Russia and any confederation organized around Russia. The initial German investment in such a partnership amounted to more than DM 60 billion earmarked for the Soviet Union. It stands to reason that Germany cannot continue to bear such a burden alone. The special relationship between Germany and Russia cannot be based only on financial contributions, however important they may continue to be. This relationship will have to assume a more political quality and, in the end, amount to a mediating role between Eastern and Western Europe. In fulfillment of this role, Germany will have to act as both a member of NATO and the European Community (EC). In contrast with the past, Germany is now fully anchored in the West, which should be reassuring to its neighbors. Certainly there is no "Rapallo" temptation today, as there was in the years following the First World War, when Germany and Soviet Russia found themselves isolated internationally.

Obviously, Germany will not be able to determine relations simply through sheer economic weight. There is no hegemonial position that Germany could assume or use. More than ever, German foreign policy will seek to promote European solutions with a view toward common interests, even if agreement between the major EC partners should remain difficult to achieve. However, since Germany has become the Eastern cornerstone of the Western alliance, and the German borders with Poland and Czechoslovakia have become the Eastern borders of the EC, the geopolitical configuration in Europe has shifted to the East. The center of political and economic gravity still lies in the West. But German policies can no longer be simply "Western" or "West European," at least not as long as Poland, Hungary, and Czechoslovakia are not yet closely associated with the EC and NATO.

Once these three Central European countries, which used to be the Eastern outposts of Western culture and civilization, have resumed their old historical ties to the West, other East European countries will also gravitate toward Western Europe. Hence the old East-West divide of continental Europe will not remain in place. Germany will have to be an integrative power as well as a mediating force for compromise and a balance of interests. This, obviously, places certain obligations and constraints on German policies in Europe; above all, they must not be confrontational. Germany has a prime interest in laying old antagonisms to rest. As long as no new confrontations arise in Europe, Germany can play this part and serve European unity, whatever its boundaries.

A second constraint lies in the anchorage that Germany must provide for the presence of American power on the European continent. Hence Germany is not free to pursue an exclusively European construction program in regard to strategic-military efforts. The same is true for other West European allies, but it is of particular importance to German-American ties as well as to the Anglo-American relationship. Germany, along with Great Britain and France, will have to act as a mediator between American and European interests.

Efforts for the internal integration of united Germany can be harmonized with efforts to promote West European unity, but while there is no inevitable incompatibility, there is undoubtedly some tension between competing demands and interests. The necessary harmonization can only succeed as a joint European operation. The risk that German strength can be overtaxed is as undeniable as is the risk that the EC could lose cohesion and unity of purpose in the process of "widening." The risks and problems of Germany and the EC are similar and run in parallel. Both must solve the problem of "deepening while widening," and in both cases, solutions will not come easily. But a true partnership in leadership requires nothing less.

6

Patterns of Partnership

*The U.S.–German Security
Relationship in the 1990s*

ROBERT D. BLACKWILL

Introduction

N ot since the 1950s has the future of the U.S.–German security relationship faced so many uncertainties.[1] These two
pivotal countries together possess extraordinary assets as they confront the end of the cold war, the collapse of communism east of
the Bug River in August 1991, and the fragmentation of the former Soviet Union. Each is a flourishing democracy based on clas-
sic Western values. Each has a political and economic governmental elite that is internationalist in temperament and habit. Each

ROBERT D. BLACKWILL is lecturer in public policy at the John F.
Kennedy School of Government, Harvard University. Previously, he was
special assistant to President Bush for European and Soviet Affairs on the
staff of the National Security Council. From 1985–87 he was U.S. ambassador and chief negotiator at the negotiations with the Warsaw Pact on
conventional forces in Europe. A career diplomat since 1967, Ambassador Blackwill has served in Kenya, Britain, Israel, and Washington in the
Department of State and on the staff of the National Security Council.
Ambassador Blackwill is the author of many articles on European security and East-West relations.

believes it has a large stake in systematic and comprehensive cooperation with the other. Each has developed over the postwar
decades patterns of bilateral consultation and even joint decision
making that have unquestionably served the two nations well. Furthermore, each has gained enormously from the seismic events of
1989–91: Germany is unified in the West in peace and freedom;
and the Soviet military threat to Central Europe and to the American homeland has lost its credibility.

Nevertheless, a certain strategic and emotional uneasiness between Washington and Bonn creeps steadily into the U.S.–German security relationship writ large. The present mutual disquiet
emanates from the largely unknown but critically important consequences that will flow in the future for the United States and
Germany from the geopolitical happenings of 1989–91.

To vivify the justifiable origins of the present nervousness in
both nations, one might compare the Second Russian Revolution
with historical events of comparable magnitude and import since
1900. The list is not a long one and includes this first approxima-
tion: World War I and the end of the Hapsburg, Hohenzollern,
and Ottoman Empires; the 1917 Russian Revolution; the great
world depression of the 1930s; the rise of fascism and World War
II; the invention and use of nuclear weapons; the Soviet occupation of Eastern Europe; the Western reaction to that occupation
(Marshall Plan, NATO); democratic transformations of West Germany and Japan; Franco-German reconciliation and the creation
of the European Community; the end of colonialism; the liberation of Eastern Europe; and the unification of Germany.

Some may find this enumeration Eurocentric. Others will wish
to add to or subtract from the list. But if the events in Central and
Eastern Europe and the Soviet Union since mid-1989 are of the
same historical dimensions of these earlier developments, at the
moment one can say only one thing with much confidence: analyses and predictions at present concerning the implications of these
changes in Europe for European and international security in general, and for the U.S.–German security relationship in particular,
are quite likely to be overly linear and thus well off the mark.

To stress how difficult it is to draw accurate strategic conclusions in turbulent times, remember only these two predictions.

The rise of the Bolsheviks was met with expectations of their quick failure as most Western diplomats and leaders believed that the demise of Lenin's faction was imminent. Woodrow Wilson termed the Bolsheviks the "fatuous . . . dreamers of Russia,"[2] repeating the judgment of his diplomatic corps that the revolutionaries would soon be overturned. Flouting continued Western predictions of communism's demise, Nikita Khrushchev, speaking at a dinner for East German dignitaries visiting Moscow in 1955, stressed that "if anyone believes that our smiles involve the abandonment of the teaching of Marx, Engels and Lenin, he deceives himself poorly. Those who wait for that must wait until a shrimp learns to whistle."[3]

In seeking to project future developments more accurately than the two figures cited above, it is tempting to move forthwith into purely contemporary questions of U.S.–German security relations. These are the matters that grip the current public debate, and they are intrinsically important in character. How will Germany and the United States influence the constituent elements of the former Soviet Union and whatever remains of the center? What is NATO's future? How will Bonn and Washington shape their policies with regard to the future of Western-stationed military forces in Germany, especially those of the United States? Will U.S. nuclear weapons continue to be deployed on German soil? In what ways will the two approach the evolution of other security institutions in Europe: the Western European Union (WEU), the European Community (EC), and the Conference on Security and Cooperation in Europe (CSCE)? And how should German policy evolve with respect to security threats to Europe from outside the traditional NATO treaty area?

While examining these prospective matters in some detail, and drawing various prescriptive conclusions as we go, it may also be useful to recall briefly the central questions and outcomes of U.S.– German security cooperation and disagreement as they occurred in the forty years before the European revolutions of 1989–91. In this way we can remind ourselves of the themes of this long and intimate bilateral security involvement, and hopefully identify trends and perspectives from the past that will inform present analysis and future policy.

Relations with the Soviet Union:
The Early Years

Policies relating to the Soviet Union were the core of U.S.–German security ties through most of the cold war period. There were two distinct phases in these bilateral discussions. In the early years, Konrad Adenauer was persistently worried that one of the allied occupying powers, especially the United States, would strike a separate deal with Moscow that would undermine Adenauer's long-term objective of unifying Germany securely within Western institutions and values. The height of Adenauer's concerns in this regard occurred during the "deadline crisis" of 1958. Presenting a six-month ultimatum to the West, Khrushchev called for an immediate set of negotiations on the status of Berlin. Demanding both the demilitarization of the city and the West's diplomatic recognition of the German Democratic Republic (GDR), he declared that West Berlin should become independent, without direct influence from either of the existing German states. Failure of the West to respond would result in unilateral Soviet action. Adenauer feared that the allies would buckle under to these Soviet demands and that "normalization" of Berlin's status would lead to a U.S.–Soviet accommodation that would codify a divided Germany. In the event, the allies held firm and Adenauer claimed victory.

It is worth noting that this incident and others like it in the 1950s set the fundamental terms of debate between Bonn and Washington on dealing with the Soviet Union. Constantly in the foreground was the question of how best to influence Moscow's policies. Adenauer and many American administrations after him believed that the men in the Kremlin only understood the calculus of pure power, and that therefore, Western demonstrations of conciliation, especially at tense moments in the East-West relationship, would only encourage further the aggressive Soviet appetite. Eisenhower and Kennedy and many German administrations after them periodically wondered whether this was too rigid and dangerous an approach, particularly in times of crisis.[4]

American Suspicion and
Rise of "Genscherism"

After the Adenauer period, the suspicion that one of the partners was soft on Moscow shifted across the Atlantic where it re-
sided securely among some along the banks of the Potomac for
many years. As Henry Kissinger's memoirs make clear, the Nixon
administration had the gravest doubts about Willy Brandt's *Ost-
politik*. Would not Bonn's overtures toward the East weaken the
Federal Republic's anchor to the West and complicate Kissinger's
own efforts to link U.S. positive policy initiatives toward the USSR
to more benign Soviet external behavior?[5] These doubts explain
Kissinger's skeptical view of the West German desire to support
the Soviet initiative to convene a Conference on Security and
Cooperation in Europe, and his disinterest in Federal Republic of
Germany (FRG) attempts to affect the outcome of the revolutionary struggle in Portugal. Most important, it was behind Washington's fury when the Brandt government was insufficiently respon-
sive to American requests during the 1973 Middle East War, a
conflict Kissinger was convinced was, at its heart, a showdown
between the superpowers. Throughout this period, although the
Nixon administration acquiesced in Brandt's efforts, which after
all produced significant results, Washington saw Bonn continually
listening too sympathetically to siren songs from Moscow. At the
same time, the Federal Republic sought to protect its own crucial
interests vis-à-vis the USSR from the effects of American policies
outside Europe, and from what the Germans sometimes perceived
as U.S. intransigence or indifference with regard to developments
on the Continent.

As the years went by, these apprehensions in Washington came
increasingly to be centered on the person of FRG Foreign Minister
Hans-Dietrich Genscher. Although in the mid-1970s Genscher
provided a moderate balance to successive Socialist led governments, as that decade progressed and until the collapse of communism and then of the Soviet Union, his peripatetic efforts to improve or at least protect West Germany's relations with the Soviet
Union often irritated U.S. policy makers. Whether it was the Federal Republic's refusal in 1980 to follow the United States and

impose economic sanctions against Moscow after the Soviet invasion of Afghanistan; or Bonn's insistence in 1981–82 on proceeding with a gas pipeline linking the Soviet Yamal fields with Western Europe despite Washington's conviction that its European allies would become too dependent on Soviet energy; or Genscher's desperate attempts to find an intermediate-range nuclear forces (INF) arms control outcome that would preclude the need in 1983 to deploy new U.S. nuclear missiles in West Germany; or Genscher's nonstop diplomacy with Moscow in 1990 during the final months before German unification; "Genscherism" came to represent for some in successive American administrations an unhealthy and myopic regard on Bonn's part for Soviet sensibilities.

Bonn Worries More about Isolating Moscow

In reviewing briefly this history with an eye to the future, a crucial theme emerges. Because they lived so much closer to the Soviet Union than Americans, and because of the roughly 400,000 troops of the Red Army deployed in the German Democratic Republic, most West Germans after Adenauer, and especially after Brandt, were extremely hesitant to isolate or otherwise weaken political and economic contacts with Moscow lest the Soviets lurch into an even deeper crisis with the West, in Berlin, or along the inner-German border. The Germans were led by geographic proximity and the balance of power in a divided Europe to wish to pursue an active approach to relations toward and involvement with the Soviet Union. Bonn believed that passivity in the West's interaction with the USSR, especially in times of trouble, would likely make matters worse for the Atlantic community, for Western Europe, and especially for the Federal Republic.

Washington was, for the most part, more willing to put relations with Moscow on hold for serious Soviet transgressions. Farther away and with many more international obligations than Bonn, and notably after the last Berlin and Cuban Missile Crises, the United States paid no grave penalty and faced no imminent danger from a downturn or an extended hiatus in its relations with the

Soviet Union. In addition, American public opinion was much more ready than its West German counterpart to accept a freeze in interaction with the other superpower. George McGovern implored in the 1972 presidential campaign, "Come home America." Germans have never had any such choice. In the center of Europe, 600 kilometers from the Polish-Soviet border, they are home.

Differing Reactions to Soviet Reform Efforts and to the August Revolution

These fundamental differences in perspective between Germany and the United States explain their contrasting policies toward Soviet reform and to the August revolution in the USSR. For the United States, its principal concern throughout the cold war, as spelled out so brilliantly by Paul Nitze and his colleagues in 1949 in NSC-68—the threat to U.S. interests represented by massive Soviet military power and consequent political intimidation—has disappeared. Many awful things might and probably will occur in the former Soviet Union. But with the exception of the loss of central nuclear command and control or civil nuclear accident, arguably none of these terrible occurrences would have a direct and immediately negative impact on U.S. national interests. Thus American politicians and citizens have so far seen no urgent strategic need or obligation to transfer significant and scarce financial resources to the former USSR, especially given existing aid commitments to other countries, the U.S. budget deficit, pressing domestic requirements, bureaucratic inertia, and extraordinary uncertainties and confusion in the former Soviet Union itself.

The turbulence at the Soviet center and in the republics has given the United States the best possible excuse to wait and see, to put its economic relationship with the Soviet Union on hold as it has done so often in the past. But initial insistence by Washington that things must clarify east of Poland before the promise of American assistance or even that of the international lending institutions has been at the bone based on strategic doubts by some in the administration and the Congress that the United States has crucial national interests at stake in the Soviet future. In short, no American consensus has as yet formed in support of a radical transformation from the compelling imperatives of NSC-68 that won the cold war to a wholly new and equally robust strategy toward that vast conglomerate and former superpower.

Germany has seen the situation in quite another way from the outset. In addition to the nuclear question, the Federal Republic has other immediate worries about developments in the disintegrating Soviet internal empire. About 230,000 Soviet soldiers remain on the soil of the united Germany, and these heavily armed forces could get nasty—or attempt to defect—if authority from Moscow breaks down. Widespread instability in the Soviet republics could easily spill over into Eastern Europe, bringing chaos to the very borders of the Federal Republic itself. Authoritarian outcomes in Soviet republics could provide problematical examples to the more impatient and less democratic elites in Eastern Europe. Hordes of refugees could come surging westward, forcing Germany to accept them or put up walls to keep them out.[6] It does not take central European grand strategists to understand the dangers inherent in these several unpleasant possibilities, none of which need be very far distant in time or space. German public opinion and politicians are seized with the future of the former Soviet Union in ways and intensities largely unknown along the Potomac and in the United States as a whole.

This difference in perspective between Bonn and Washington has produced unusually frank words on the subject from Chancellor Kohl directed partly at his friends in the American administration. Bonn has already earmarked more than 60 billion marks ($34 billion) for aid to the Soviet Union, including funds for trade financing, bank credits, the removal of Soviet troops from German soil, and the subsequent construction of additional military quarters in the Soviet Union.[7] (Moreover, 140 billion marks was spent in 1990–91 by the FRG to shore up the economy of Eastern Germany.)[8] After warning the West for two years that extensive aid was critical to maintaining political stability in Eastern Europe and the Soviet Union, Bonn now argues, with increasing candor, that the burden for supporting reform to its east must now shift westward. "We are not the paymasters of everyone in the world," Kohl advised following the attempted Soviet coup.[9] "This huge task cannot be left to us Germans alone, or just to the Europeans. Every country—and I mean every country—must carry a fair share of his joint responsibility."[10] Assailing continued Western hesitancy, he stressed, "The most foolish possible policy now would be for us simply to sit back as interested onlookers and say, 'So, what are they up to in Moscow?' "[11]

Stabilizing the Former Soviet Union

Kohl is right in his strategic judgment that the West must deeply engage in the future of the former Soviet Union. This would seem to be close to self-evident if the Second Russian Revolution is one of the transcending historical events of the last hundred years. Although Germany will feel first the effects of disintegrative turbulence to the east, history and two wars this century should teach Americans that if there is widespread instability and conflict on the European continent, the United States will eventually be drawn in. In the wake of the attempted Soviet coup, it was striking how events on the other side of the Bug could quickly weaken the foundations of Western economic interdependence. Reacting to reports from Moscow, the Frankfurt stock market suffered its worst one-day loss in two years as foreign investors fled Germany. Among the hardest hit were German companies with considerable ties to the Soviet Union, and leading German banks, particularly Deutsche Bank, which suffered from widespread fears that the putschists would interrupt repayment of money owed for their multibillion dollar credits.[12] With American investments on the Continent totaling over $200 billion in 1990, and European ventures in the United States surpassing $250 billion the same year,[13] the ties of the Atlantic community go tangibly well past abstract strategic identities of interest or even profound cultural and moral bonds. So the real policy question before Washington is whether the United States will actively commit the vision and the resources necessary to confront the Soviet situation and its critical impact on the rest of Europe and Northeast Asia in time to affect the short-term outcome.

What, then, should the United States, Germany, and the rest of the West do, and do urgently, to try to promote a positive future for the lands beyond Eastern Europe, to avoid the return of dangerous and destabilizing external policies by the Soviet center or the republics, or the violent disintegration of the former Soviet state?

We should recognize that events in what used to be called the Soviet Union present a historic window of opportunity. People there have concluded that their society has failed. They believe that the economic and political democracies of the West have succeeded. They truly aspire to be "normal societies." They know that they do not fully know what that means, or how it can be achieved. They believe that people in the West do know. They truly stand at a "learning moment," eagerly receptive to the lessons of Western experience in normal societies. The West must not abandon the brave Russians, Ukrainians, and others fighting for reform. If it gives up, many of them will prudently do the same. If the West can pause to recall the central values on which its economic and political institutions were founded, it should make a major effort to distill and communicate these core truths to citizens from the former Soviet Union whose entire lives have been confined to a prison of distorting mirrors. The conversion of a military-industrial society must occur most importantly in the minds of key people: one by one.

The West should pursue a strategy of building infrastructures for democracy. What remains of the Soviet center and the republics is today open to printing presses, copying machines, personal computers, fax machines, and satellite dishes. Specific assistance can make the opening of the Soviet consciousness irreversible. Western support, however, must be differentiated. Assistance should be given to those whose actions will help bring democracy and a market economy, not to those who wish to use violence as an instrument of their political objectives. Democratic change, yes. Repression, no. Encourage a new union of sovereign nations. Discourage anarchy surrounding the disintegration of the Soviet state.

In the management of what will remain a dangerous international environment, the United States, and Germany as well, should continue active attempts to engage what is left of the central Soviet government and, increasingly, the republics. Recent decisions by Moscow to withdraw its troops from Cuba and, along with the United States, end military support to the sides in Afghanistan, as well as the November 1991 U.S.–Soviet chaired Middle East Peace Conference all attest to the benefits of this approach.

A Series of Bargains, Some Perhaps Grand

Most important, in an effort to forestall Soviet futures that would most deeply threaten Western interests and global stability, Western governments led by the United States and Germany should immediately design and offer a variety of bargains, some of which could be grand,[14] totaling Marshall Plan proportions to the former Soviet Union. The terms: massive technical and substantial financial assistance to reforms conditional upon continuing political pluralization, a coherent economic program for moving rapidly to a market economy, and adherence to fundamental and pertinent international agreements.[15] The strategy: create incentives for leaders at the center and in the republics to choose a future consistent with our mutual best interest by promising real assistance for real reform and responsible security and human rights policies.

The Western side of the bargains should entail well-designed, step-by-step, strictly conditional programs of assistance provided to the center and in many more cases directly to the republics and localities to motivate and facilitate rapid transition to a market economy. Core elements of the programs of incentives would include:

• A clear signal of the West's commitment to help in this peaceful transformation in any way Western assistance can have an impact upon the probability of success.

• Massive technical assistance distilling lessons of international experience and providing those lessons in an array of intense, on-the-ground training programs. In the first instance, emphasis should be placed on agriculture, food distribution, defense conversion, energy exploitation, transportation, communication, privatization, macroeconomic policy, banking, and the overall legal framework.[16]

- Major financial assistance only if and as the center and the republics are committed in their respective separate economic policies to realistic programs for the transition to the market economy.[17]
- Full membership for the union in the International Monetary Fund (IMF) and World Bank. As the union and republic governments, in conjunction with Western assistance, undertake the necessary structural changes in their economic and financial institutions and policies, they should become eligible for billions of dollars of aid from these institutions.
- Financial assistance of many billions of dollars per year for the years 1992–94 in grants and loans,[18] the cost to be shared by the United States, Europe, including importantly through the European Community, and Japan. The grants should be allocated appropriately between the center and the republics, and especially directly to Russia and the Ukraine, the most populous and important of the republics. Funds would go for large-scale technical assistance as indicated above, general balance-of-payments support, project support for key infrastructure (like transportation and communication), the maintenance of adequate safety nets as part of a general "conditionality program" that followed basic IMF–World Bank principles, and, when conditions permit, a currency stabilization fund for the union and perhaps for the Ukraine as well if it insists on a separate currency.

Some in the West today declare the former Soviet Union to be a lost or at least losing cause, asserting that it should be quarantined to stop the spread of its infection. It is too early to draw such a fateful conclusion. Recall that it was not until two years after the end of World War II that George Marshall called for a massive coordinated program to assist the reconstruction of Europe. The founding fathers of the transatlantic relationship on this side of the ocean persevered against what many at the time believed were very long odds, knowing that to do otherwise would be to consign generations to come to a world less stable and less safe. A Western effort championed by the United States and Germany to help transform the former Soviet Union would certainly be significantly more difficult than the challenge undertaken by the Marshall Plan. Nevertheless, there are more than enough reasons of self-interest and values to try.[19] As this is written, Western assistance to the reform effort in the former Soviet Union is far too little. Even if that changes, one hopes it will not be too late.

What Next for NATO?

U.S.–German defense cooperation within the context of the North Atlantic alliance has been one of the great success stories of the postwar period. From the creation of the *Bundeswehr* in 1955, through the integration of increasingly capable West German forces and their able military leadership into the NATO command structure, through the initial deployment and then maintenance of large numbers of U.S. troops on German soil, the defense relationship between Bonn and Washington was the key for over thirty years to NATO deterrence of the Warsaw Pact. The size of U.S. forces in the FRG varied greatly over the decades depending on whether U.S. preoccupation had shifted for a time elsewhere, such as to the Indochina peninsula. In the 1970s, the U.S. Army in Germany was wracked by race, drug, and morale problems. The regard in which these American forces were held by the West German communities in which they were stationed therefore fluctuated over the years. Support in the United States for the continued deployment of U.S. troops in the FRG came under occasional pressure, especially when East-West relations were good, the U.S. economy was bad, or both. Occasionally there was a brief bilateral crisis over how West Germany was to be defended in case of attack, as in 1977 when a document leaked from the Carter administration that suggested allied troops might have to fall back quickly from the inner-German border and thus give up large chunks of FRG territory in order to have any chance of holding even part of the country.[20] Throughout the period, the two governments argued periodically about offsets, and later burden sharing, and whether each was doing its full share in maintaining Western defense, a disagreement fought on both sides as required with statistical manipulation and self-righteous complaint. Nevertheless, the endurance and quality of this defense relationship overcame all such passing problems and in the end was triumphant in the cold war.

But what now for NATO, and for U.S.–German defense cooperation? Beginning with the alliance, it is difficult to exaggerate the conceptual challenge to NATO's existence that has been caused by the collapse first of the Soviet military occupation of Eastern Europe, then of the Warsaw Pact, then of communism in the USSR, and finally of the Soviet Union itself. (Perhaps it needs to be stressed here to a few nostalgic pessimists, especially in the United States, that these new difficulties for NATO, born of supreme organizational success, should hardly excite agony among us.)

NATO's Core Functions

NATO foreign ministers in June 1991 in Copenhagen indicated the alliance's four core security functions:

I. "To provide one of the indispensable foundations for a stable security environment in Europe, based on the growth of democratic institutions and commitment to the peaceful resolution of disputes, in which no country would be able to intimidate or coerce any European nation or to impose hegemony through the threat or use of force.

II. "To serve, as provided for in Article IV of the North Atlantic Treaty, as a transatlantic forum for Allied consultations on any issues that affect their vital interests, including possible developments posing risks for members' security, and for appropriate coordination of their efforts in fields of common concern.

III. "To deter and defend against any threat of aggression against the territory of NATO member states.

IV. "To preserve the strategic balance in Europe."

Looking closely now at these four core NATO principles that were so sensible before the three days that shook the world in August 1991 and at the outcome of the November 1991 NATO Summit in Rome, one must ask how these principles apply to the current situation. With regard to the first operational component of Principle I, that NATO should seek to reduce the likelihood that any European nation could intimidate or coerce another, one

wonders how the alliance might accomplish this worthy goal.
NATO is unlikely to involve itself any time soon if Rumania attempts to coerce Hungary or if Russia tries to intimidate the
Ukraine (as Boris Yeltsin has already sought to do by linking the
Ukraine's participation in the union with its borders with
Russia).[21] There is also the problem in contemporary Europe of
what is a nation? Serbia has certainly done its best to coerce and
intimidate Slovenia and then Croatia, and at this writing is brutal-
izing Croatian territory by force of arms. The alliance has had no
role in the Yugoslav crisis other than to exchange information. So
it would appear that in fact NATO is unlikely to be in a position to
implement this important element of the first of its core reasons for
existence.[22]

What about the alliance's function of thwarting hegemonic ambitions on the Continent, the other major objective in Principle I?
This goal was the glue that held history's most successful alliance
together. No matter how inflamed relations became between and
among NATO allies, the Soviet threat always made alliance considerations over time return as the hub of transatlantic relations.
But after the fragmentation of the USSR triggered by the Second
Russian Revolution, given the disastrous state of the Soviet economy, and in view of the inevitable very large reductions in armed
forces in the former Soviet Union, it will be many years and probably decades, if ever, before another hegemonic threat could
emerge from east of the Bug. Here, then, NATO's preoccupation
seems happily overtaken by events, as made clear by the virtual
absence of this theme at the Rome NATO Summit.

Principle II's emphasis on the alliance as a vehicle for consultation among its member states continues to have utility. Only in this
forum can the West examine in detail the security implications of
the break-up of the internal Soviet empire and only at Evere can
Western arms control policies be developed and agreed. However,
the 1989–91 revolutions in Europe have starkly shifted the emphasis of Western concerns, discussions, policies, and actions from
military deterrence of a clear and present adversary to issues of
political economy concerning how best to support the nascent
democracies beyond the Oder-Neisse in ways that reduce the dangers of violent instability including in the former Soviet Union

with its 27,000 nuclear weapons.[23] This change in the substance of the problem in Europe that the West worries most about has resulted in a consequent alteration of the most active channels of transatlantic communication. It is the G-7, the G-24, the U.S.–EC mechanisms, the Organization for Economic Cooperation and Development (OECD), and the international lending institutions that are best suited to deal with the daunting difficulties of Eastern Europe and the Soviet center and republics. It will be in these institutional frameworks, and not in NATO, where most decisions will be made regarding crucial political and economic policies of the West toward the ex-Communist nations to the east. In the arms control area, an entirely new conceptual basis for negotiated arms reductions in Europe must be developed, if that proves possible, before arms control efforts can resume their former important place on the NATO agenda. In short, the stress given in Principle II to NATO as the preeminent means of intimate transatlantic exchange on the most important matters facing Europe already seemed somewhat behind the pace and direction of events on the Continent, even before the August attempted coup and its stunning aftermath.

The "deter and defend" language of Principle III is an old NATO formula aimed at the threat of an old Soviet Union that no longer exists against the territory of an old Federal Republic of Germany that also no longer exists. This concept would now appear to apply only to threats from the Middle East against Turkey as during the war with Iraq, and perhaps in the worst case in future years from weapons of mass destruction based in countries on the southern rim of the Mediterranean. It is unlikely that these new threats against alliance territory, now largely either potential or hypothetical, will produce the same level of enduring interest and commitment on the part of major NATO allies, including the United States and Germany, that did the all-embracing and much clearer Soviet case.

As for Principle IV, one has reason to ask after the August revolution, what is the "strategic balance within Europe"? It is not East-West in character as we have known it for almost half a century, since most or all of the former East is trying desperately to join the West. It is not centered on or animated by conflicts of the

Serbs against the Croats, or the Armenians against the Azeris, or the Georgians against the Georgians, or prospectively the Czechs against the Slovaks, or even the Ukrainians against the Russians. Some of these conflicts could theoretically affect the strategic balance in Europe if we could first find it, but none are of a dimension or weight to define it. This balance-of-power concept regarding the European continent has centuries of refined thought and bloody action behind it, and no doubt contains regional and local security applications in the new Europe. But at least for the moment, no grand "strategic balance in Europe" seems in sight. This is no bad thing, by the way, since the concept is deeply adversarial in nature. So NATO will be hard put in contemporary circumstances to explain to Western publics exactly how its existence contributes to a continental balance of power that does not now exist, and that NATO governments do not wish to see emerge.

Is NATO Still Relevant?

To do this brief textual analysis of a single NATO communique is not to argue that the alliance no longer has a purpose. It will not be clear for some years whether the democratic experiments in the Soviet republics, and especially in Russia, will take root and succeed. If NATO were to be allowed to lapse, in which case American troops would almost surely go home, and if Europe was then faced with a resurgent and aggressive Russia and/or a Russian-Ukrainian war that spilled westward, who believes that the uniquely collective NATO treaty obligations, intimate U.S. security involvement in and commitment to the security of Europe, and allied integrated military cooperation could all be re-created in time to avoid another catastrophe on the Continent? Moreover, while U.S. officials can never so testify to the Congress or make the argument to the American people, Europeans want U.S. troops in Europe because they believe an American military presence reduces the likelihood that historical patterns of intra-European rivalry and conflict that produced war after war over the centuries will again resurface. In addition, the alliance is the sole plausible vehicle for continued U.S. military deployments in Europe, the only institutional framework for that purpose that Americans know, understand, and at least to this point, support. (To say that Americans have never heard of the CSCE understates the case.)

Finally, the West needs a vital NATO because of a point President Bush has made thoughtfully since the European revolutions began in 1989. Given the utterly unforeseen nature of the events of the early 1990s, what policy makers or analysts can be so confident of the eventually benign shape of the new Europe, so sure that new and better European security institutions can be conceptualized and then quickly created, that they would undermine or even dismantle the single organization that has been most responsible for producing the longest peace in Europe's history?

No New NATO Members, Please

Here a word of caution is in order. NATO not only will have to change dramatically to cope with the new Europe, it is already doing so. Major revisions in its military doctrine, alert procedures, and command structures; multinational integration to the division level; large cuts in conventional and nuclear force levels; a change in NATO's nuclear doctrine; and much less frequent and intrusive exercise patterns are in place or well underway and were an important part of the Rome Summit and the alliance's sixteen-page "New Strategic Concept" unveiled there. However, it would be a mistake to go further and widen the membership of the alliance at this time to include at least some of the countries of Eastern Europe. NATO's decision at Rome to keep well short of that and instead offer the ex-Communist nations an enhanced consultative arrangement was just right.

It is entirely understandable that these new democracies should feel vulnerable in an unstable region and wish to attach themselves formally to the only existing and enormously successful European alliance. But undue creativity and experimentation on NATO's part with regard to East European membership, at least in the near term, would severely weaken the political integrity of the alliance; complicate beyond recognition NATO decision making; call into question the current and future practices and capacities of the integrated military structure; and immediately raise the issue of Estonian, Ukrainian, or even Russian membership. At that point Western publics could be excused for failing to recognize why such a diverse institution should command their support, and particularly their defense dollars. For the foreseeable future, East Europeans should make do with broad expressions of NATO's interest in their security. This might not represent the perfect answer for Warsaw, Prague, and Budapest, but Eastern Europe would certainly not profit from an alliance that had lost its self-identity and thus its capacity to act.[24]

The Danger of Hollow Armies

In the radically changed European security environment, and given the disappearance of the Soviet military threat to Western Europe in general and Germany in particular, a serious issue arises concerning the future readiness of NATO forces on German soil.[25] For decades, West German citizens were willing, if increasingly reluctant, to accept the notion that deterring the Red Army required disruptions and irritations in their daily lives caused by frequent NATO military exercises. U.S., British, and other Western tanks from time to time clogged and sometimes tore up roads in the Federal Republic. Long convoys of NATO vehicles tied up traffic as Western troops moved from their permanent garrisons to exercise areas. German farmers, though compensated, accepted with no enthusiasm the environmental damage done to their fields by tank treads, heavy artillery pieces, and other armored vehicles. And, most politically contentious of all, the citizens of West Germany suffered the discomforting effects of low-level training flights by NATO, and especially U.S., aircraft as allied pilots sensibly sought to establish the advantage of terrain familiarity over their potential Soviet adversaries.

German support for these activities was waning rapidly before German unification, the end of the cold war, and the collapse of Soviet communism. Ordinary Germans increasingly ask why they should continue to tolerate the significant interference in their lives that these NATO military activities represent. All this occurs in a country without the vast, empty spaces found in the American West and Southwest where the United States primarily holds these sort of exercises. German voters point out ever more often to the government in Bonn and to their local political representatives that the people of no other industrial democracy, including the United States, are asked to make such tangible sacrifices affecting negatively the quality of their daily lives in a European security environment without a Soviet military threat.

With these German sentiments in mind, NATO military authorities are steadily reducing the number and size of Western military activities in Germany, and are relying increasingly on computer simulations to capture the requirements, challenges, and uncertainties of modern warfare. Low-level flying has all but stopped. However there is a limit to how far training inside the garrison can go. Contemporary armies cannot adequately maintain their readiness, much less their fighting edge, if they are mostly confined to their caserns. If this were to occur in Germany, the professionalism and morale of all forces, allied and German, would be sure to fall. This could be particularly true of American servicemen and women an ocean away from home. This unhappy situation would certainly not escape an American military leadership determined to maintain smaller, but ready forces with fewer defense dollars, not to say the vigilant eyes of the U.S. Congress.

Indeed, the difficulties of retaining a militarily plausible force in a united Germany and in Western Europe as a whole in the 1990s without an external threat has led some analysts to predict the emergence of a hollow NATO army deployed in the FRG, even given much smaller alliance forces in Germany. It appears probable in such circumstances that sentiment would grow in Washington to bring the troops home from Germany if they were prevented from doing their jobs there in a professional way. Discussions commenced in Bonn in September 1991 with the aim of negotiating new Status-of-Forces Agreements between Germany and the allied nations that have troops on German soil. Although compromise should in the end be possible, these are bound to be tough negotiations because of the domestic political pressures on Bonn, and the equally stringent technical requirements of allied armies and air forces in Germany. In any event, a weak and unready NATO force dependent on exceedingly long warning time to meet any threat that might emerge in the future might well find that this loose approach could fail disastrously in an unexpected or extended crisis.

How Long Will Allied
Armies Stay in Germany?

The potential emergence of technically deficient U.S. forces in Germany is not the only serious military problem that may arise between Bonn and its NATO partners, including the United States, in the years ahead. All Soviet forces are scheduled to be withdrawn from Germany by 1994, but in view of the developments in Moscow, it could happen sooner. Until Soviet forces leave, it seems likely that the German public will support the continued deployment of Western, and especially American, military personnel on German soil. How much longer after the mid-1990s this German willingness will continue to accept foreign forces of any militarily significant size is uncertain. Although there is presently no important lobby in Germany for U.S. troop withdrawal, that could change if instability to the east diminishes as the 1990s progress, and if Germans begin to feel more confident and secure. But this is a global trend that goes well beyond the Federal Republic. In the post–cold war era, it is likely to be increasingly unusual for national ground forces to be deployed in sizable numbers on foreign territory, not least because host countries will find it more and more difficult, in the absence of an immediate threat, to justify such deployments to their publics. Why should Germany necessarily be any different?[26]

Added to this uncertainty is one generated by sharply decreasing defense budgets in the United States and Britain, the two NATO nations most heavily engaged during the postwar period in the defense of Germany. In the United Kingdom's case, Her Majesty's Government has announced that the British Army on the Rhine will be cut at least in half from its 1990 size of 66,000, and its garrison in Berlin, which currently numbers 3,000, will be reduced until its projected departure at the end of 1994.[27] Whether the British public will support, even in the medium term, a force of twenty-odd thousand in a Germany bound to be richer and more prosperous than the United Kingdom is an open question. The same is true for the smaller Belgian and Dutch contingents. Canada has already announced the withdrawal of all but 1,200 of its ground forces from Germany.[28] France has indicated its intention to bring home most, and perhaps all of its three divisions from the FRG within several years.[29]

As for the United States, the size, character, and location of future military deployments in Europe, and especially in Germany, remained unclear as 1991 drew to a close. At least one-half, and perhaps two-thirds of the 330,000 U.S. troops deployed in Europe at the beginning of 1990 will be returning to America in the next few years. According to press reports, the Pentagon would like to keep a corps structure and two Army divisions in Germany, with three or four air wings based in Western Europe.[30] This would mean a total U.S. force in Europe of 100–125,000, in addition to a smaller Sixth Fleet in the Mediterranean. For the reasons mentioned above, this downsized but still significant United States military presence in Europe would be an important contributor to European security and to U.S. interests in the period ahead. But U.S. domestic political pressure is rising fast within the Congress to make further large cuts in the defense budget beyond the 25 percent reduction already planned for the years 1992–96. Led by the president, the Bush administration is sensibly resisting these calls for greater slashes in the Department of Defense (DoD) budget until the European landscape becomes somewhat clearer, but the outcome of this debate remains in doubt. If it goes badly for the administration, the result could be larger and more rapid U.S. troop withdrawals from Europe than are currently being planned. That would be bad for Europe, bad for Germany, and bad for the United States, but it is not impossible.

The Future of U.S. Nuclear Weapons in Germany

The issue of U.S. nuclear weapons deployments in Germany and the doctrine for their possible use has been one of the enduring, and frequently contentious, issues in U.S.–German relations. In the 1950s, these weapons were introduced by the United States into West Germany without a great deal of forethought concerning their numbers, their purpose, and their effects on German territory and on the German population if they were ever used. For the U.S. Army and later the Air Force, it seemed logical and prudent to increase steadily the number of U.S. nuclear weapons in Europe, and especially in the FRG, for the purpose of deterring the huge Soviet conventional force. As the years passed, thousands of American nuclear artillery shells, surface-to-surface missiles, air defense weapons, mines, and bombs arrived in the Federal Republic, most with ranges sufficiently short that they could only be detonated on German soil, East or West. By the mid-1970s, there were over 7,000 U.S. nuclear weapons deployed in Europe, with well over half of them in the FRG.[31]

West Germans naturally had the greatest ambivalence about this American nuclear protection. If these weapons truly would prevent a Soviet attack, and thus by definition never have to be used, then perhaps they served a useful and solely deterrent purpose. But if deterrence failed, if nuclear weapons deployed in the Federal Republic became instruments of war fighting and actually began to explode on German soil, the outcome would be catastrophic for Germans, whether or not the Soviet Army was eventually driven back across the inner-German border. Each change in NATO nuclear doctrine from Massive Retaliation in the early 1950s to Flexible Response in 1967 to Last Resort in 1990 provoked the greatest possible scrutiny and often anxiety from Bonn, lest the change mean that the United States did not intend credibly to threaten nuclear use, thus weakening deterrence, or conversely that Washington really did intend to employ these awful weapons early, recklessly, and massively on German territory in the event of a conflict.

From the American side, there was sometimes the suspicion that German governments hoped that if war came, the superpowers would fight a strategic nuclear conflict from homeland to homeland and over the heads of Europe, thereby sparing the two Germanies from the nuclear holocaust. If this was an objective of at least some Germans, it explained in part their desire to remove all, or at a minimum most, U.S. nuclear weapons from the Federal Republic. Such a West German approach, or at least occasional temptation, was unacceptable to succeeding U.S. administrations, and provoked the crude threat from some in Washington of "no nukes, no troops," or in its more recent civilized form, a U.S. call for the FRG to participate responsibly in "nuclear risk sharing."

These differing attitudes produced a prickly nuclear relationship between the two countries, and periodic bilateral crises on the subject. After the Multilateral Force fiasco was finally ended by Lyndon Johnson in 1964, the Nuclear Planning Group was established in NATO to give the West Germans a greater voice in alliance nuclear decision making. Jimmy Carter in 1978 canceled the neutron bomb deployment to the FRG without consultation after the Helmut Schmidt government had reluctantly agreed to accept it;[32] responded positively in 1979 with a two-track INF deployment/arms control proposal to meet Schmidt's concern that a deterrence gap was emerging in Europe because the Soviet Union had intermediate-range missiles and NATO did not; and reached a strategic arms control agreement with Moscow that, to the dismay of the FRG, he could not persuade the U.S. Senate to ratify.

Ronald Reagan traumatized the FRG by talking casually of limited nuclear war; demonstrating that he had only the faintest grasp of nuclear matters; delaying nuclear arms control until the end of the first year of his administration and then coming up with the INF Zero Option that most West German experts thought was utterly non-negotiable; proposing his Strategic Defense Initiative without discussion with Bonn; and then, at the 1986 Iceland Summit, suggesting the abolition of all nuclear weapons, again without seeking FRG views on this fanciful idea. During the same period, however, Reagan worked with Chancellors Schmidt and Kohl to successfully deploy Pershing II and Cruise missiles in West Germany in 1983; near the end of his two terms negotiated, signed, and ratified the Zero Option INF Treaty with the Soviet Union; and oversaw with Mikhail Gorbachev the beginnings of the fundamental transformation of U.S.–Soviet relations.

As President George Bush took office, several predominant trends had emerged from this long history of the U.S.–German nuclear relationship. The number of U.S. nuclear weapons in the Federal Republic and in West Europe as a whole was in steady decline, dropping to about 4,000 in 1990.[33] German public opinion was increasingly opposed to these deployments on West German territory and particularly to any modernization. The U.S. Congress, too, was ever more skeptical of the technical utility of short-range nuclear forces, and of FRG willingness to accept them. After Gorbachev's progressive if selective implementation of Soviet "new thinking" in foreign and national security policy from 1987 onwards, it became less and less obvious to ordinary citizens in both the United States and the FRG that these weapons played a useful role. These factors led the Bush administration to first postpone and then cancel plans for modernization of the Lance short-range missile that was to have been deployed in West Germany, and then in 1990 to propose arms control negotiations with the Soviet Union to eliminate some of these short-range nuclear forces (SNF) systems. During the same period, President Bush pushed hard for a START agreement on strategic forces, and that treaty was completed and signed in Moscow in June 1991. (At about the same time, the Conventional Forces in Europe [CFE] Treaty was also finally agreed.)

All of this was before communism ended its terrible long run in the Soviet Union. In rapid response to those events, President Bush announced *inter alia* on September 27, 1991, that the United States would unilaterally eliminate all short-range nuclear weapons on land and at sea in Europe, because a Soviet attack on Western Europe "was no longer a realistic threat."[34] In one dramatic move, the American president ordered the withdrawal of most, but not all, U.S. nuclear weapons from FRG territory and removed most, but not all, of the immediate bilateral nuclear substance from the U.S.–German security relationship. The United States will bring home and destroy its nuclear artillery shells and short-range ballistic missile warheads from Europe.[35] But the decades-long discussion on these matters between Bonn and Washington does not end here because in his speech, the president also included these two potentially portentous sentences: "We will, of course, insure that we preserve an effective air-delivered nuclear capability in Europe. This is essential to NATO's security."

These sentences mean at a minimum that the United States would like to keep hundreds of air-delivered nuclear weapons in Germany,[36] a prospect that may not seem immediately sensible to every German politician and citizen. As Joint Chiefs of Staff Chairman Colin Powell put it in an October 9, 1991 speech, "While we are altering considerably the mix of theatre nuclear weapons available to NATO commanders in Europe, we are not eliminating them. The essential nuclear linkage remains, in the form of our dual capable aircraft."[37] Moreover, the president may be seeking to retain the option of modernizing these forces in the mid-1990s by deploying in Germany and elsewhere in Western Europe a new tactical air-to-surface missile (TASM) with a range of just under 500 kilometers. Given the Second Russian Revolution, the negative trends in Germany described above concerning nuclear weapons, and the serious technical problems that TASM has experienced in its development stage,[38] it seems problematical that this new system will actually ever be deployed on German territory. The more pressing question is whether, despite the many uncertainties of the shape and character of the new Europe and the consequent need for the United States to retain some nuclear capability on the European continent, the people of a united Germany will agree any longer to the placing of nuclear weapons in their country.

Other Security Institutions from the Atlantic to the Urals

The problem of a separate European defense identity and its impact on the alliance is now well up on the U.S.–German agenda. This issue, too, has a long and sometimes painful history. Since President Kennedy's famous "Two Pillars" speech, American administrations have always favored more defense effort from the European allies to lessen the U.S. burden. However, Washington has never demonstrated its willingness, in return for an increased commitment of defense resources from its European partners, to cede some of its authority within NATO to the other side of the Atlantic. Some of the allies, and particularly the French, have for years sought, at the expense of U.S. influence within the alliance, a much greater West European voice in NATO decision making in particular, and European security in general, without a commensurate willingness to spend the money and create the military forces necessary safely to allow some American troop withdrawals from the Continent.

At the beginning of 1991, when European defense cooperation

appeared to have considerable momentum within the European Community and the Western European Union, the Bush administration brought its weight to bear heavily, and some thought clumsily, in allied capitals.[39] Washington was determined to avoid a shift in transatlantic decision making on security matters from NATO to one or both of these European institutions; to protect NATO's integrated military structure against French arguments that such tight command arrangements were no longer required because of the dramatic decline of the Soviet threat; to overcome France's objections and increase the alliance's political profile in the new Europe; and, as always, to maintain control through NATO structures of any conceivable crisis with the Soviet Union in Europe that might lead to a potential nuclear exchange.

In the Mitterrand government's view, these American objectives would, if accomplished, ensure continued U.S. dominance of the alliance and smother yet again the nascent European defense impulse. As this argument ground on through the spring, and with U.S. diplomats busy with their allied counterparts, especially in London and Bonn, EC and WEU members could not reach agreement among themselves concerning the shape of this invigorated European defense entity or its proper relationship with the alliance. (As German columnist Josef Joffe has put it, "The WEU is a sleeping beauty that has been kissed many times but never awakened.") At the same time, the Community's attention was diverted to issues concerning the powers of the Council versus the Commission versus the Parliament, and the question of extending majority voting to additional political subjects, including those of foreign policy. So yet another "Second Pillar" initiative from the allies trailed off. By September Germany and Britain were at such odds regarding the future nature of European integration that it appeared uncertain that the Community deadline to agree on the terms of European political union by the end of 1991, including increased security cooperation, would be met.[40]

This transatlantic row was reignited in mid-October 1991, when France and Germany announced their intention to create a joint army corps that would be open to other WEU members and serve as the hub of an eventual European army. They did not at that moment indicate whether this proposed force would or would not be within the NATO integrated military structure, but the French quickly made clear that France had no intention of rejoining NATO's military arm and that this new force would proceed without the alliance and without the United States. Britain's Foreign Secretary Douglas Hurd immediately warned that it was "useless and dangerous to overlap what NATO is doing."[41] Dick Cheney, U.S. secretary of defense, added that "it is our very strong feeling that whatever is done in the arena of developing the European security identity should not detract from or undermine or in any way weaken . . . the cohesion or coherence of the NATO structure that's been so effective for the past 40 years."[42]

With Germany in its nightmare position of being trapped between Paris and Washington, and as the Germans tried to reassure both of its closest allies simultaneously, the dispute simmered on until the early November NATO Summit in Rome. There, the U.S. called and raised the French bid. President Bush told allied leaders that "our premise is that the American role in the defense and the affairs of Europe will not be made superfluous by European Union. If our premise is wrong, if, my friends, your ultimate aim is to provide individually for your own defense, the time to tell us is today."[43] This challenge produced the predictable flood of reassurance from the allies, and France once more bitterly found that when the allies are forced to choose between Paris and Washington on fundamental NATO defense issues, it is no contest. Despite this further delay in developing European defense cooperation, over time the EC will return to the subject, and Washington and Bonn will again have to balance the prospective benefits of a more vital European defense identity against the inevitable loss of U.S. military presence and influence on European security issues that this would produce. Here, it is instructive to notice that both EC and U.S. traditional views on this subject have recently been altered by the Yugoslav crisis.[44] When Western governments and experts in 1989–90 discussed future European architecture, the debate centered—especially in Germany—on whether NATO or the CSCE would be the most desirable hub of a new European security system. As noted above, the alliance hoped it could indirectly provide a stabilizing influence on Eastern Europe. The CSCE created a Crisis Resolution Center to the same end. In the tragic Yugoslav event, it was neither of these institutions that took the lead in seeking to negotiate a stop to the violence. NATO remained on the sidelines, no doubt exchanging information but no more. The CSCE provided a useful umbrella for negotiation done by others elsewhere.

The European Community has emerged as the West's last best hope to resolve the crisis. Even though the EC has so far been unsuccessful in this attempt, the implications of this purposeful EC effort for European security and U.S.–German security cooperation could be long-lasting. Some might have argued before the shattering of the Soviet Union that the Yugoslav case was unique: no border with the former USSR; not a member of the Warsaw Pact; thus no traditional East-West dimension and no NATO role; and besides, the Americans were otherwise engaged trying to arrange a Middle East peace conference. Thus some might have believed that another explosion in Eastern Europe would mark a return to the familiar East-West pattern of the United States and NATO in the forefront.

With the Second Russian Revolution at full speed and the Soviet military threat to Europe ended, and especially if EC peace efforts in Yugoslavia succeed against expectations, might not the European Community become the arbiter of Eastern European security disputes? After all, these countries want EC membership. The Community and its member states (Germany easily leads that list in pushing money into Eastern Europe) are by far the largest aid donors to them. This EC leverage is very much greater than that of the United States and will grow. And the United States may again be hesitant to put itself into the middle of Eastern European nationalisms and ethnic hatreds, not to mention all-out wars in the region, when it will be so much less immediately affected than EC member states.

With these dimensions of the Yugoslav crisis in mind, and in view of the Soviet collapse and the major reduction of U.S. troops in Europe scheduled for the next few years, it is now time for the United States to abandon its traditional opposition to rapid and real European defense cooperation and to work with the allies, beginning with the British, to push constructive European defense cooperation (not the kind sometimes favored in Paris) forward in the context of political union. This seems to be the approach President Bush took during his November 1991 summit with the EC in the Hague.[45] Not only should Washington gracefully accept that the American role in NATO should recede in importance over time, though remain substantial, if a robust European defense identity and military capability can be achieved, this should precisely be the U.S. objective after Europe's glorious revolutions of 1989–91.

One last comment concerning present and future institutions of European security. As mentioned earlier, some in the Federal Republic and fewer in America hoped that the CSCE could become the core of a new European security order. That seemed both unlikely and unwise a year ago. Now it appears close to impossible. This organization has no military forces at its disposal. It has no experience in collective threat assessment or deterrent action. It operates entirely on the basis of unanimous consent, and it is shortly likely to have something like fifty exceedingly diverse members. The CSCE will certainly remain the preeminent European human rights organization. And it may be that the CSCE can at the margin serve the cause of European security, but certainly not at the expense of a weaker NATO or lessened security role for the European Community. If the alliance and/or the EC were to erode seriously in the 1990s, the CSCE would not be an inheritor of their mantles, but a parallel victim of their decline.

Germany's Military Role Regarding Threats from Outside the NATO Treaty Area

That there have been recent problems between the United States and Germany regarding security threats to the West emanating from outside the alliance treaty area should come as no surprise. Unless the immediate defense of German territory was involved, successive FRG governments have always been highly uncomfortable and sometimes publicly or privately critical when other NATO members undertook or threatened military actions, the former having always been thankfully not in the Soviet context. Whether it was French and then U.S. involvement in Vietnam, U.S.–Soviet confrontation during the 1973 Middle East War and over Afghanistan, the British liberation of the Falkland Islands, or American use of force against Libya, Nicaragua, Grenada, and Panama, most Germans have instinctively believed that international problems could be resolved without resort to force if only enough patience and good will were applied. "Negotiate harder" was the constant advice from Bonn whenever an ally, usually the United States, indicated it was about to undertake violent action against a transgressor. Many outsiders and Germans alike explained this deeply held and emotional aversion to force as an instinctive reaction against Nazi bestiality, and earlier Prussian deification of military virtue. As Thomas Kielinger has pointed out, Germans appeared to believe that being obviously peace loving was their primary international obligation.[46]

But even within this understandable historical context, the German government's initial response to the U.S. led coalition's military operation to drive Iraq out of Kuwait was lamentable. The issue was not whether German troops should be sent to the Gulf to fight. The German Basic Law prevented that.[47] Nor was it the FRG's interest in a diplomatic solution to the crisis that met UN objectives, although Foreign Minister Genscher may have been a bit too willing to take into account Saddam Hussein's point of view. Most of the international community wanted the dispute settled peacefully. Nor was it even the previous assistance German business gave to Iraq's programs to produce weapons of mass destruction,[48] even if the federal government's failure to stop that activity was mystifying and indefensible. Rather, it was the slow, delay-ridden German reaction to the U.S. request for financial assistance in carrying out the war as if this was just another offset negotiation of the 1960s,[49] and its extraordinary reluctance to send eighteen aging Alpha jets and air defense units to defend Turkey, a NATO ally on NATO territory, after Turkey had committed itself for decades to come to the aid of West Germany if the Soviets attacked.[50]

But that was then and this is now. The crucial question for the Federal Republic today in this regard is whether it will amend its Constitution to allow deployment of German forces outside of NATO territory.[51] Although this is not a pressing issue at the moment, it has everything to do with Germany's evolving self-image, its place in the new Europe, and most important, the capacity of the European Community over the years to mount a plausible and effective military force to defend EC interests worldwide. Without a change in FRG policy that would permit an indispensable and unambiguous German military contribution to future WEU and EC defense arrangements and policies, it is difficult to see how the Federal Republic can escape the "free rider" accusation. Much more crucial, if Germany shrinks from undertaking new defense obligations, it would have to accept a major part of the blame for slowing the pace and strength of European integration in its most important manifestations. This delay would not be in the long-term strategic interest of the United States.

Conclusions

Several broad generalizations with regard to the future of U.S.–German security ties follow from the above analysis:

- With the Soviet military threat to German territory gone, and especially after complete Soviet troop withdrawal from Germany in 1994, the most salient reason for Bonn and Washington to cooperate in matters of European security has disappeared as well.
- The classical East-West political-military issues that for decades have so preoccupied the two nations, and the intimate and productive patterns of bilateral cooperation they engendered, are much less relevant after the recent European revolutions.
- For better or worse, Germany will increasingly find its future on the Continent in the company of its European partners and without intense day-to-day interaction with far-away Washington.[52]
- For its part, the United States will continue to have preeminent security interests with respect to developments in Europe, but over time will have significantly less capacity, and perhaps desire, to influence events from the Atlantic to the Urals.
- For these reasons, it will be an uphill struggle to keep this bilateral security relationship intact and of central importance to the two countries, but

• If U.S.–German security cooperation seriously atrophies in the 1990s, both Europe and the world will be more dangerous places.

Notes

[1] This is a particularly poignant fact given the remarkable cooperation between Washington and Bonn to bring about German unity. See Robert D. Blackwell, "German Unification and American Diplomacy," forthcoming.

[2] *New York Times,* November 13, 1917, p. 1.

[3] *New York Times,* September 18, 1955. Hear those piping crustaceans.

[4] See especially, Allison (1971). Allison's exhaustive work remains one of the most comprehensive discussions of American efforts to avoid military confrontation with the Soviet Union.

[5] Kissinger (1979), pp. 408–412.

[6] *Financial Times,* September 25, 1991, p. 2.

[7] *Wall Street Journal,* August 20, 1991, p. A10.

[8] *Wall Street Journal,* August 20, 1991, p. A1.

[9] *New York Times,* August 25, 1991, p. A11.

[10] *New York Times,* September 5, 1991, p. A13.

[11] *New York Times,* August 22, 1991, p. A13.

[12] *Wall Street Journal,* August 20, 1991, p. A1.

[13] *Survey of Current Business,* August 1991, pp. 47, 81.

[14] My Harvard colleague, Graham Allison, and I coined the term "grand bargain" in early 1991 long before the Soviet Union shattered. Things have changed, but even then we stressed that the republics, as well as the center, would have to be participants in the bargain. Now, of course, the republics will dominate.

[15] I have in mind the Non-Proliferation Treaty, START, CFE, and the 1990 Paris CSCE Declaration on Human Rights.

[16] For more detail, see Robert D. Blackwill and William Hogan, "An Army of Experts-in-Residence," *New York Times,* September 11, 1991, p. A27.

[17] See the *New York Times* editorial especially endorsing rapid Western assistance in support of Boris Yeltsin's announced reforms in Russia, November 12, 1991, p. A24.

[18] The exact figure would have to be worked out in talks among the parties.

[19] This argument is developed at length in Allison and Blackwill (1991). See also, Allison and Blackwill (1992); Allison and Blackwill, "On with the Grand Bargain," *Washington Post,* August 27, 1991, p. A23.

[20] Barnet (1983), p. 372.

[21] *New York Times,* August 27, 1991, p. A6.

[22] I say this with no relish. In fact, NATO is the best candidate to provide the hub for a new European security system, and perhaps even of a European military intervention force for Eastern European contingencies. But that would appear to be a long shot and in any case far in the future.

[23] At the Rome NATO Summit, the alliance urged Soviet republics to "refrain from any steps that would lead to proliferation of nuclear weapons or other means of mass destruction." *Washington Post,* November 9, 1991, p. 1.

[24] A Bush administration official is reported to have told allied governments at

the Rome NATO Summit that with regard to Eastern European wishes to join NATO as full members, "in the long run we'll let them in." *International Herald Tribune,* November 8, 1991, p. 1.

    [25] This section and the next draw on Blackwill (1991).

    [26] A senior German official reminds me that if Europeans do build a Political Union, then this sort of stationing on foreign soil within the EC should be entirely routine.

    [27] *Arms Control Reporter,* June-July 1991, p. 407.E-2.27.

    [28] *Arms Control Reporter,* May-June 1991, p. 407.E-2.26, and author's exchange with senior NATO official.

    [29] *Arms Control Reporter,* June-July 1991, p. 407.E-2.28.

    [30] *Arms Control Reporter,* March-April 1991, p. 407.E-2.22.

    [31] Barnet (1983), p. 370.

    [32] Barnet (1983), p. 376.

    [33] International Institute for Strategic Studies (1990), p. 214.

    [34] *New York Times,* September 28, 1991, p. 4.

    [35] According to the *New York Times,* this will total worldwide 1,300 ground based artillery shells and 850 short-range ballistic missiles. Reprinted in the *International Herald Tribune,* September 30, 1991, p. 1.

    [36] NATO announced October 17, 1991 that it would reduce its European nuclear arsenal to 700 weapons, a cut of 80 percent. *Boston Globe,* October 18, 1991, p. 1. Despite being opposed to the elimination of nuclear weapons carried by tactical aircraft in Europe, however, the United States has canceled a nuclear version of Boeing's short-range attack missile.

    [37] *Boston Globe,* October 10, 1991, p. 11.

    [38] *Defense News,* November 26, 1990, p. 4.

    [39] *Washington Post,* June 7, 1991, p. A17.

    [40] *New York Times,* September 26, 1991, p. A17. See also, *Washington Post,* September 28, 1991, p. A18.

    [41] *The European,* October 18–25, 1991, p. 1.

    [42] *Washington Post,* October 19, 1991, p. A19.

    [43] *New York Times,* November 8, 1991, p. 1.

    [44] For an earlier discussion of this subject, see Robert D. Blackwill, "United States and European Community Defense and Foreign Policy Coordination," paper prepared for "United States/European Community Relations: Towards a Global Partnership," Westfields Conference Center, Virginia, September 20–22, 1991.

    [45] *Financial Times,* November 11, 1991, p. 3.

    [46] Kielinger (1991), p. 246.

    [47] Kielinger (1991), pp. 246–248.

    [48] *New York Times,* January 26, 1991, p. 8.

    [49] *New York Times,* January 25, 1991, p. A11.

    [50] Sked (1991), pp. 53–54. Bonn similarly received criticism for waiting until the third week of the war to rescind its official September 1989 ban on low-flying Tornado practice flights in Germany.

    [51] Sked (1991), pp. 54–56.

    [52] Some thoughtful Europeans believe that Germany as the leading power on the Continent may find it in its overall interest (as part of its prestige) to be seen as *the* European interlocutor for the only superpower in the world.

7

Patterns of Partnership

Security Relationships: Germany

KARL KAISER

T hroughout the postwar period the relationship between the United States and West Germany represented an important, if not central, element of the cold war structure. It was on German soil that East and West confronted each other through two opposing alliances that spanned the globe. Germany, its orientation, and resources were one of the main stakes in the East-West conflict. In the same vein, the relationship between East Germany and the Soviet Union was of strategic importance for the structure and maintenance of the Soviet empire.

The crucial factors that once shaped the American-German relationship are now fundamentally altered or, indeed, no longer present: the cold war and the East-West conflict in Europe have disappeared; Germany is united; and the European security environment is a radically different one. The United States itself is no

---

KARL KAISER has been the director of the Research Institute of the German Society for Foreign Affairs (Bonn) since 1973. He is also professor of political science at the University of Bonn, and the author of numerous books and articles on German foreign and security policy.

longer the same country that once built up the anti-Soviet coalition. The impact of these changes on the German-American security relationship is likely to be profound. What form will these
changes take and what will be the consequences for the roles and
policies of both countries?

The United States and Germany:
The Evolving Centrality
of the Relationship

To understand the essence of the American-German relationship it is useful to compare the terms of this relationship as they
existed at the beginning and the end of the cold war. When after
World War II the East-West conflict became the dominant consideration of American policy toward Europe, Washington opted for
rebuilding a democratic state on the Western held territory of
war-ravaged Germany. As the European country with the largest
population (except for Russia) and a considerable economic and
technological potential, Germany occupied the geostrategic center
of Europe. To prevent its takeover by the Soviet Union clearly had
first priority; to transform that part of Germany controlled by the
Western allies into a force for extending Western influence to the
East came second.

As the events of 1989 and 1990 demonstrated, U.S. policy was
ultimately successful on both counts. But in the course of this
process West Germany's position evolved from that of an utterly
dependent client, an occupied country devoid of even the minimum attributes of sovereignty, to the second largest Atlantic democracy, to which President Bush saw fit to offer a "partnership in
leadership" in 1989 when the old order was beginning to crumble.

In the late 1940s West Germany desperately needed help from
the U.S., above all, protection against the Soviet Union, and especially so in Berlin. It required assistance in rebuilding democracy
and its economy, and it depended on Western support to become
a respected member of the international community. As time went
by, success set in, and West Germany's need for help decreased.
The relationship became less asymmetrical; indeed, as the Federal
Republic grew stronger, multiple dependencies developed in both

directions, and the number of areas in which Washington needed support and help from Bonn increased.

The collapse of communism, the dissolution of the Soviet empire, the unification of Germany, and the success of European integration efforts corresponded to the visions of American, German, and European statesmen of the early postwar period and testified to their farsightedness. Naturally, some of the intermediate stages and by-products of this process would have been hard to predict. The first goal in rebuilding democracy in West Germany was primarily to unroot any remnants of Nazism and then to immunize the West Germans against the ideological onslaught of communism emanating from Soviet occupied East Germany. The success and stability of West German democracy ultimately turned out rather to have quite an erosive impact on all of Eastern Europe by weakening its fear of Germany and the felt need for protection by the Soviet Union. In East Germany, the continuous, daily impact of a functioning democratic model ultimately encouraged the people of Leipzig and Dresden to take to the streets and shake off the Communist system.

Germany's economic miracle is hardly imaginable without the generous aid extended through the Marshall Plan, continuous American support for the establishment of a market economy (in particular before 1949), and the liberal openness of U.S. markets for German exports. By the late 1980s Germany had become Europe's leading economy and the Deutsche mark Europe's primary currency. But that was not all that had changed. During the same period economic factors grew in importance in defining the power status and influence of states in the modern world; ironically enough, this development favored the losing countries of the Second World War, Germany and Japan. When the Soviet Union collapsed as a military adversary, the world was suddenly able to perceive the relative weakness behind America's military strength. By then the United States no longer occupied its early postwar position as the dominant force in the world economy that could practically dictate its rules. It had instead become a normal participant in a complex international economy of mutual dependencies and vulnerabilities. Worse yet, its deficits had transformed what was once the world's biggest creditor nation into the largest debtor

nation that found itself increasingly dependent on outside financ-
ing at the very time when economic means became more and
more important in dealing with the crises of the post–cold war
world.[1]

Germany by then was more than just a leading economy in
statistical terms. The country had reentered world politics by way
of its economic strength. The economic giant had long remained a
political dwarf. Yet it was in the economic area that German
statesmen began to translate economic power into political influence. The instrument of economic summitry grew out of an initiative by Chancellor Helmut Schmidt and French President Valery
Giscard d'Estaing. Not only did economics become the first and
main currency of German diplomacy, but at the end of the cold
war period Germany had emerged as the primary Western trading
partner of every single East European country; it thus enjoyed a
privileged position for the era that followed the collapse of Soviet
rule and socialism in the East.

As the post–cold war era begins, we find the United States
weakened while Germany is significantly strengthened in the very
areas that will count more than military factors in dealing with
many of the security problems of Central and Eastern Europe:
economic links, political influence, and financial resources to draw
on. Between 1989 and late 1991, Germany had provided 56 percent of all Western aid to the Soviet Union and 32 percent of aid to
other East European countries.[2]

European integration is another area that owes a great deal to
the United States. American policy makers vigorously supported
early efforts at European unification. By making Marshall Plan aid
conditional upon a joint European administration they laid the
foundations for close European cooperation. In the end, West
European integration did achieve two of its most important goals.
First, it transformed the relationships of society and states so that a
new basis for a permanently peaceful conduct of affairs was guaranteed, and second, European unity provided the framework in
which the re-creation of a potentially powerful united Germany
became acceptable.

But the failure to extend European integration to a common
defense effort through the European Defense Community, which

faltered in 1954 because of British and French shortsightedness, resulted in a structural shortcoming that has had an increasingly negative impact during the transition from the rigidities of the cold war to a new set of relationships in Europe. The absence of a strong European structure in the security field turned the issue of European versus Atlantic approaches into a constant bone of contention and burdened the efforts to adapt international security structures to the requirements of the post–cold war era.

Yet another shortcoming made itself increasingly felt as the cold war approached its end. Americans had never completely realized that the eventual success of European unification efforts ultimately implied a growing European identity as well as European definitions of interests that would, in some areas at least, differ from those of the United States. To be sure, such a development lay in the logic of unification, but where it took form it generated seemingly neverending disagreements, be they over trade, relations with Eastern Europe, or new security structures.

The European Community and its various predecessors originally were envisaged as the centerpiece for a new and democratic Europe destined to overcome communism; but nobody in the United States or Europe apparently dared to predict what eventually happened. The European Community became the central pole of attraction for a reordering of the entire European state system, an island of stability and prosperity amid growing chaos, poverty, and violence. Practically every one of the old and new states in Central and Eastern Europe looked to the Community as a model for its own development and as a center of political and economic power with which it wanted to enter into close relations. At the time of transition from the cold war to a new international system, Germany is the leading economy and the largest member state of an integrated Europe that is bound to play a crucial role in dealing with Eastern Europe's political and security problems, while the United States, unfortunately, still has a number of unresolved difficulties with the European Community.

Toward the end of the cold war period the relative weaknesses of the United States in dealing with the new problems of Eastern Europe became increasingly evident. At the same time, however, its remaining strength was impressively demonstrated in two subsequent and partially overlapping developments: Germany's unification and the Iraq crisis. American leadership was decisive in resolving, within a strikingly short period of time, the complex international issues of German unification. During the Iraq crisis, which initially appeared to be the opening event of a new era of major conflicts in the Third World, the United States succeeded in organizing a global coalition against the Iraqi aggressor and sketched the first elements of what President Bush called a "new world order" after the traditional East-West antagonism had been overcome.

Conversely, the end of the cold war not only highlighted the growing assets and strengths of Germany, it also exposed united Germany's remaining weaknesses. The very Iraq crisis that demonstrated the United States' power and resolve as the last military and diplomatic superpower revealed that Germany was far from being able to translate its substantial resources and growing status into a commensurate posture of practiced international responsibility.

European Security after the Cold War

The European environment that shaped the patterns of German-American security relations for more than forty years has changed so radically that any discussion about the future shape and substance of security policies must start with an assessment of remaining threats and new challenges. Given the breathtaking pace of change, any such analysis is constrained by uncertainties and can only attempt to extrapolate from trends presently apparent.

Security begins at home. Western societies enter the post–cold war period in a state of high technological development, an advanced division of labor, constantly expanding networks of exchanges, and a general condition of interdependence that make them vulnerable to disturbances from outside that can more easily spread throughout the system. The intensive information link-up of Western societies inherently accelerates the spread of such disturbances. Given the internal integration and removal of barriers within the European Community, disturbances from outside tend to affect the Community as a whole with particular intensity.

Possibly the most important change for Western security ironically lies in the very removal of the East-West barrier in Europe, generally most longed for in re-creating a "Europe whole and free" (President Bush). The East-West border running through Germany and Europe not only separated two opposing alliances and value systems, but it also insulated the West for several decades from the internal repression, upheavals, and large-scale use of violence within the Soviet realm. Though this dividing line began to be pierced in the mid-1970s as a result of the process initiated by the Conference on Security and Cooperation in Europe (CSCE), it still provided "stability by division." The stability thus created was an integral part of the overall confrontation with the Soviet Union, allowing the West to build its island of prosperity and democracy behind a relatively effective barrier.

That partition has now disappeared. Democracies have been set up east of NATO, and the struggle for fundamental reforms of political, social, and economic systems has spread throughout the former Soviet empire. It is in the nature of liberal societies not to remain insensitive, but, on the contrary, to generate empathy with regard to developments in countries with shared values and aspirations. Moreover, openness to the flow of ideas, persons, and goods is one of the characteristics of Western systems. Even without any recurrence of outright military threats, the West will thus be profoundly affected by developments in the East.

"Classical" Threats

In reviewing potential challenges to European security in the future the first obvious question is: what has become of the "classical" threats stemming from massive Soviet military power stretching all the way into the heart of Germany, capable of surprise attack and large-scale invasion into Western Europe? After all, the formation of NATO, its strategy of flexible response, its posture of forward defense in Germany, and its complex organization of integrated command structures had been developed in response to these Soviet capabilities. But now the Warsaw Pact has disappeared and along with it the enforced allegiance of the armed forces of the Soviet Union's allies. Mikhail Gorbachev reversed decades of Soviet opposition to on-site inspections and thus made possible disarmament agreements and verification provisions of unprecedented scope.

The 1989 treaty on conventional forces in Europe (CFE), the agreements in connection with German unification providing for the withdrawal of Soviet forces from East Germany by the end of 1994, the retreat of Soviet forces from the territory of Moscow's former allies, as well as the unilaterally undertaken reductions of forward deployed military equipment have already eliminated the Soviet Union's capacity for surprise attack and large-scale offensives even before existing agreements are fully implemented. In the future a large-scale invasion would require months of preparation, which, in turn, would provide ample warning time to the West. But such an eventuality has become increasingly unlikely, as much for political and economic reasons as for more strictly military ones. With pluralism and democratization growing apace, the Soviet Union loses its capacity to attack other states. The disintegration of the Soviet Union, spreading internal conflict, the ever worsening economic crisis, as well as the breakdown of order and the lack of loyalty to existing authorities accelerate this process. Limited conventional options will be subject to the same constraints. This even applies to NATO's northern and southern flanks, now the only areas where alliance members and the Soviet Union share a common border.

Another threat that NATO used to perceive—the theoretical option of nuclear blackmail designed to obtain compliant political behavior—is also diminishing with the dismemberment of the Soviet Union and the democratization of its successor republics. In sum, all of these threats vanish along with the Soviet Union as a unified actor capable of aggressive action. It is the combination of dismemberment, decay of authority, and democratization that removes these potential threats to the West. Only the total reversal of this trend and the restoration of a neo-Stalinist regime with aggressive tendencies, even if confined to the Russian Federation, might pose a new problem for the West. But such a renewed threat would be unlikely to exist very long, since it would be thwarted by all the economic, social, and ethnic problems faced by a Soviet empire or a Russian Federation in decay.

The New Nuclear Problems

Some of the very developments that have eliminated the threats emanating from the Soviet Union as a single actor tend to create new security problems for the West at other levels. The future fate of some 27,000 Soviet nuclear weapons is portentous and consequently most important for Western policy. The problem arises at two levels: the potential proliferation of nuclear actors and a loss of control over weapons. With regard to proliferation, the split-up of the Soviet Union into numerous independent or semi-autonomous republics with varying degrees of independence in foreign and security policies threatens to create several new nuclear powers where there was once one nuclear actor in command of an immense tactical and strategic arsenal. Besides the Russian Republic, Byelorussia, the Ukraine, and Kazakstan hold nuclear weapons on their territory. Efforts on the part of the Soviet leadership to retain central command over nuclear weapons as one of the main functions of the union they seek to maintain (with some participation of the republics in nuclear decision making possible) may well fail.

During the last decades, in a complex process of interaction with the West, the present Soviet elite in command of nuclear weapons has learned how to live with nuclear weapons and how to control them. During many years of negotiations, through arms control agreements, after constant dialogue, and as a result of participating in joint institutions, this elite has developed certain concepts and rules that it shares with the West, all of them conducive to prudent behavior. The West has been able to count on their adhering to these rules, which laid the groundwork for the indispensable predictability that helped to safeguard the nuclear stability that the world enjoyed over the past decades. The creation of additional independent nuclear actors on the territory of the former Soviet Union may hand over control of these weapons to leaders not sharing this learning experience, who may, therefore, be unpredictable and basically incapable of handling such a potential in a responsible manner. Moreover, these successor republics are likely to be unstable, threatened by economic crises, internal strife, and putsches from the right and the left.

But the proliferation problem also exists on the international level. The clandestine efforts of Iraq to obtain nuclear weapons of its own have demonstrated that the nonproliferation regime, based on the Non-Proliferation Treaty (NPT), the control activities of the International Atomic Energy Agency (IAEA), and various other arrangements, requires substantial strengthening. This will become all the more necessary since the Non-Proliferation Treaty expires in 1995. In the past the Soviet Union has always been a supporter of a vigorous nonproliferation policy. Now the question arises whether the remnants of a central government are still *capable* of supporting an international policy of nonproliferation and whether the potential nuclear republics are *willing* to do so. In any case, if autonomous republics become nuclear weapon states, present treaty arrangements will require fundamental revisions.

Whereas the proliferation of nuclear weapons through the emergence of independent republics within the former Soviet Union at least presupposes governmental control, however inexperienced it may be, the potential consequences become even more dangerous and unpredictable should nuclear weapons escape the control of such governments. Many of the nearly 18,000 tactical nuclear weapons in the Soviet arsenal are relatively easy to handle, and a large number of them do not have the sophisticated technical devices that prevent their unauthorized use. The erosion of authority, growing political chaos, and possibly even civil war could produce conditions under which nuclear weapons might fall into the hands of secessionist groups or mutinous military units. Though their actual use in such situations seems somewhat improbable, their mere appearance under such circumstances is likely to have a profoundly destabilizing effect. Matters would get worse if some of these weapons were to slip out of the country and end up in the hands of radical governments or terrorist groups. In such a case they could resurface very soon under conditions that would directly threaten vital interests of Western nations.

Destabilization

Among the new threats to European security, the processes and likely results of the destabilization of Eastern and Southeastern

Europe, as well as of the entire Soviet Union, are most frequently cited. These have a particularly diffuse and yet potentially very momentous dimension. It arises from the combination of several factors.

• Independence movements in and fragmentation of currently multinational states will produce in the region between the NATO area, the Caucasus, and Vladivostok a collection of twenty to thirty more or less independent states. These will replace the monolithic structure of decision making in the formerly Socialist world, where, aside from Moscow, only Yugoslavia and, to a lesser degree, Albania and Rumania pursued some measure of independence in foreign policy.[3]

• All of these newly independent states, most of which are striving for democracy, have neither elites nor populations experienced in democracy; they also suffer from an inadequacy, if not total lack, of institutions capable of managing public affairs. In all likelihood an extraordinary variety of different regimes, ranging from incomplete democracies to semi-authoritarian states and outright dictatorships, will emerge to the east of Western Europe's democracies that, by stark contrast, are engaged in a process of ever deepening integration.

• In all of these states the extraordinarily difficult transition from decades of command economy to a market economy results in protracted crises, chronic shortages, and thus misery for millions.

• Practically all of these states already have or will seek to acquire armed forces of their own. At the same time their politics will be marked by a phase of assertive ethnic nationalism. The presence of minorities on their own territories or of minorities within the territories of neighboring states with whom they share borders of disputed legitimacy makes the situation all the more explosive. In sum, states within this vast region have both the instruments as well as some strong motives to transform internal disputes into interstate conflicts.

In general, the destabilization of a particular region in the world is not necessarily a problem for American, German, or Western security. But in this case a number of factors make these develop-

ments relevant to the outside world, and their identification deline-
ates the tasks for Western security policy.

• As already mentioned, Western democracies will experience a
great deal of sympathy for countries and peoples now struggling
for democracy, human rights, and a decent standard of living;
Western political processes will seek to translate such sympathy
into supportive measures. The West has a stake in the success of
the struggle for democracy in this vast region, for it is a fact
that democracies are more peaceful and cooperative in their external behavior than autocratic or dictatorial regimes, which in
this case would, moreover, dispose of a significant military potential.

• The worsening economic crisis associated with the transition
from command economy to market economy not only has a potential external impact because it undermines the chance of developing democracy, but it could also create such a degree of dislocation and misery that those most affected might begin looking for
better living conditions elsewhere. Especially in combination with
political chaos and civil war, this could result in waves of migration
so large as to swamp the receiving countries and undermine stability there.

• Violence is unlikely to remain restricted to its area of origin.
The vast amount of military equipment accumulated during
decades of wasteful and excessive armament, in particular the
presence of nuclear weapons in the area, gives every conflict a
significant destructive potential. These conflicts can spill over into
neighboring democracies close to the West or even lead to the kind
of hegemony NATO promised to prevent in its 1991 Copenhagen
Statement on the "Fundamental Tasks of the Alliance." In addition, violence might also spread to other adjacent areas, as support
for prosecuted minorities widens into an interstate conflict, for
example. Among the areas susceptible to such a spread of violence
are the Middle East and Southeast Asia, that is, unstable regions of
critical importance, where such conflicts would immediately assume wider strategic implications.

• Developments within this volatile group of twenty to thirty
states that are all experiencing various forms of crises and that find

themselves involved in numerous conflicts can have a considerable impact on the outside world, particularly through the transfer of all kinds of arms, know-how, or personnel from the huge Soviet military-industrial complex. Such transfers, especially of weapons of mass destruction or missile technology, would obviously have a destabilizing regional or global effect.

• Certain types of catastrophies that might result from internal turmoil are likely to have an impact far beyond the borders of the former Soviet Union, notably another explosion of a nuclear reactor as occurred in Chernobyl or the actual use of nuclear weapons.

• The loss of all or most of the former Socialist states (or their successors) as partners who are politically capable, resourceful enough, or willing to cooperate responsibly in dealing with global problems may possibly have the gravest long-term impact on world politics. For instance, commitments to act on global climate affairs are being made, but they remain ultimately irrelevant for lack of finances, appropriate technology, or adequate enforcement capacity. How can these states help combat terrorism or support a vigorous nuclear nonproliferation regime when they turn into the supply centers for large amounts of weapons and, possibly, technologies of mass destruction? How can they make a significant contribution to the development problem when what was once the Second World is increasingly turning into a variation of the Third World?

Global Challenges

When analysts occasionally characterize the cold war period as one of stability they tend to neglect the repeated large-scale use of violence within the Soviet bloc and the continuous occurrence of internal conflict and interstate war in the Third World. International politics in the Third World were highly unstable since the end of the Second World War with more than one hundred wars and many million killed as a result. All trends point in the direction of a continuation of this trend of instability in the post–cold war era. Although democracy has spread in some parts of the globe, notably in Latin America, there are still many authoritarian regimes and dictatorships to be found that tend to be less prudent and peaceful in their external behavior. Moreover, conventional military potentials have grown throughout the Third World, including an increasing capacity to produce and trade relatively sophisticated weaponry. Given the many unresolved conflicts in these regions, their destructive potential increases steadily.

Not only the eastern part of the Northern hemisphere has turned into an unstable, problem-ridden region; things are not much better with regard to the general global environment. Four trends are likely to be of particular concern to Western and therefore to American and German security policies in the future.

• The spread of weapons of mass destruction and of missile technologies represents the most portentous and thus urgent problem. The worldwide advancement of science and technology (not least due to development programs promoted by the industrialized countries) has not only increased the capabilities of mastering weapons technologies themselves, but also furthered the facility of individual states effectively to hide their patterns of acquisition and to conceal the true state of development in these fields. The discovery of Iraq's clandestine acquisition of considerable capabilities in the fields of chemical and nuclear weapons as well as missile technology (preceded by the open use of chemical weapons in the Iran-Iraq war) has provided new insights into a problem of increasingly global proportions. Unlike the East-West conflict, where nuclear weapons helped to deter war, the presence of nuclear potentials in the Third World is likely to have a profoundly destabilizing impact, because many of the factors that helped to secure peace between East and West (such as decades of detente, common rules and institutions, bureaucratic handling of politics, etc., are missing in the Third World. Weapons of mass destruction will affect Western interests because of their destabilizing effects within regions. But they can also challenge Western interests more directly by threatening Western states or forces directly. The spread of missile technology in combination with chemical or nuclear weapons only underscores this point.
• Increasing poverty and political chaos in the developing world

could cause waves of refugees sweeping north. Together with potentially large numbers of refugees moving from east to west, south-north migration could turn the problem of migration into a global issue of immense proportions. The relative failure of development policies and incessant population growth (which adds roughly 1 billion people every decade) are likely to increase poverty; at the same time, global information networks communicate the realities of wealth in the prosperous North to the hungry and miserable crowds in the South. Migration pressure will therefore almost certainly become one of the major problems for developed Western societies.

• The global ecological deterioration is increasingly assuming crisis proportions. As the scientific evidence grows that burning of fossil fuels causes global warming, and that the use of chlorofluorocarbons results in the destruction of the earth's protective ozone layer, immediate action to reduce these emissions becomes a matter of long-term survival. In this respect the United States and Germany, as highly developed countries that not only contribute significantly to the problem but also command relevant ameliorative technologies, carry particular responsibilities.

• International terrorism unfortunately continues to be a threat to Western societies. The increasing technological complexity and the growing interdependence of advanced industrial societies increase their vulnerabilities and hence offer a wide variety of points of attack to any terrorist offensive. The spread of unresolved conflicts in world politics, the existence of radical and fundamentalist movements, as well as the potential availability of weapons of mass destruction all make terrorism a continued threat for Western societies.

Roles and Policies
for the U.S. and Germany

The task of adapting their security policies and roles to the new circumstances of the postwar period finds the United States and Germany under the impact of almost opposite trends. The American posture in the world appears to be undergoing a phase of contraction, whereas newly reunified Germany, the reluctant late-comer, is expanding its posture as it tries to define the scope of its new responsibilities. The interaction of domestic pressures and external needs makes the outcome of both processes uncertain, though the results of the American reassessment may be more predictable than those of Germany's where the divergence be-tween external requirements and internal readiness is wider than in the American case.

Domesticism vs. International Responsibilities

Both the United States and Germany enter the post–cold war era with domestic handicaps. In the case of the United States, increasingly pressing social and economic problems require more attention and resources. Many Americans see in their solution a prerequisite for a renewed American security policy.[4] In the case of Germany, the reconstruction of East Germany and its integra-tion in a competitive German and European economy consumes enormous energies and resources and diverts political processes toward domestic issues. Nevertheless, a number of factors suggests that in both countries the pressures for domesticism will not eradi-cate a posture of sensible international responsibility.

In the United States, the breakdown of the Soviet Union as its primary military adversary, together with the collapse of commu-nism, has provided additional arguments to the old isolationist coalition of conservatives and liberals that wants the United States to withdraw from the quarrels of the world in order better to be able to satisfy domestic wants and needs. Although the strength of isolationism should not be underestimated, it is hard to believe that the United States would abandon its present posture as pur-sued by President Bush, described by one observer as a combina-tion of Wilsonian idealism and Bismarckian realism.[5] The remark-able, at times even outstanding, performance of the United States as a leader in the postwar world not only served the causes of democracy, human rights, and prosperity around the world, but it also of course served American interests. What logic could be found in a policy that commits America's resources during the cold war in the name of stability, democracy, and the protection of American interests, but then turns toward isolationism with the transition to a post-cold war world that is likely to be even more unstable, given expanding destructive potentials and a growing number of unresolved conflicts? Why should it be in the United States' interest to turn inward at a time when its dependence on a functioning international environment has grown, when its own public participates more than ever in outside affairs via the information revolution, and when American citizens will immediately be threatened by any breakdowns in an interdependent global environment?

In the case of Germany, powerful factors focus the political process inward, especially since the reconstruction and integration of almost totally run down East Germany has turned out to be infinitely more difficult than was assumed at the time of unification. In tackling these problems, Germany now transfers to East Germany annually the rough equivalent of the entire U.S. Marshall Plan aid to Western Europe. Needless to say, such a massive effort generates many problems and much domestic controversy.

Nevertheless, Germany cannot afford a prolonged posture of domesticism. No country will be affected as profoundly by developments in Central and Eastern Europe as Germany. Strategically located in Europe's center, and as the West's most eastern prosperous country, Germany is most exposed and, more important, most intensively linked by tradition, culture, and involvement to developments in the eastern half of Europe. For these reasons, German policy vis-à-vis Eastern Europe is under strong pressures to be internationalist, even though the military dimensions of Germany's "out-of-area" posture remain uncertain.

The Need for U.S. Involvement in Europe

American involvement with, and some military presence in, Western Europe continues to be of vital importance for dealing with potential conventional conflicts. To be sure, such an American role would be one of strategic reinsurance, since conventional aggression against NATO territory that would trigger the American commitment appears extremely unlikely, and use of force outside NATO territory in Europe will be only of limited interest to the United States, as the Yugoslav case has demonstrated. But as a reinsurance—and thus reassurance—against a reversal of policies in Russia, which will constitute a formidable conventional power in any case, the American role remains vital. The newly established East European democracies in particular attach great importance to a continued American involvement, not only as a guarantee against Russia, but also as a welcome counterweight to a potentially domineering role by Germany in Europe.

The United States also remains an indispensable partner in guaranteeing nuclear security. Here, two problems have to be distinguished. First, over the course of the cold war the United States contributed to the maintenance of peace in Europe and the world through its nuclear arsenal and its cooperation within NATO. Though nuclear weapons have lost their function of deterring conventional war unleashed by the Soviet Union, they do remain an instrument of reinsurance against a reversal of policy in that country or its potential nuclear successor states, and against massive conventional attacks. However, both contingencies are of highly remote probability. Moreover, a small nuclear capacity would remain necessary to deter future nuclear proliferators. These functions could be fulfilled with a fraction of the present nuclear arsenal and eventually even without U.S. tactical nuclear weapons on European soil. The nuclear disarmament policies of the United States and the Soviet Union point in this direction; hopefully, they will soon be joined by Great Britain, France, and China.

A second nuclear problem is of equal importance. Given the confused and partially chaotic internal state of the former Soviet Union, not deterrence, but the disarmament of its vast nuclear arsenal is the main task of the future. To prevent internal proliferation and a concomitant loss of control, a drastic reduction in the number of some 27,000 warheads and the establishment of effective controls over remaining ones are imperative. President Bush's radical disarmament proposals in this field have to be seen in this context. At present the Soviet Union does not have the industrial capacity to dismantle such a large number of nuclear warheads. Moreover, a system has to be devised to control the large amount of weapons-grade materials after disassembly. Only the U.S. has the industrial, scientific, and political experience properly to deal with this problem, which is of truly global importance. Other industrialized countries may be of help, including Germany, but their role can ultimately be only marginal.

The United States also retains a vital role in further transforming the European system of states through arms control and the CSCE mechanisms. Given the potential volatility of conflicts in Europe, notably on minorities and borders, arms control and disarmament approaches remain an important means for constant dialogue and, hopefully, for reductions of existing military potentials. The CSCE framework has been useful in pushing for the protection of human rights and the advancement of democratic procedures; both of these issues very much remain in the Western interest.

The crisis mechanism adopted by the CSCE member states in 1991 has since been of some value, even though it ultimately proved unable to prevent the outbreak of ethnic hostilities in Yugoslavia or to stop the resulting civil war. Its basic weakness is due to the fact that it was developed as a crisis mechanism for conflicts *between* states, and not for conflicts *within* states. Only the European Community, with the full support of the United States and other powers, is in a position to play a potentially useful role in mediating such European conflicts, because its political and economic resources provide a certain degree of leverage.

To support economic and political reforms in Eastern Europe remains a major task of all Western states; it will require not only a substantial transfer of resources, technical assistance, and training, but also a good deal of political encouragement. Though the main work will have to be done by the West European countries, notably through the European Community, a substantial American (and Japanese) contribution in establishing the general framework and in providing the necessary resources is absolutely essential. The new NATO tasks that the alliance set for itself in Copenhagen in June 1991, of supporting democracy and preventing hegemony in Europe, require a significant American participation.

For the international community to deal effectively with such global challenges as the proliferation of weapons of mass destruction, ecological deterioration, terrorism, and mass migration, an American role is vital and indispensable. To prevent further proliferation it is imperative that the international control regime be strengthened substantially. Such an improvement can only be achieved through a coalition of states that includes the major suppliers as well as potential supporters of international institutions capable of decisive action where necessary. Needless to say, American participation is vital on both counts. As the Iraq case has clearly demonstrated, where measures to prevent proliferation fail, recourse to sanctions or even the application of military force under international law must remain available options. It is hard to imagine how this can be done without drawing on American military power. On the other hand, it is doubtful whether a strengthening of the international regime to control proliferation can succeed as long as the U.S. continues to reject, as a general rule, challenge inspections in the field of chemical weapons.

The Iraq crisis demonstrated both the necessity for American involvement and leadership and the need for multilateral cooperation and support. To uphold vital principles of international law, the United States took the lead in setting up a coalition of forces, for which it made available its own military infrastructure and most of the necessary materiel; it also organized diplomatic support from the international community and obtained the financial means without which the United States could not have succeeded in defeating the aggression of Iraq. If similar challenges arise again, only multilateral action with substantial American participation is likely to remedy the problem.

In the field of environmental deterioration, but especially in regard to climate policy, the United States at present appears to be reluctant to enter into strong commitments. Yet it is obvious that without a substantial American contribution to a reduction of emissions and concomitant support for an adequate international regime, the further deterioration of the environment is unlikely to be stopped; much less can improvements be achieved.

In the field of international terrorism, American interests are not different from those of other Western countries in making every possible effort to combat its origins and activities. The destabilization taking place in the former Soviet sphere of influence and the growing danger that technologies of mass destruction may become widely available make international cooperation even more imperative in the future.

Finally, mass migration in Europe may appear to be a remote problem for a country that is protected by two oceans and has a fairly elaborate policy in place regarding its southern neighbors. But if mass migration does become a phenomenon of international politics, it is bound to affect rather substantially the economic, social, and political environment on which the functioning and well-being of the American social and economic system depend.

The end of the cold war offers new opportunities to enhance the role of the United Nations as the international community's principal organ in dealing with violations of international law. The handling of the Iraq crisis with the essential help of U.N. mechanisms provided a hopeful beginning. In order fully to develop the potential of the United Nations, it will be necessary, however, to activate the institutions envisaged in its charter, notably the Military Committee. This will require deliberate efforts on the part of the leading powers, and in particular the consent of the United States, which has in the past hesitated to pursue such an approach.

Germany's Expanding Role

In response to the dramatic changes in Europe, Germany has reconfirmed its adherence to the well-proven structures that have guaranteed its security throughout the postwar period. In that context it also expressed its firm belief that the continued involvement and a minimum military presence of the United States remain necessary to safeguard peace in Europe. Although survey research shows a decline in the public's acceptance of American troop stationing in Germany and the need for NATO,[6] the political consensus among the major parties regarding the importance of NATO and an American presence for dealing with Soviet uncertainties remains strong. Moreover, Germans generally share the belief widely held in Europe that throughout the postwar period the United States played an important, though barely acknowledged, role of rendering the old rivalries among the West European powers irrelevant through its mere presence. Despite the success of European integration, that role continues to remain important in light of European-wide dangers of renationalization and the increased power of a united Germany.

The crises in Eastern Europe affect Germany more than any other country in the West. Germany has, therefore, amply demonstrated its willingness to assist Eastern Europe through transfer of resources and involvement. But Germany's political and economic elites share the conviction that it would be undesirable for Germany to act more or less alone. Unless there is a European policy, backed up by a transatlantic approach, Germany in the long run would have no choice but to pursue a policy of its own: it cannot long tolerate disintegration, chaos, and violence in the East that would affect Germany most severely. Indeed, what was once a *Drang nach Osten* (a compulsion to turn eastward) could then be replaced by a *Zwang nach Osten* (a compellence to do so).[7]

For reasons of history, inclination, and expediency, Germany has a deeply felt preference for conducting its security policy in a multilateral context. Since the United States has traditionally been Germany's main partner in this area, the American role is considerable, not only in dealing with remaining "classical" threats, but also in creating the framework for a redefinition of Germany's role in meeting the new problems of the post–cold war world. To be sure, the main task of redefining Germany's role in the new environment falls to the Germans themselves, though allies and friends can be helpful. Since unification, Germany has become one of the world's largest and most resourceful democracies. Consequently, Germany has to assume a significant share of the responsibilities for maintaining security and peace in Europe and around the world.

During the cold war, Germany contributed significantly to the containment of the Soviet Union, to the restructuring of West European relations, to East-West cooperation, as well as to a more efficient management of the world economy. Throughout this period Germany chose not to be involved in military conflicts "out-of-area." It was considered unwise to employ German military units outside the NATO area, particularly as long as memories of the exploits of German troops under Hitler were still alive. Moreover, as long as Germany was divided and the meeting point of two highly armed and very hostile alliances, any involvement on the part of West Germany in a Third World conflict carried with it the danger of a spill-back into the German and European situation. Unfortunately, over the years various German governments of different political orientation referred to alleged constitutional constraints as a justification for German restraint, where arguments based on realpolitik would have been completely sufficient. In subsequent years, that justification increasingly tied down German policy, even though the Federal Republic's Basic Law does not explicitly prohibit out-of-area activities if undertaken as part of collective security efforts.

The Iraq crisis caught Germany in the midst of unification. Though hopes for a German commitment of military forces were expressed here and there, Western governments did not formally make any such requests. In any case, Germany wisely chose to offer its support of the coalition effort in the form of military equipment, substantial financial contributions, and the use of Germany as a major supply base for all military activities.[8] In the final stages of the crisis, however, German reluctance and public disagreements about the necessary solidarity with Turkey, and, most of all, an inadequate expression of solidarity with the coalition effort as a whole revealed that, despite the new circumstances, Germany's political class was by no means prepared to revise the policy of complete abstention from military responsibilities outside of NATO.

In democracies a redefinition of a country's role in external affairs can only come about as the result of public processes. Responding to new challenges from outside, policies must be revised accordingly and subsequently legitimized through public support. Unification, the Iraq crisis, developments in Eastern Europe, and global challenges have set in motion an intensive debate in Germany as to the country's future international roles and responsibilities. The Social Democratic party, in opposition since October 1982, would like to confine any "out-of-area" role of the *Bundeswehr* exclusively to peacekeeping functions. The ruling Christian Democratic parties tend to favor an active role of German armed forces either as part of a European intervention force or under the provisions of Chapter VII of the U.N. Charter. Foreign Minister Hans-Dietrich Genscher of the Free Democratic party (the Christian

Democrats' coalition partner) has already promised, in his September 1991 address to the U.N. General Assembly, that Germany will actively participate in U.N. peacekeeping missions and that any necessary constitutional adjustments will be made. Final determination of Germany's course is fraught with domestic difficulties, as a consensus of all political forces is not in sight. For the time being, however, a pragmatic evolution of the role of the *Bundeswehr* is taking place without much public controversy: after the fighting had stopped in Iraq, mine-sweeping units worked in the Gulf, air force units supported humanitarian actions in Iran and Turkey, and German military personnel participated in the work of the U.N. Disarmament Commission in Iraq.

If the redefinition of Germany's role outside of NATO remains consistent with the majority view of turning the United Nations into the principal organ enforcing international law, an enhancement of Germany's role in the U.N. is likely. Making Germany a permanent member of the Security Council, as has on occasion been suggested, is only thinkable—leaving aside all other problems that would have to be resolved—if Germany agrees to take part in U.N. military missions just as any other permanent member would. The post–cold war world is likely to witness many conflicts, proliferation of weapons of mass destruction, aggressive dictators, and numerous violations of international law. German abstinence in dealing with such conflicts made sense as long as Germany was divided. Now that it has become unified, however, and turned into Europe's largest and richest democracy, such reticence can no longer be its answer. Destabilizing developments in European or global politics will affect Germany particularly strongly. If Germany were to leave the handling of difficult and unpleasant affairs to allies, while it prefers to concentrate on the more agreeable and profitable aspects of international affairs, it would eventually find itself isolated and despised by the international community.

A European Security Structure

The development of a European security structure will be increasingly important for Germany's security policy. During the cold war Germany pursued its security policy primarily in the context of NATO, while the Western European Union (WEU) fulfilled some coordinating functions at the political level. The European Community assumed increasing weight in the nonmilitary dimensions of security policy through the instrument of European political coordination, at the CSCE level, for instance. Not surprisingly, the question of the respective roles of European and Atlantic security structures in the aftermath of the cold war has turned into a subject of increasing controversy. Though the alliance on various occasions—most notably during the Copenhagen meeting of June 1991—restated that NATO will remain of crucial importance for all affairs relating to security in Europe, including the future of democracy, American policy and that of several of its European allies has been based on the fear that the build-up of European security structures might undermine the American involvement in European affairs and thus lead to the demise of NATO.

For Germany the relevance of European structures to its security policy will increase for a number of reasons.

• Europe's historical disasters had their origins in failures of security policies and structures. At a time when nation-states experience a spectacular revival in Eastern Europe, while the danger of a renationalization of security policies emerges in the West, the preservation and strengthening of the European framework—with the Franco-German relationship at its core—remain as important as ever.

• The Atlantic framework of security cooperation retains its importance; indeed, it seems more indispensable than ever. But it is based on intergovernmental relations among sovereign nationstates. European security cooperation, however, is of a different quality insofar as it aims at integration and the pooling of certain elements of sovereignty.

• The European Community is likely to become the focus of European efforts to deal with European security issues in the post–cold war era, such as supporting Eastern European reform efforts or mediating newly arising conflicts, for only it can muster the necessary resources and carry out appropriate policies at the operative level.

• A genuinely European security policy that implies a common posture and a certain pooling of sovereignty is the only conceivable avenue, other than a strengthening of the United Nations, available for offering Germany a responsible military role outside the NATO alliance. For all of these reasons, Germany is committed to strengthening emerging European security structure within the framework of the Atlantic alliance. The same reasons strongly argue in favor of revising American policies, which have tended to express support for European security structures on a rhetorical level, while on a practical level more often than not they opposed such efforts. Support of a European defense identity would clearly be in the long-term interest of the United States. It could pave the way not only for a new transatlantic division of labor, but it would also help to secure the kind of long-term American role in European security affairs that the United States and Germany both consider vital to their own interests. Above all, American support of a European security structure would, in the end, strengthen the American-German partnership, for the benefit of both.

Notes

[1] These trends have been analyzed in my contribution "Directions of Change in the World Strategic Order," Adelphi Papers No. 23, International Institute for Strategic Studies, London, 1989, pp. 3–20.

[2] Helmut Kohl in a speech at the University of California, Berkeley, September 13, 1991.

[3] The exact number of future state actors is hard to predict. They will comprise the five former allies of the Soviet Union (Poland, Czechoslovakia, Hungary, Rumania, Bulgaria), the three Baltic republics, Albania, at least three successor states to the Yugoslav Federation, the Soviet Union plus its remaining twelve republics, and a certain number of the twenty additional autonomous republics that are likely to seek independence.

[4] See Allison and Treverton (1992).

[5] Gordon A. Craig, "Zu stark, um sich zurückzuziehen. Die Zukunft der Vereinigten Staaten nach dem Ende des Kalten Krieges," *Frankfurter Allgemeine Zeitung*, October 26, 1991.

[6] On this problem see Rattinger (1991), pp. 445–475.

[7] Ronald D. Asmus, "German Unification and Its Ramifications," Santa Monica: RAND Paper R-4021-A, 1991, p. 70.

[8] The case is examined in Kaiser and Becher (1991).

8

Patterns of Competition

United Germany and the United States:
A New Partnership for the 1990s

ROBERT D. HORMATS

U nited Germany and the United States—two countries that for decades have shared a deep sense of common purpose and been bulwarks of the Western alliance—should be pillars of the emerging world economic and political order. But they are

ROBERT D. HORMATS is vice chairman of Goldman Sachs International, with responsibility for development and execution of the firm's business in Western Europe and Canada. Mr. Hormats has a long career of government service in the executive branch, beginning in 1969, when he was staff member for international economic affairs with the National Security Council, a post he held until 1973. After a year as guest scholar at the Brookings Institution, on a fellowship from the Council on Foreign Relations, Mr. Hormats returned to the NSC as senior staff member for international economic affairs. From 1977 to 1979 he served as deputy assistant secretary of state for economic and business affairs, and from 1979 to 1981 as deputy U.S. trade representative, with the rank of ambassador. In 1981 and 1982 Mr. Hormats was assistant secretary of state for economic and business affairs. His publications include several books on international monetary and financial issues and articles in *Foreign Affairs,* the *New York Times,* the *Washington Post, American Banker,* and the *Financial Times* of London.

currently finding it hard to bring their policies into harmony. In 1990 and 1991 significant differences of opinion emerged between the two nations on matters ranging from interest rates, to trade, to aid to the USSR, to Operation Desert Storm.

Frictions between Bonn and Washington reflect neither German ingratitude toward the U.S. for its longstanding support of West German security and its more recent support for unification, as Germany's critics in the U.S. charge, nor are they simply a series of minor misunderstandings, as those wishing to minimize policy frictions suggest. They result from conflicting near-term priorities and preoccupations.

The importance of close German-American relations is constantly reaffirmed by leaders and public opinion in both countries. Chancellor Kohl has genuine affection for the U.S., and doubtless President Bush has a similar feeling toward Germany. Moreover, the August 1991 coup attempt by Soviet hardliners underscored to Germans the importance of an American defense presence in their country and to Americans the importance of an effective alliance with Germany and other Western European allies. The possibility that the former USSR will experience dangerous instability for years to come has served to strengthen this perception. The security, economic, and political interests of both countries continue to be similar in many ways. But the policies both countries would have had to pursue in the early 1990s to achieve harmony between them would have been inconsistent with their more pressing domestic and regional agendas.

This chapter describes, and attempts to put in perspective, the reasons for recent policy differences between Bonn and Washington. It goes on to propose an economic and political agenda for future German–U.S. relations—an agenda that can also lead to a revitalized transatlantic economic partnership and a new transatlantic balance of responsibility based on a new balance of economic as well as political power between the U.S. and Western Europe.

The ability and willingness of Germany and the U.S. to rebuild their bilateral relationship and tailor it to changed international circumstances will be a pivotal factor in future U.S.–European relations and in the future of the global economy. For forty years the U.S. and Germany have been twin cornerstones of the Atlantic alliance and leaders in building Western prosperity. Their future partnership will be indispensable not only to shaping a constructive course for U.S.–European economic cooperation in the 1990s but also to preserving stability and security in Europe, the Atlantic region, and other parts of the world.

The Germans are a people placed by history in the middle of Europe and conditioned by both history and geography to look East and West for trade and security; for centuries the Germans saw themselves primarily as a Middle European power. After World War II, Germans who had a choice, those in West Germany, opted—for the first time in their modern history—to plant their flag and their destiny firmly in the West. Chancellor Konrad Adenauer understood that membership in the European Community and in NATO would envelop his country in a fabric of strong Western economic, political, and security ties that would ease concerns among its neighbors about its future course and restrain any possibility, however remote, of future unilateralist instincts.

Yet Germany continues to have important interests in the East. And the 16 million citizens of the new Eastern states did not grow up with the same institutional ties to the West as their brothers and sisters on the other side of the Wall. Western relationships must remain strong enough and comfortable enough to ensure that both groups of Germans continue to see their future prosperity, security, and cultural fulfillment as being realized through solid ties with the West. This will be far less of an issue now that the cold war is over and Eastern and Western Europe are drawing closer together. But these changes do not lessen the importance of Germany's Western links and its involvement in Western centered institutions; they only make them less contentious vis-à-vis its neighbors to the East. Indeed they also make such institutions more attractive to nations to the East.

The European Community has proved to be of enormous economic and political benefit to Germany. It is likely to continue to be so through enhanced economic, monetary, political, and perhaps ultimately security cooperation. NATO, or a successor institution in which the U.S. and Germany are involved, is likely also to play a stabilizing and supportive role in German defense. Indeed security concerns did not die with the end of the cold war, and the prospect that not only Russia but also the Ukraine and Kazakstan will retain formidable strategic arsenals, if only for internal bargaining purposes, should reinforce the importance of NATO.

But the West must also recognize the importance that Germany attaches to ties to nations of the East and its desire to maintain close relationships with them. The U.S., along with Germany's other Western partners, must try to establish a framework for multilateral Western economic and political cooperation with Eastern and Central Europe, as well as the USSR, in which German interests can be incorporated and broadly served. Kohl has correctly asserted that the job of supporting reform in Eastern Europe and the former Soviet Union "cannot be left to us Germans alone, or just to the Europeans." The Germans should not be made to feel that they must shoulder virtually the entire financial and political responsibility for the future prosperity and stability of the East. The rest of the West, most especially the U.S., risks major recriminations within Germany, if due to its lack of financial support for Eastern Europe and the USSR, the Federal Republic's bill for assisting those nations is so onerous that it causes major difficulties for the German economy or if the collapse of democracies in Eastern Europe is blamed by the German populace on insufficient support from Germany's allies.

An American policy priority in the 1990s must be to revitalize its ties to a united Germany and an increasingly united Europe. That means providing strong support for the enhanced unity of the European Community and encouraging Germany to use its economic influence to ensure that the Community evolves on the basis of market principles and does not dwell on internal matters to the degree that it fails to shoulder its responsibilities in the global economy. Without a strong consensus between the U.S. and Germany on such matters as trade, financial stability, and burden sharing, the two nations risk becoming embroiled in mutually disruptive economic conflict and contributing to U.S.–European economic tensions.

Recent History

In 1990 and 1991 relations between Germany and the U.S. were
like those between two orchestras simultaneously playing different
symphonies in the same concert hall, each so preoccupied with its
own performance that it could scarcely make out, much less ap-
preciate, the music of the other.

Monetary Issues and Interest Rates. It is now painfully
clear that October 3, 1990, the day on which German unity was so
joyously celebrated at the Brandenburg Gate, was only the beginning of the process of bringing the two parts of Germany together.
That process has been painful, slow, and expensive, requiring
enormous social, political, and economic adjustment by peoples
on both sides of the old inner-German border. The economic
challenge has been formidable. And it is understandable that Germans would be so preoccupied by this historic task that other
matters—including its relations with the U.S.—would receive less
attention.

While Americans were anguishing over how to persuade other
nations to finance the $50 billion price tag for Operation Desert
Storm, Germans were engaged in an exercise over how to raise
funds to pay a bill perhaps ten times larger to finance the multiyear
process of German unification and East German reconstruction.
In 1991 alone the German government committed roughly $60
billion to the rebuilding of Eastern Germany. This it financed in
part by imposing a 7.5 percent personal and corporate income tax
surcharge—touted as a "contribution to unification"—and raising
the gasoline tax by 25 pfennigs per liter (67 cents per gallon). Gas at
the pump in Frankfurt and Halle rose to roughly $3.00 per gallon,
of which $2.00 was accounted for by taxes.

During much of this period the U.S. urged the Bundesbank not
to raise interest rates. It feared that a rate increase would slow
German growth, thereby reducing German imports, and would
put pressure on the U.S. Federal Reserve, as well as other foreign
central banks, to raise (or at least not lower) interest rates; Washington argued that these developments together would jeopardize
America's recovery prospects and those of much of Western
Europe as well.

The Bundesbank had other priorities. In the face of high German budget deficits and surging consumer demand, it sought to counter inflationary pressures and expectations. The combination of large fiscal deficits and high inflation is a dangerous one in a country with a past that includes the Weimar Republic. Just as the U.S. seeks to avoid a reemergence of its historical economic demon, the Great Depression, so Germany is determined to keep at bay its own demon, the hyperinflation of Weimar.

Far from responding to American pressures, the Bundesbank *raised* interest rates periodically in 1990 and 1991. On one particularly embarrassing occasion for the U.S., during the April 1991 meeting of the Group of 7 finance ministers and central bank governors in Washington, Germany rejected an attempt by President Bush himself to twist its arm to lower rates. This was but the latest example of a longstanding proclivity of the U.S. and Germany to hector one another on proper economic policy. On this particular matter, of such enormous domestic importance to Germany, deference to the American view was simply a nonstarter. Moreover, many German leaders, observing America's inability to reduce its own budget deficit, reckoned that the U.S. had little standing to offer economic advice to the Federal Republic.

Trade Relations. On the matter of trade, American pressures also bore little fruit. The chief American trade objective for several years had been completion of the Uruguay Round of multilateral trade negotiations. The biggest block to progress was agriculture. For several years the U.S. had pressed the European Community to slash its subsidies of farm prices and agricultural exports while cutting tariffs on imported food and feed. In the past, Germany had supported (with some grumbling from Bavarian farmers) liberalization of the European Community's common agricultural policy. In 1991 Germany did not abandon its basic principles on agriculture. Indeed toward the year's end Bonn indicated support for agricultural reforms similar to those proposed by the EC Commission; Kohl reportedly had told his cabinet that it would be "a catastrophe" if the Uruguay Round failed. But Bonn's reformist zeal had been weakened by internal and intra-European considerations.

Domestically, higher taxes and the cost of reunification, among other factors, had cost the government significant political support; most stunning was the early 1991 Christian Democratic Union (CDU) loss in state elections in Chancellor Kohl's own home of Rhineland-Palatinate. The chancellor simply was not as strong domestically in 1991 as he had been a year earlier. Farmers in Western Germany are politically powerful, especially in Bavaria. And farmers represent a far larger portion of the population of the more agrarian states of the former German Democratic Republic (GDR). The chancellor was unwilling to confront these voters for the sake of accommodating the U.S., however important agricultural trade was to the Congress and to his friend, George Bush.

There was another reason for Kohl's reluctance aggressively to champion EC agricultural liberalization. Germany's second priority, after making unification succeed, was the construction of the Community's single market, planned for completion by the end of 1992, as well as the framing of agreements for Economic and Monetary Union (EMU) and for European Political Union (EPU). Kohl's support for those enterprises was meant in part to offset concerns among Germany's Western European neighbors that the Federal Republic would turn its back on them because of preoccupations with unification at home and a desire to strengthen ties with Eastern Europe. Bonn, therefore, would not lightly confront Paris on agriculture. It needed to demonstrate to the French its desire to work with them on issues they considered important, and it wanted President Mitterrand's support for its objectives in Western and Eastern Europe.

The Uruguay Round was not unimportant to Germany. Indeed the Kohl government strongly supported its overall objectives. But in 1991 it was simply not as high on Bonn's priority list as domestic political considerations or intra-European relations.

Helping the USSR. Assistance to the Soviet Union was another source of friction between Bonn and Washington. By mid-1991 Germany had committed $33 billion to the USSR—ten times that pledged by the U.S. Much of this was to "purchase" Soviet agreement to expeditious German unification, to the removal of the Red Army from German soil, and to Moscow's acquiescence in a united Germany remaining in NATO. Kohl's decision to press for quick unification (which many at the time regarded as impossible) and to pay Moscow whatever it took to win its acceptance was surely one of the most brilliant policy moves by a leader of any nation in this century. Kohl's wisdom in employing this strategy has been demonstrated repeatedly since then—especially by the events of August 1991 in the USSR. And the economic cost was, in the final analysis, quite small.

While not seeking to prevent Germany from providing such assistance, which would have been fruitless in any case in light of the prizes this aid won for Germany, Washington itself was unwilling to commit new funds to the USSR. Its help in early and mid-1991 was provided in the form of guarantees to support the export of U.S. farm products to the Soviets. The U.S. also resisted efforts by Chancellor Kohl to have the Group of 7's Houston Summit in 1990 and London Summit in 1991 pledge large amounts of new assistance to the USSR. After the abortive August 1991 coup, German spokespersons strongly implied that had more assistance been forthcoming from the West the takeover attempt might have been averted. While such an assertion is of dubious validity, it illustrated the bad blood that existed between the two nations on this matter.

Washington insisted at both economic summits that major economic reforms must be undertaken by the USSR before large-scale assistance could be considered. It felt that while technical assistance and emergency food aid would be useful, sizable loans or grants would simply be wasted because the USSR had no structure or program for using the money wisely. Germany was considerably less preoccupied than the U.S. with the need for the Soviets to make immediate and dramatic economic reforms or to use financial assistance with maximum efficiency. Not that reform and efficiency were unimportant to the Germans; rather Bonn put higher priority on achieving political goals and on considerations like helping Gorbachev consolidate his position against reactionary forces, averting political or nationalist instability, and avoiding a massive westward exodus of Soviets, especially of the 2 or 3 million ethnic Germans in the USSR. Senior German officials also were sensitive to Gorbachev's concern that a Polish-type, radical reform program would disrupt Soviet society, provoke a challenge from the right, exacerbate ethnic tensions, and further weaken his control.

Chancellor Kohl and Foreign Minister Hans-Dietrich Genscher both had concluded that Gorbachev's continuation in power was greatly in Germany's interest. Had he not permitted and indeed encouraged reforms in Eastern Europe—reforms that ultimately led to the democratization of nations of that region (although arguably he did not expect his policies would lead to that, but only to a more liberal form of communism)—stayed the repressive hand of the despised Honnecker, and agreed to withdraw the Red Army from Eastern Germany while accepting membership of the united Germany in NATO? The Germans could not take the risk of what could happen if Gorbachev were forced from power. It was they who most feared the consequences of a successful coup by hardliners, men who might have balked at complete removal of the Red Army from Eastern Germany, or manipulated it to extract more concessions from Bonn, and resorted to repressive actions that could have triggered a flood of Soviet and Eastern European refugees onto German soil.

There were other reasons for helping. Bonn also feared economic collapse in the USSR because of its impact on Germany's own economy. The USSR had been the main trading partner for all of Eastern and Central Europe. An implosion of the Soviet economy would directly and indirectly harm the economy of the united Germany. It would raise the already high cost to Bonn of rebuilding the new Eastern states and could trigger a massive flow of migrants to Germany that would put even greater strain on Germany's already overburdened apparatus for coping with refugees and on its social system as well—exacerbating xenophobic sentiments already surfacing in the form of nasty, if now isolated and limited, antiforeign incidents in Germany itself.

Germany and the U.S. had different historic perspectives. Many Germans, among them Helmut Kohl, recalled vividly the humiliation and privation that their nation had experienced as the result of the Versailles Treaty, reparation requirements imposed by the victorious powers in World War I, and the lack of economic help to rebuild after that war. German leaders did not want to see the USSR (or Russia) turn into a slavic Weimar characterized by hyperinflation and high unemployment leading to a slavic Third Reich—a bitter, resentful, authoritarian threat to its neighbors. Nor did they want the Soviet Union to collapse into feuding republics that took out their frustrations on one another and retained large, in some cases nuclear, armies. These developments could increase pressure on the Federal Republic itself to maintain a large military force and to become more politically involved in Eastern Europe.

Desert Storm. There was yet another divisive issue in U.S.–German relations during this period. When Iraq invaded Kuwait the U.S. sought to rally political, economic, and military support first for Operation Desert Shield to protect Saudi Arabia and then for Operation Desert Storm to push Iraqi forces back within their nation's borders. American pressure on Bonn to commit forces to the effort met with resistance by the German government. German objections were based in part on constitutional grounds; it was prohibited by the German Basic Law. But even without this constraint, reluctance to act would have been strong. Germans had convinced themselves for over forty years that their nation should not deploy troops outside of the NATO area, and they had been strongly reinforced in that view by their neighbors and by the U.S. as well.

On the economic front, many Germans believed that their country already was bearing a gigantic financial burden for rebuilding Eastern Germany and Eastern Europe. Only after an agonizing period of indecision did the German government commit financial aid to the Gulf. Although ultimately the amount was substantial—amounting to roughly $11 billion, or about 0.7 percent of the country's GNP, with about $6.6 billion going to Washington—the delay caused considerable bitterness in the U.S.

The damage done to U.S.–German relations on this matter resulted not so much from Bonn's failure to commit troops, which was largely understood, but from a feeling among many Americans that having received U.S. defense protection against the Warsaw Pact for forty years, Germany was slow to provide even financial support to the U.S. to defend another part of the world against attack and to protect its oil supplies. The negative perception was compounded by German reluctance to send aircraft and air defense equipment to defend Turkey, a NATO ally, against a possible attack. Sporadic anti-American demonstrations in Germany, particularly in Berlin, although involving relatively few people, shocked Americans as well.

Germans, for their part, felt that they were being pushed to reverse overnight a long-held policy against sending troops out of the NATO area by countries that for years had insisted on that policy. And many Germans believed that having already made major financial commitments to rebuild the states of former GDR, to Eastern Europe, and to the USSR, large-scale financial support for the military eviction of Iraq from Kuwait was inappropriate, especially in view of the lack of broad popular enthusiasm in Germany for the war itself and resentment at what they considered relatively thin U.S. consultations with Bonn.

The U.S.–European Agenda

The above mentioned problems in 1990 and 1991 suggest a compelling and challenging future agenda for the U.S. and Germany: trade, monetary policy, East-West relations, and burden sharing. Germany and the U.S. will need jointly to address these issues not only because they affect important common interests but also because they are of overwhelming, indeed pivotal, importance in future U.S.–European relations.

During the cold war the need to preserve allied unity in order to counter Soviet power served as a compelling argument for resolving economic disputes and reaching compromises between the U.S. and Western Europe on potentially acrimonious trade and monetary issues. Now such constraints have all but evaporated.

Management of economic issues will be all the more difficult because consultative and problem-solving arrangements between Europe and the U.S. on such matters are less defined and less institutionalized than those that have long existed with respect to security. An "organic link" exists on defense between the U.S. and Western Europe in the form of NATO. Economic consultations constantly take place between Western European nations and the U.S. in the Group of 7, the Organization for Economic Cooperation and Development (OECD), and other forums, and there are increasing numbers of high-level discussions and negotiations between the U.S. and the EC. But there is no bilateral *organic* link on economic issues, no common U.S.–European *institution* or even a formal agreement (as in the case of the U.S. and Canada) to compel U.S. and European officials on the basis of mutually accepted principles and procedures to try to coordinate policy or to resolve differences. Moreover, neither Americans nor Europeans appear to believe that their economic destinies (or their security destinies) will be as intertwined in coming years as their defense ties have been in the last forty years.

With security ties less of a preoccupation, and no institution with political authority to compel U.S. and European officials to deliberate about and seek to resolve economic differences (in contrast to a network of intra-European economic consultative and decision-making arrangements), the potential for transatlantic commercial, monetary, and financial friction runs high.

The future shape of Atlantic relations will depend heavily on how the U.S. responds to Western Europe's desire for greater independence of economic and political action, on how Western Europe responds to the U.S. desire that it assume greater responsibility for its defense and for the health of the world economy without marginalizing U.S. interests in these areas, and on how the two work together to manage the momentous transition now taking place in Eastern Europe and the USSR.

Institutional adjustments will be inevitable. On an increasing number of matters the appropriate U.S. interlocutor will be a Community institution. The Community has become the central and preeminent institution in Europe; the U.S. will need to relate to it at high levels and on many fronts. These contacts will be both bilateral and in the major international institutions and groups— the Group of 7 being among the most important.

On the pace and nature of U.S.–European relations, Washington most likely will take its cue from Europeans themselves. Where Europe speaks with one voice the U.S. will need to engage in negotiations with the institution or individual representing European policy. The semiannual U.S.–EC consultations started by President Bush and Commission President Jacques Delors (which

include on the EC side the president of the European Commission
and the head of state or government of the nation holding the
rotating EC presidency) should be given increasing prominance by
both sides—and address a broader and deeper substantive
agenda—as should consultations initiated by Secretary of State
James Baker and his Community counterparts.

On the other hand, Europe is a collection of democracies. It will
continue to be characterized by political pluralism. There will be
wide scope, and a need, for the U.S. to work with different power
centers in individual nations, and within EC institutions, to influence Community policy. Ties between Washington and capitals of
individual EC members will remain important channels for coordinating positions and resolving differences. Close and frequent
consultations between Bonn (Berlin) and Washington will be vital
not simply because there will be bilateral issues to resolve but also
because Germany will continue to play a significant, and in many
cases a decisive, role in EC decision making.

Unless the U.S. and Germany can agree on their essential common interests—e.g., maintaining an open multilateral trading system, promoting an improved global monetary order, finding cooperative approaches to assist reform in Eastern Europe and the
USSR, and developing a sustainable formula for global burden
sharing—and make their realization a common priority, the potential for divisive U.S.–German and U.S.–EC disputes will grow.
The U.S. also must work closely with officials in other EC capitals
both to avoid putting Germany in the embarrassing position of
being seen as its Trojan Horse in the EC on specific issues as well
as to enable Washington to mobilize support elsewhere, particularly in the event that Bonn and Washington disagree.

Germany, Western Europe, and the U.S. must also come to
terms with a problem of inner-German transition. During forty
years of Communist rule, Eastern Germans developed attitudes
and practices that differed sharply from those of their relatives to
the West. That is a problem for the Bonn government and a challenge for U.S.–German relations. The psychological division of
Germany will be a significant factor in the country's foreign and
international economic policy for years to come. Citizens of the
former GDR have been thrust into a dramatic economic transi-

tion; it has led many to see themselves as second-class citizens of the new Germany. Easterners had become used to their former government delivering social benefits, however modest, and protecting their job security; many believe the government of the unified Germany has done too little of both. Conversely large numbers of Western Germans see Easterners as an unexpectedly heavy economic and social burden.

Easterners also have different attitudes toward foreign policy. Significant numbers of Easterners have strong pacifist feelings and an aversion to things military. They have been taught for two generations to see the U.S. as a military threat and a potential aggressor. And American society was widely regarded in the East as highly and excessively materialistic. These internal considerations could complicate Germany's relations with the U.S. and its security ties with NATO. It must be the task of West Germans, Western Europeans, and Americans alike to see to it that Easterners discover the benefits of the European Community and the Atlantic relationship; failure to do so could mean that they will exert their political power to the detriment of both.

Trade

Trade differences between the U.S. and the EC lie primarily in three areas: 1) general economic philosophies, particularly over the role of government in the economy; 2) the contribution each should make to improving the global trading system; and 3) the degree to which each should be permitted to shield economically or politically important sectors (e.g., agriculture, textiles, telecommunications, and government purchases) from foreign competition or to artificially boost the international competitiveness, through subsidies, of certain types of products (vanguard technologies, civil aviation, and agriculture, again).

In its broadest manifestation, trade policy reflects domestic policy, which is why a number of differences between the U.S. and the EC are so difficult to reconcile. U.S. economic policy, shared in the U.K. and other nations whose economic policies claim Adam Smith as intellectual forefather, places a high premium on individual freedom, a minimal government role in the economy, relatively open trade, and unfettered entrepreneurialism. Germany and most of its continental neighbors adhere to variants of a "social market" philosophy. German policies combine a high level of personal and economic freedom, and a commitment to market principles, so successfully implemented after the war by Ludwig Erhard and subsequently by a string of German governments, with a high "social safety net," government influence to avoid sharp swings in the economy, as well as encouragement of corporate cooperation enabling major players in the economy to support one another.

Trade conflicts between the U.S. and EC center on the appropriateness of certain types of government intervention and the degree of support that government legitimately may provide to key economic sectors. Such differences will not be resolved entirely by the Uruguay Round, however successful it might be, or by any other single negotiation. They will require ongoing and intensive consultations among European and U.S. authorities for years to come. The U.S. should use such influence as it has through this process to influence the direction of EC policy in favor of minimal economic regulation and intervention by member governments and by the institutions of the Community. Likewise the U.S. should be willing to entertain similar representations by the EC; it already has reflected some Commission concerns about the U.S. banking system in consideration of legislation on financial reform.

The U.S. sees the Uruguay Round as a test of whether the EC is committed to building a more open *global* trading system as it tears down internal barriers to trade, financial flows, services, and people and improves trade links with the nations of the European Free Trade Association (EFTA) and of Eastern and Central Europe. Will it pursue "open regionalism" or "restrictive regionalism"? Accomplishing the former means negotiating agreements that will expose more of its sectors to competition from outside Europe (in return, of course, for similar concessions by its trading partners). This will be done just as many of those same sectors are being exposed to intensified competition from *within* Europe due to elimination of internal restrictions to commerce in the 1992 process or new arrangements to expand access to the EC market for products of Eastern Europe and EFTA.

EC industries that have become accustomed to high levels of protection or government subsidy are likely to resist an increase in their exposure to imports from outside of the EC, as have French farmers to the import of Eastern European meat, especially during the current economic downturn. European governments, in this environment, might be tempted to help businesses in their countries by slowing the internal unification process, declining to open EC markets further to outside competition, or insisting on unreasonable compensation for further liberalization. They might dig in their heels by, for example, resisting further liberalization of non-EC access to the enormous government procurement market in the Community.

If Europe is perceived by Americans to be dragging its feet in the Uruguay Round, or creating new EC barriers where no international rules as yet exist (e.g., certain types of services, intellectual property, and investment), Washington will find itself beset by domestic pressures to take retaliatory or coercive measures against Europe—as it is now pressed to take such measures against Japan. The EC is likely to resist or retaliate, leading to a series of major trade disputes.

It would have been desirable had the Uruguay Round reached a successful conclusion in Brussels in December 1990, when it was supposed to end. But there is a silver lining to that otherwise dark cloud of failure. The continuation of the Round in 1991 encouraged the EC to remain more conscious of its responsibilities to the general trading system as it worked to create its single market; it also enabled nations outside of North America to monitor and influence negotiations on the North American Free Trade Area. In addition, the delay has bought time for Western nations to recover from their present economic slump, providing a more propitious environment for them to make trade concessions.

The Uruguay Round represents the first major test of post–cold war economic cooperation among major trading nations. Completing it successfully with a big trade liberalization package is the single most important step they can take together to ensure their continued prosperity and that of other nations in coming decades. Their willingness to make bold concessions in the interest of a more open trading order, which exposes their economies to the often painful disciplines of the world market while providing them increased export opportunities, is the *sine qua non* of real progress. A significant European contribution to a successful outcome of the Round, more than any single act, would dispell the notion that the single market will limit the access of foreign goods and services to the EC.

The implications of failure would go well beyond economic matters. It could be the 1990s equivalent of Smoot-Hawley. In an environment poisoned by trade disputes, the process of building the much heralded post-cold war order would become increasingly difficult. Far from being a time during which the U.S. and its friends advance democratic values and constructively engage former adversaries, the period ahead could see the global trading and political system weakened by intense trade friction, economic nationalism, and restrictive regionalism. That would, *inter alia,* strengthen pressures in the U.S. for a wholesale reduction in troop levels in Western Europe and embolden the neoisolationists. These possibilities put a high premium on the success of the Round.

If, however, the Round should fail, the major trading nations, with Germany and the U.S. playing leading roles, must map out a strategy for preserving key features of the current trading system, especially trade nondiscrimination and generalized most favored nation treatment, and establish a game plan for resuming some type of trade negotiations on subjects such as protection of intellectual property, treatment of investment, and government procurement—utilizing the General Agreement on Tariffs and Trade (GATT) or the OECD.

For the Uruguay Round to succeed, the U.S. and Germany (the latter utilizing its formidable influence in the EC), along with other major nations, must establish clear trade priorities and commit at the head of state or government level to reach an agreement based thereon. They will need to devote similar efforts to selling the results to domestic constituencies. German and American trade officials must reconcile their own differences over agriculture, services, and other prominent issues as a precondition for success in the talks.

For Germany and the U.S., internal pressures to limit import concessions will have to be reconciled with external needs. Both countries have an enormous interest in access to global markets for the products of their companies. Germany also must reinforce in the minds of its EC partners and its own people that even though 71 percent of European trade is intra-European (compared to the Western Hemisphere where only about 10 is intraregional), 13 percent of Europe's GNP depends on exports outside of the European region (compared to roughly 11 percent for Western Hemisphere nations). That trade, along with Europe's growth prospects, will be jeopardized if the Uruguay Round fails. The U.S. needs to emphasise to its citizens that millions of American jobs and the profitability of many American companies depend on exports, and in so doing attempt to counter inward-looking pressures.

Germany cannot hope to see recovery in Eastern Europe unless the exports of that region have greater access to global markets; that will be difficult unless the Uruguay Round succeeds. The more constrained Eastern European trade opportunities are, the greater the likely German aid burden in the East. Nor can the U.S. expect to see Latin America accomplish its economic reforms and achieve prosperity—which are needed to finally put the debt problem behind them—without growing global trading opportunities.

The evolution of the European Community's legal and social structures as they relate to internal and international competition will have a long-term effect on U.S.–EC trade relations. The U.S. and Germany both have an interest in creating a Europe with minimum regulation in order to infuse more competition into markets within Europe and avoid the resource distortions and inefficiencies that result from overregulation and subsidies. The U.S. has an interest in encouraging Germany to use its voice in the Community to avoid new regulations that increase labor costs and business rigidities or augment local content and other similar requirements on foreign firms. Rejecting such tendencies will be critical to the ability of American companies to do business in the single market and their willingness to invest in the new Eastern German states.

At the same time, Germany has an interest in an internationalist minded U.S. and in encouraging sound U.S. domestic reforms. If the U.S. economy falters, not only will German and EC exports be adversely affected but there also will be a risk that the U.S. will turn its back on its international responsibilities because it lacks the resources or the domestic political consensus to support them. That could remove a strong international voice in favor of freer trade, virtually isolating the Germans on this subject.

Germans are not blind to the fact that in recent years the roots of America's economic strength have been neglected. The pace of investment in the U.S., the key to future productivity and growth, has slowed. The political process has sidestepped or postponed decisions on urgent economic issues: budget deficits, growing entitlements, and financial reform. And the U.S. educational system has failed to turn out the large numbers of highly trained men and women who will be needed in this age of information and technology. (For a fuller discussion of the subject of the interrelationship between the U.S. economy and America's future international role, see my article entitled "The Roots of American Power" in the Summer 1991 issue of *Foreign Affairs*.)

The pendulum of U.S. public opinion is clearly swinging away from foreign involvement toward greater emphasis on domestic affairs. To some extent that is not only inevitable but appropriate. There is not a general mood of isolationism in the U.S.—yet. But a weak economy coupled with lack of a perceived foreign threat, plus a failure of the Uruguay Round, could push the pendulum very far in that direction. An America in retreat militarily and politically, and withdrawing from international economic leadership, could provide fertile ground for those in the U.S. seeking protectionist measures in a misguided attempt to boost America's domestic prospects; it could also generate pressures for aggressive measures to force other nations to conform to unilateral (as opposed to GATT based) trade and other commercial demands. They might obtain support from those who believe that America's international interests were so modest that the risk of a major trade confrontation with Europe or Japan would cost the U.S. relatively little on other international fronts.

Monetary Issues

The history of U.S.–German monetary relations is one of general cooperation punctuated by periods of often very public conflict. In recent years the U.S. and Germany have worked harmoniously in the Group of 7, and before that in similar forums, to pursue, at various times, balance-of-payments adjustments and currency stability.

But there have been periods of intense friction. During the Carter administration the U.S. pressed Germany to become the "locomotive" of the world economy, or at least Europe, by adopting more stimulative policies. It believed this would help, *inter alia,* to reduce the U.S. trade deficit. Germany's willingness to give in to these U.S. requests (in return for which the U.S. deregulated oil prices) has been cited subsequently by German officials as a prime cause of the increased inflation Germany experienced in the early 1980s. Under the Reagan administration the combination of loose fiscal policy and tight monetary policy was regarded by Germany as the main cause of a sharp rise in U.S. interest rates, which in German eyes pushed up interest rates in the Federal Republic and drew capital away from its financial markets, exacerbating the slowdown in German growth.

Germany's influence in the international monetary system derives in large measure from the credibility of the fiercely independent Bundesbank, the consistent soundness of its domestic monetary policy, and the historical strength of the Deutsche mark. In recent years its influence also has been enhanced by the fact that German monetary policy has induced monetary policies in other European nations to march in step with it. Germany wields the greatest influence in the European Monetary System (EMS) and exercises a preeminent role in negotiations aimed at creation of an Economic and Monetary Union. Although details of such a union remain to be worked out, the general thrust is toward much greater coordination of economic and monetary policy followed by creation of a single European currency and a single central bank.

Change in European monetary institutions foreshadows change

in U.S.–European monetary relations. Germany has acted successfully as Europe's economic "anchor" because of its long-sustained and strong anti-inflationary performance. It has been instrumental in the international monetary system's evolution from a dollar-centered order to an increasingly multicurrency order; over time the U.S., Germany (perhaps soon the EC in its place), and Japan have come to share monetary leadership.

These three leaders of the international monetary system will find their task complicated by the intense global competition for capital in the 1990s. Demand for capital will grow in Eastern and Central Europe, the USSR, Latin America, and much of Asia; Germany will devote more of its domestically generated savings to rebuilding its new Eastern states; Japan's savings are likely to continue to slip, and it will invest a larger portion of those savings at home and in East Asia; and the U.S. will continue to borrow heavily abroad. Germany, the U.S., and Japan will need to maintain interest rates high enough and inflation low enough to attract foreign capital and keep a relatively large portion of domestic savings at home. Successful anti-inflationary policies in these countries in turn can influence other nations seeking price stability and capital to emulate their performance. Their goal should be to ensure that inflation in their own regions and in the international monetary system converges on the best inflation rates rather than on the average.

Much of the monetary friction of the past can be averted in the future if the U.S., Germany (the EC, as EMU evolves), and Japan do what sound economic policy and their future capital needs will require them to do in any case: make price stability the top priority for their policy coordination efforts. This focus on holding down inflation does not deny that growth and high unemployment are important; it suggests only that these goals are unlikely to be attainable *without* price stability. Indeed countries like Germany, with consistently low rates of inflation and a strong currency, have been able to achieve very low rates of unemployment and stable growth over the years.

If price stability is clearly established as the common priority for these three nations, they could become "anchors" or centerpieces of three currency zones. Germany already plays such a role. The ultimate goal would be tight currency relationships among nations with similar types of economies within these zones. Intraregional trade then would be more insulated from currency volatility. Exchange rate flexibility could be somewhat greater among the three currency zones. Simply put, tighter exchange rate commitments would apply to regional currencies and more flexible ones to the three anchor currencies vis-à-vis one another. The anchor countries would nonetheless try to maintain significant currency stability among themselves—and thus among their respective currency zones—through anti-inflationary monetary policy, fiscal policy aimed at steadily reducing budget deficits, and structural policy harmonization aimed at reducing regulatory and other government impediments to market efficiency.

The USSR and Eastern Europe

The third area in which the U.S. and Germany share common interests is promoting reform in Eastern Europe, containing the fallout from the disintegration of the Soviet Union, and coping with ethnic and nationalistic hostilities throughout the region. Differences must be resolved on several subjects: how much economic support to give Eastern Europe; how much help to extend to the former USSR and how to apportion this between the center and the republics; how to cope with separatist pressures from ethnic groups throughout the region; and how to avert massive westward migrations.

The Community is the major pole of stability in Europe. Its prosperity and unity have had an enormous attraction for the nations of Eastern and Central Europe, as have its democratic and social values. It has a special role in and responsibility—different in kind and degree from that of the U.S.—for countries like Poland, Czechoslovakia, and Hungary by virtue of culture, proximity, and history. Although the U.S. has a moral obligation, and a broad set of interests, in supporting reforms in these nations as well as others in the region, it is upon Western Europe that history and geography have thrust the heaviest burden and greatest responsibility.

The democratic process is still fragile in Eastern and Central

Europe. Stability there is threatened by a host of economic problems including high inflation to high unemployment. Events in the
Gulf and the USSR took this region off the front page in 1991; yet
many of the gains of 1989 and 1990—trumpeted widely as a triumph for the West and for liberal democratic values—could be
reversed if growth and employment do not pick up. This probably
would not lead to a resurgence of old-style communism, which has
been thoroughly discredited there, but it could lead to the rise of
old-style autocracies—hardly advocates of freedom or free markets.

In the 1960s and 1970s the West would have paid tens of billions
of dollars to bring about the collapse of communism in the region,
a bargain price considering the resulting reduction in the Soviet
threat to Western security and thus the saving of tens of billions of
Western defense dollars. Now, having realized the desired collapse, the economic needs of the region are forced to compete—
especially in the U.S.—along side other pressing domestic and
international economic priorities; they are no longer seen as a
security priority.

Germany has demonstrated a profound understanding of the
inherent dangers of economic and political collapse in Eastern and
Central Europe. More than any other Western European nation,
Germany is vulnerable to massive immigration should things go
wrong in the East. It has closer trading relations with the East than
does any other major Western nation. And its security is more
closely linked to developments in the East than that of any of its
NATO allies.

It is not surprising, then, that Chancellor Kohl has been the
Western leader most enthusiastic about supporting reforms in the
Soviet Union as well as in Eastern and Central Europe. But the
U.S. and the rest of Western Europe share an interest in averting
turmoil in the region. They also have an interest in not placing
Germany in the position of carrying a disproportionate political or
economic burden in that area, which would provoke charges of
"excessive German influence" or cause Germans to believe that
the West is generally unsupportive of their goals of stability and
prosperity in that part of the world. If things go wrong in the East,
Germans could hold their Western neighbors partially responsi-

ble; some might argue emotionally if not accurately that ties with the West were harming the ability of Germany to pursue its Eastern interests.

Utilization of Community institutions, the Group of 7, and the Group of 24 have broadened the aid-giving and monitoring process. These groups together can permit Germany to avoid becoming so deeply immersed in the domestic affairs of nations in the region, by virtue of its having to provide large amounts of direct aid and unilaterally to monitor conditionality, that it is the target of criticism in Eastern Europe if economic reforms, or their failure, lead to social or political pain in these nations. A more forthcoming Western response, one that embodies a multiyear strategy for providing technical and financial assistance to the major reforming nations of the East, would enable Germans to see their Western partners as more supportive of their broader goals in Eastern Europe and the Soviet Union.

The U.S. and Western Europe will be most successful in influencing change in Eastern and Central Europe if they can establish common political principles to guide their decisions on whether and under what conditions to provide or withhold economic assistance. A few simple concepts appear reasonable: the EC and the U.S. should underscore opposition both to the unilateral or forceful redrawing of borders in the area, and to the use of force to suppress regions, minorities, or nationalities seeking greater autonomy or rights. Assistance should be conditioned on protection of minority rights by recipient governments and linked to establishment of institutional lines of communication by which the West can encourage responsible treatment of minorities as well as moderation by them, utilizing the European Community, the Conference on Security and Cooperation in Europe (CSCE), or the Council of Europe to monitor and mediate developments.

EC influence would be greater in Eastern and Central Europe, and chances for reforms to succeed would be enhanced, if the Community were more forthcoming in allowing exports from that region more liberal access to its market. In negotiating association agreements, the EC has been reluctant to significantly reduce import barriers on a number of items that the Eastern Europeans could sell to Western Europe in larger amounts to earn hard currency, e.g., steel, textiles, and especially agriculture. German leadership will be vital to establishing a more liberal Community position.

The question of the magnitude and type of financial assistance that should be provided to the USSR, or successor nations, is likely to be an ongoing issue between the U.S. and at least some members of the EC, including Germany. There is danger that the U.S. and Germany will work at cross purposes—with the U.S. being less forthcoming than Bonn and the Germans providing large sums to which they attach relatively weak conditions. Conflict between the two nations would reduce Western influence over Soviet and republic economic reforms.

The West needs a strategy to ensure that assistance promotes, rather than serves as a device to permit avoidance of, Soviet reform. It should insist that the republics cooperate on economic issues even if they choose to go their own ways politically or resist creation of a strong central economic authority—which many republics feel would be dominated by Russia. A common plan involving the key republics on one hand and the World Bank, International Monetary Fund (IMF), European Bank for Reconstruction and Development, and the OECD on the other could mobilize the best of the West's technical resources and permit pledges of funds to be made on a stand-by basis (like an IMF stand-by agreement) so that reformers in the republics would have confidence that preagreed sums of funds would be available if promised reforms were undertaken. A multirepublic economic plan, although not necessarily one organized by central authorities, is needed to address questions of currency convertibility, debt, and fiscal stability, but reforms such as military conversion, demonopolization, and privatization can be accomplished at republic level.

Burden Sharing

The focus on burden sharing during the Gulf War dwelt more on how to share financial burdens than on why burdens should be shared. Without a broader understanding among major nations of the West on common security, political, and economic goals, orderly and fair burden sharing in future Gulf-type situations, or any others, is unlikely to materialize. Agreement on common goals will require a more intense U.S.–EC–Japan dialogue on foreign policy objectives and interests leading to an understanding of how to share responsibility for pursuing them. Without this exercise in anticipation of a crisis (recognizing that the inherent inability to predict the precise nature of a future crisis in advance makes detailed planning impossible), intra-Western relations during periods of crisis will be subject to acrimony, cross-charges of unfairness, and excessive demands being hurled across the Atlantic and Pacific.

Genuine responsibility sharing will require the major industrialized nations to agree on the special roles of each, so that there is at least a notional concept of fairness—balancing the benefits that a nation or group of nations receives from the global system and the contribution it makes to its stability and prosperity. The U.S. would of necessity continue to be the ultimate guarantor of Western defense; Western Europe would assume greater responsibilities for its own defense and for the health of the global trading system; Japan would do likewise, while also sustaining its already preeminent position as the world's largest aid donor.

It remains to be seen whether Americans will agree to carry the preponderant security burden of the West—which entails potential loss of life by its men and women—while permitting other countries like Germany and Japan to make only, or largely, a financial contribution. It also remains to be seen whether the U.S. will agree to continue to be the ultimate guarantor of the West's defense if Americans believe that competitors like Japan and Germany (the EC) are challenging it economically through "unfair" practices. Such issues must be worked out before, and in anticipation of, the next crisis.

Agreed standards for sharing responsibility, backed up by collective moral suasion, could be established and monitored by the annual Seven Nation Summits; these summits could evolve into the primary political/economic consultative group among the U.S., Germany, and the other major industrialized nations. That should be attractive also to the European Community, which has a seat at the summits and can represent Europe's interests where a consensus among EC members exists. The Seven Nation Summits, and the subcabinet level groups that support them, could become central institutions of the "new world order."

A better organized process of responsibility sharing involving active U.S. cooperation with Germany and Japan would help dispel American concerns that the burden for supporting democracies and strengthening the global economy was being inequitably shared. It would also shield other nations—Germany being at or near the top of the list—from what they on occasion consider arbitrary American demands, and give them greater credit for the responsibilities they do shoulder. The U.S. would be obliged to accept greater power sharing as the natural handmaiden of greater burden sharing if this process is to succeed.

Conclusion

In these four areas the U.S. and Germany have enormous roles to play. The factor most critical to their success is whether they can establish a common agenda for the future, rooted in a perception of shared long-term interests. The relationship between the two nations cannot and need not be what it was from 1950 until 1989. But it is important that leaders of both nations recognize the historic opportunities and responsibilities they share to build institutions and systems in the post–cold war world that embody their common democratic and market values and tie them together with like-minded nations in a new democratic commonwealth. The future of U.S.–European relations—and much of what Germany and the U.S. have attempted to create together since World War II—hangs in the balance.

9

Patterns of Competition

Economic Relationships:
Germany

NORBERT WALTER

R ecent revolutionary transformations in Eastern Europe and in the Soviet Union have not only changed the face of Europe. They have also laid the groundwork for a new global order. The East-West conflict is over, the failure of communism manifest. The Soviet threat, for years the glue that helped hold the West together, is a thing of the past. The result is a fundamental change in relations between Europe and the United States. Whereas the Western European–American alliance was once a strategic necessity, it is now a matter of political choice. Consequently it will require greater cultivation and care. Will Germany be able to meet this requirement?

Obviously Germany will be strongly preoccupied with its own

NORBERT WALTER is chief economist, Deutsche Bank Group. He was previously associated with the Kiel Institute of World Economics, and in 1986–87 was John McCloy Distinguished Research Fellow at the American Institute for Contemporary German Studies in Washington, D.C. Dr. Walter would like to thank his colleagues at the Deutsche Bank Economics Department, Barbara Boettcher and Dieter Braeuninger, for their valuable contributions to this chapter.

concerns in coming years. It is faced with the historic task of rebuilding the economy in the new federal states, an area that covers
30 percent of German territory, and of raising the living standards
of 16 million people in the Eastern part of Germany to the level
enjoyed by their fellow citizens in the Western part. Nonetheless,
Germany will also have to pay particular attention to events in
Eastern Europe. Of all big Western industrialized countries, Germany is closest to Eastern Europe and thus particularly affected by
the economic and political reform process in the region. Countries
such as Hungary, Czechoslovakia, and Poland, as long as they
continue on the road to reforms, could eventually turn into promising markets and attractive industrial locations for German companies. In the long run, the same will be true of the Baltic republics. On the other hand, Germany's economic perspectives would
worsen considerably were the reconstruction of these economies to
be delayed or even to fail. In that case a wave of immigrants might
wash over Germany—exceeding by far the country's capacity for
integration. Growing social tensions as well as a stronger burden
on public finances would be the result.

Does this imply that the German economy will in future years
direct a considerable part of its resources to the East? Or will
economic perspectives continue to be most favorable in the West,
where dramatic changes are also taking place? Integration in
Western Europe is progressing at high speed. By the end of 1992,
the single European market will open its doors. The way has been
paved for a European Economic and Monetary Union. In North
America a large free trade zone is emerging that will extend from
the Arctic to the Caribbean. Economies in Eastern Asia are also
growing at a rapid pace and are becoming increasingly interdependent. Japan, with its many trade links and its strong commitment to direct investments abroad, is the engine of this process.
Soon the world economy will be divided into three major regions.
Within this triad, Japan is seeking to play the leading role.

What effects will these developments have on the transatlantic
alliance? Will Germany—will Europe—still need a partner on the
other side of the Atlantic Ocean?

America and Germany—Partners or Rivals?

Economic ties between Germany and the United States remain strong, even though over the past four decades the United States has declined in importance as Germany's trading partner. This is particularly apparent in regard to imports. While the United States accounted for 18.5 percent of German imports in the early fifties, its share has now dropped to 7 percent, roughly the same level as German imports from Belgium and Luxembourg. Forty years ago, of course, the European Community (EC) did not exist, and the industries of Germany's European neighbors, still crippled in the aftermath of the Second World War, were in no position to export significantly to Germany. Quite the opposite was true for the American economy, which had not been damaged during the war, but rather had expanded its capacities and therefore was able to meet the growing import demand in the years of the German *Wirtschaftswunder* (economic miracle) in the 1950s. German exports to the United States approached DM 47 billion in 1990, a solid 7 percent of overall German exports. After topping 10 percent at times, German exports to the United States have thus returned to the level of the 1950s. Over the same period of time, the share of exports bound for EC countries rose from 35 percent to over 54 percent.

Direct investments are an especially impressive indicator of the economic linkage between Germany and the United States. For the Federal Republic of Germany, the main target as well as the source of direct investments is the United States. Bilateral German-American corporate links are of a magnitude unmatched elsewhere. By the end of 1989, German direct investment in the United States amounted to DM 55 billion (about 30 percent of total German direct investment abroad), while American investment in Germany rose to nearly DM 40 billion (a solid 30 percent of all foreign direct investment in the Federal Republic). The second leading target country, France, lags far behind, with an investment volume of DM 15 billion, or just over 8 percent of all German foreign investment.

German investments in the United States at the end of 1989 encompassed nearly 2,400 companies, mainly in the chemical industry and in electrical engineering. These companies—with a payroll of almost 500,000 employees—registered an annual turnover in excess of DM 170 billion in the United States. American investments in Germany are concentrated in the manufacturing sector as well, primarily office and data processing equipment and automobiles, followed by holding companies and property administration.

Inevitably, transatlantic economic relations are beset by certain problems. Tensions stem, above all, from the high U.S. foreign trade deficit. The United States posted its last trade surplus in 1975, and has been in deficit ever since. This is reflected by American foreign debt, which exceeded $400 billion at the end of 1990; ten years earlier, the United States still had net foreign assets on that order of magnitude. The United States recorded its last trade surplus with the Federal Republic—measured in dollars—in 1966. Following high levels in the 1970s, its trade deficit with West Germany contracted briefly during the early 1980s, only to climb to a record $16.3 billion in 1987. Since then, the shortfall has been diminishing gradually.

In Washington, huge American trade deficits have sparked increasing criticism of the Japanese and the Europeans—and the Germans in particular. Germany, so goes the allegation, is importing prosperity and jobs to the detriment of the United States. American dissatisfaction has largely centered on three areas: trading practices, macroeconomic policies, and the issue of burden sharing.

On the trade policy front, American wrath has been directed primarily at Japan, but the EC has also come in for criticism regularly. The history of trade conflicts between the United States and the European Community traces back to the "chicken war" in the 1960s and is closely bound up with the EC's protectionist agricultural policies. Its system of import duties and export subsidies has placed American farmers at a disadvantage not only within the EC, but in other markets as well.

Conflicts also simmered over other issues. Since the mid-1980s, U.S. administrations have catalogued the United States' leading trade partners' worst violations to free trade in the *National Trade Estimate Report on Foreign Trade Barriers*. The list of EC trading sins in the 1991 report (little different from earlier compilations) includes obstructions to agricultural trade, discriminatory standards and inspection procedures, and subsidies granted to the European aerospace industry. At the same time, the report credits the EC with progress in liberalizing its telecommunications markets. Another problem area is EC local content requirements for motor vehicles and copying machines produced in the United States by companies from the Far East. Even though the EC and Japan have concluded a bilateral trade agreement on car imports, it remains controversial whether these restrictions will be extended to imports of Japanese cars assembled elsewhere, such as in the United States.

American demands for a reduction of subsidies have been directed most strongly at Germany, the main trading partner on the European mainland. Such appeals have evoked little sympathy in Germany, not least because influential politicians and public figures, not to mention the public at large, consider government intervention entirely justified. Germans tend to overemphasize social goals in their own country. As a result, subsidies and other forms of state intervention in the economy are usually veiled in the rhetoric of social policy. In implementing such measures, German legislators are fond of invoking a "greater good," such as consumer safeguards or the protection of the socially disadvantaged. Rarely do they perform cost-benefit analyses. Once introduced, state protection is regarded by its beneficiaries as an inalienable social right. That makes it extremely difficult to roll back subsidies or to liberalize markets. In the past, German legislators have been little swayed by foreign criticism, unless supranational authorities such as the EC or the European Court expressly obligated Germany to dismantle regulations.

Germany and its European partners have generally countered American accusations by pointing to U.S. measures to restrict trade. Since 1985 the EC has replied to the U.S. white paper by compiling its own *Report on United States Trade Barriers and Unfair Practices*. The 1991 report documented some seventy measures designed to obstruct European exports or investments in the United States. The spotlight fell on two general trends. One was the U.S. government's approach to trade legislation, which allows unilateral retaliatory measures and thus flouts General Agreement on Tariffs and Trade (GATT) principles of multilateral world trade. The other concerned the growing fragmentation of the American market due to varying legal and administrative provisions at the state level. This has a particular impact on the awarding of public contracts, an area further complicated by a wide range of buy-American guidelines and local content rules. The Community will have no such regulations once its public procurement markets are liberalized in 1993.

A second thrust of U.S. criticism focuses on Japanese and, most of all, on German fiscal and monetary policy. A number of American administrations have repeatedly branded German macroeconomic policies as overly restrictive. The Carter, Reagan, and Bush administrations have all argued that Germany, as the world's pre-eminent exporter, shares a special responsibility to pursue lower short-term interest rates in order to stimulate domestic demand. U.S. officials have made this appeal with particular vigor whenever the economy was tailing off and unemployment rates rising sharply, as was the case in the late 1970s or again in the early 1990s. The Germans, whose *Bundesbank* (federal bank) is renowned for its commitment to price stability, have generally resisted such proddings. These differing monetary philosophies apparently stem from different historical experiences. The Germans are still impressed by the ruinous hyperinflation of the 1920s, and determined above all never to sacrifice the stability of the German mark. American politics, in contrast, is still influenced by the terrible unemployment of the Great Depression during the 1930s.

The dispute over macroeconomic policy reflects differing appraisals of Germany's role in the world economy. The United States regards Germany as a spare locomotive of sorts, ready to go into service whenever the world economy runs out of steam. However, Germany hardly has the economic clout to fulfill this function alone. German gross national product (GNP) of roughly $1.65 trillion in 1990 amounted to only 7 percent of world aggregate GNP (barely a third of U.S. GNP). Viewed on a European scale, though, a far different situation emerges. Germany has, however inadvertently, acted as a powerful locomotive for the economies of its Western European neighbors in 1990 and 1991. The surge in domestic demand as a result of German unification exerted a strong tug on goods and services from abroad.

Viewed more narrowly, past differences over global burden sharing centered primarily on an equitable European contribution to the common defense effort. Many Americans argued that their own high level of defense spending, one of the main causes of the swelling budget deficits, was driven principally by the military commitment to Europe. Voices in the U.S. Congress frequently accused Europe of enjoying a "free ride" and argued that the Europeans should contribute more. This issue will be of secondary importance in the future. The end of the cold war clears the way for reductions in defense spending around the globe. The United States plans substantial cutbacks in its military presence in Europe. Soon Europe will have to bear considerable responsibility for orchestrating and funding its own defense.

United Germany: Economic Outlook

American observers have responded to recent international developments with varying assessments of German economic performance. In the tumultuous months after the Berlin Wall was breached, many felt that a unified Germany, with a population of almost 80 million, would capitalize on the thaw in Eastern Europe to become an economic force ready to dominate all of Europe. To no small extent, this forecast was reflected in trading on the Frankfurt exchange, where prices soared to record highs in early 1990. Fears of a newly potent Germany were rife in Europe, and even in the United States. Those fears were quickly dispelled, however, when it became evident that the desolate shape of the East German economy would hamper efforts at a speedy merger of the two economies. German hesitation during the Gulf conflict further sapped the market's confidence. German stocks, reflecting that lack of confidence, tumbled again during the second half of 1990.

As Lord Ismay once put it, the original goal of NATO was "to keep the Americans in, the Russians out, and the Germans down." Many who once scoffed at this set of objectives now claim that it has been achieved. Its one-sided triumph in the Gulf War has turned the United States into the world's undisputed leader.

America has impressively underscored its political leadership and military superiority. The now-defunct Soviet Union, in contrast, is mired in a serious economic crisis compounded by political disintegration. The Baltic states have left the union for good, to be followed by other republics. What will remain is a confederation largely preoccupied with solving its own massive problems.

Furthermore, less than a year after unification, many observers feel that Germany has lost out. The country seems to have squandered its credit in the Arab world, which now provides less business for German companies. East-West trade, with Germany at its center, has been shrinking markedly as a result of economic problems in the East. Worst of all: Germany seems to be struggling under the economic burden of unification. After a decade of, at times, enormous surpluses—as much as DM 108 billion in 1989— Germany is set to post a major balance-of-payments deficit—in the range of DM 25 billion—in 1991. The budgets of local, regional, and federal authorities also went deeply into the red; the overall 1990 deficit of DM 90 billion reached DM 120 billion, or 4.2 percent of GNP, only one year later. As a proportion of GNP, the German public deficit considerably exceeds that of France (an estimated 1.4 percent of GNP in 1991) or the United Kingdom (2.1 percent), and is approaching the deficit level of the U.S. federal government (5.3 percent). In the year before unification, the German budget shortfall had amounted to only DM 21.5 billion. No wonder, then, that the Deutsche mark is also showing signs of weakness. Fears of an all-too-strong Germany have given way to growing doubts about German economic strength. Are those doubts legitimate?

The twin deficit and the recent cooling off of the economy in West Germany are likely to be only temporary. They do, in any case, obscure the very real potential for growth. Since the mid-1980s, the fundamental dynamism of the (West) German economy has been boosted by four factors, which will continue to have an impact in the future: the EC single market program; the presently favorable age structure of the German population; immigration, especially from Eastern Europe; and the gains from rebuilding East Germany.

The EC project of establishing a unified internal market by the end of 1992 has given new zest to Western European economies. Companies throughout the EC are preparing to seize the opportunities that will be opened up by the removal of all internal trade barriers. The dismantling of border controls promises to expand markets and to facilitate more cost-effective production. This will go hand in hand with lower procurement costs. Of course, competitive pressures will rise as well. Unless capital investment is increased, business firms will be unable to take advantage of these opportunities and to maintain their market positions. Not surprisingly, Western Europe witnessed an extraordinary investment boom in the late 1980s. A prime beneficiary of this investment wave was the German economy, with its high-caliber capital goods sector. While investment activity in Europe has eased off since 1990, it is bound to bounce back after a brief respite. The investment pace will quicken no later than early 1993, when the single market finally opens for business. Of course, mobility of labor, capital, goods, and services within the Community will benefit not only German producers of capital goods, but many other sectors of a German economy strongly dependent on exports. Finally, deregulation efforts set in motion by the single market program have also given new impetus to the German economy. National interest groups are losing their influence in a supranational Europe.

The postwar baby boom is responsible for Germany's currently favorable population structure. It hit Germany later than the United States, stretching from the mid-1950s to the late 1960s. Germany's baby boomers have been entering the job market in large numbers in recent years. This young segment of the population is well-educated, open-minded, and highly motivated. The older ones among them have already established families and are enjoying the prime of their working life. This substantial growth in its labor force's size, quality, motivation, and flexibility will greatly increase the innovative capacities of the German economy in the 1990s and thus holds out a promise for inflation-free growth in Germany.

Germany also stands to benefit from the large numbers of Eastern European immigrants. Some 1.3 million ethnic Germans emigrated to the Federal Republic in the period 1986–91. In light of the economic difficulties facing Eastern Europe and the Soviet Union, this influx is set to continue, though at a somewhat slower pace. Their willingness to adapt and their high degree of mobility will enable the immigrant workers to enhance the efficiency and flexibility of the German labor market. Overall productivity will benefit from improved utilization of capital equipment. Moreover, during their initial phase of integration these workers will have a marked propensity to consume due to pent-up demand, which provides additional impulses to the consumer goods industry and to the construction business for years to come.

After the period of rampant euphoria in late 1989 and early 1990, Germans began to dwell on the presumed burdens imposed by unification. Indeed, there is a danger that the high costs of unification might have a serious adverse effect on the German economy. These costs are due primarily to the enormous investments required to modernize East German capital stock, which proved to be far more obsolete than initially assumed. But costs have also been driven up by a wide range of subsidies and transfer payments designed to ease the social dislocation caused by the transition to a market economy.

The difficulties of adjustment have been exacerbated by the near-total collapse of trade among the former COMECON (Council for Mutual Economic Assistance) countries. Exports to COMECON countries once accounted for 10 percent of East Germany's GNP. To no small extent, though, the current East German need for high subsidies is also the result of a misguided wage policy. Substantial wage increases have struck a significant blow to the competitiveness of East German companies while seriously reducing the number of cost-efficient jobs. Labor and management must now steer a different course. Wages and working conditions in Eastern Germany should be brought up to Western levels only in a gradual, step-by-step process. At the same time, wage settlements in West Germany must take the situation in East Germany into account.

A number of factors suggest that future wage increases will be somewhat more moderate. Economic activity in West Germany has entered a spell of weakness. In this situation enterprises will be more determined to oppose union wage demands than was the case in early 1991 at the end of a long boom. Moreover, the unions' position will suffer from a strong increase in the supply of labor. Many of the ethnic German immigrants from Eastern Europe, gradually finishing up their language and training courses, will soon be entering the labor market. In addition, there are numerous East Germans resettling in, or commuting to, the western part of the country. Finally, a growing number of companies are not organized in any of the employers' associations and are, therefore, not subject to wage agreements negotiated by unions and employers. This trend can be noticed particularly in East Germany.

So far, German economic policy has not responded adequately to the challenges posed by unification. Economic development in East Germany must be given top priority, without, of course, weakening growth prospects in the western part of the country. Only sharp reductions in public debt will make it possible to lower high interest rates hampering investment in all of Germany and prompting a great deal of foreign criticism. Substantial cutbacks in the wide range of subsidies are essential. Nor can a reduction of social transfer payments be off limits. Plans to lower corporate tax rates should be pursued vigorously, as such a measure would bolster German growth potential in a European market that is becoming more integrated every day.

In short, were Germany to learn from past mistakes—and indications are strong that it is learning the right lessons, not only in economic policy—it stands to profit greatly from unification. Eastern Germany not only offers an attractive market, it also has great potential for industry. The inadequacy of its infrastructure tends to blind Western observers to the tremendous benefits offered by a large pool of well-trained workers. Moreover, Eastern Germany will play a crucial role in the future as a bridge for trade with Eastern Europe. Geographical proximity is one obvious factor in Eastern Germany's favor. In addition, many Eastern Germans have acquired an excellent working knowledge of East European languages and are familiar with local mentalities and customs.

The Germans have no monopoly on the benefits of economic development in Eastern Germany. German imports rose nearly 12 percent in 1990 and another 10 percent in 1991. According to an econometric simulation of the impact of German unification on the world economy,[1] increased German imports will likely have an expansive economic effect on members of the European monetary system in particular; this effect should more than offset the contractive impact of rising interest rates. Even the United States stands to register favorable growth effects approaching 0.4 percent per year. Of course, German imports will decline as Eastern Germany expands its manufacturing base. But for some time to come, foreign investors can take advantage of the favorable opportunities afforded in Eastern Germany; indeed, foreign capital is more than welcome, as is immediately obvious to anyone who tours the region and follows the activities of the *Treuhandanstalt* privatization agency.

Germany's Future Role in Europe

From the very beginning, German unification has been closely tied to the process of Western European integration, partly in order to expedite the breakaway of Eastern Germany from the Soviet sphere of influence, but mostly in order to dispel any lingering doubts that a united Germany would remain anchored in the Western European community of nations. Bonn continues to forge ahead with the organization of a European Economic and Monetary Union (EMU), and, together with France, is spearheading the push for a European Political Union (EPU).

Political factors aside, the German strategy has been influenced chiefly by economic considerations. In the end, the German economy can only thrive in the future if it remains closely tied to Western Europe. Almost 55 percent of all German exports, which together account for roughly one-third of Germany's GNP, went to other EC countries in 1990; taking into consideration all of Western and Northern Europe, that share rises to 70 percent. It is thus wholly in Germany's interest that the single EC market be implemented on schedule. The same holds true for swift moves to realize EMU. After all, only in a unified currency region can Europe enjoy all the benefits of its single market.

The EC has made major progress toward EMU since the Wall came down. A first phase, which began on July 1, 1990, aims at the complete liberalization of capital movements, along with integrating all EC currencies into the European Monetary System (EMS) and enhancing economic and monetary cooperation. A second phase, slated to begin in 1994, will mark the transition to a unified currency region by focusing on the harmonization of monetary policies and by pursuing a higher degree of economic convergence (aligning inflation rates at a lower level). Finally, a third phase will actually introduce a common European currency, the stability of which will be monitored by a politically independent central bank along the lines of the *Bundesbank*.

The German mark, linchpin of the European currency system for over a decade, is slated to be absorbed into a stable European currency that will gradually reflect Europe's economic strength and may well emerge as a rival to the dollar. At present, the German mark is still second to the dollar as an international investment and reserve currency. Over 20 percent of the $770 billion currency reserves of the world's central banks are maintained in German marks, with the dollar accounting for 55 percent and the yen for just under 10 percent.

In contrast to the monetary union, the contours of the political union have yet to come into sharper focus. Europe must still decide what its political landscape will look like at the end of the decade. Not surprisingly, the process of political integration is proving to be much more complicated than economic cooperation. Countries with a strong centralist tradition, such as France, are especially reluctant to transfer elements of political sovereignty to supranational EC institutions. This behavior is hardly logical in view of the fact that preparations for the single market and EMU have already entailed a substantial transfer of national authority to Community-level decision making. And the Community will obtain larger powers in the future. At issue is a joint foreign and security policy—a prospect that challenges the self-identity of the member states more than anything else. Special interests also come into play. Two cases in point are Spain and France, both of which must contend with serious ethnic problems at home; thus they view various movements for national autonomy in Southeastern Europe with a particularly wary eye. The Yugoslav conflict, however, clearly demonstrated the need for an enhanced coordination of European foreign policies as well as the importance of a truly European security policy.

Long before the "old" European Community completes the

process of integration, it faces new challenges as countries aligned with the European Free Trade Association (EFTA) and various East European states wish to join the club. Austria and Sweden have already formally applied for admission; Norway and Finland are expected to follow suit. Switzerland shows signs of moving toward the EC, although the restricted access to its labor market still poses a stumbling block. In general, the seven EFTA states could be absorbed without economic dislocations, since the project of establishing a "European Economic Area" foresees EFTA largely adopting EC single market guidelines by 1993. Yet France, Ireland, and the poorer EC members states in Southern Europe are resisting efforts to expand the Community, as they fear economic handicaps and the dominance of "Northern" interests.

Germany, which stands to profit greatly from intensified trade, has much at stake in future EC relations with Eastern Europe. By the same token, Germany has the most to lose should Eastern European economic reforms be delayed or should they fail altogether. Throughout Eastern Europe, initial steps toward a market economy have generated much friction and have been accompanied by declining standards of living. This development, aggravated by the Gulf conflict, resulted in Eastern European economic performance dropping an average of 14 percent in 1990. The shift to convertible currencies and world market prices at the beginning of 1991 spelled the downfall of numerous bilateral trade relationships within COMECON, which, in turn, triggered further slumps in output and pushed up unemployment levels. If these negative trends persist, the West—and Germany in particular—could be confronted by a large wave of immigration from Eastern Europe. A massive influx into Germany, however, would generate social conflicts, potentially reversing the positive effects of moderate levels of immigration. With these considerations in mind, Germany has been in the forefront of those who argue that the West, and especially the EC, cannot afford to turn its back on Eastern European pleas for aid and closer economic cooperation with the European Community.

The burdens of rebuilding Eastern Europe are rather unevenly distributed among the industrialized nations. Having pledged 38.9 billion ECU up to 1991 (exchange rate in September 1991: 1 ECU = 1.21 US $), Germany is thus far providing nearly 60 percent of total Western aid to the Soviet Union. The Japanese share of 0.3 percent and the British share of 0.12 percent hardly show up in the statistics. Even the United States with 2.1 percent and France with 2 percent are making but a minimal contribution. Of course, a sustantial part (approximately 7 billion ECU) of the German funds earmarked for the Soviet Union is in payment for the costs of troop withdrawals from Eastern Germany. Bonn has also assumed a mammoth share of Western aid under the PHARE program to support fledgling democracies in the region; Germany is providing 8 billion ECU or nearly a third of the 24.7 billion ECU in aid pledged by the twenty-four largest industrial states (G-24). If one adds these commitments to the high costs of German unification and Germany's share in underwriting the costs of the Gulf War, it is evident that an equitable worldwide sharing of burdens cannot be said to exist. Germany has clearly reached the limits of its resources. Other Western industrial nations, notably Japan, but other EC countries as well, must now contribute their fair share.

Over the medium and long term, however, a liberal EC trade policy will be far more important than immediate financial assistance in aiding Eastern European countries. These are in obvious need of free access to Western markets, given COMECON's collapse and a generally oppressive debt burden. Long-term economic improvements are fully dependent on the successful reorientation of Eastern European exports. A number of agreements concluded between the EC and Eastern European countries foresee wide-ranging cooperation and the reduction of import restrictions. However, trade restrictions have yet to be sufficiently relaxed in certain key areas, such as coal, steel, textiles, and farm products. Bonn is called upon to press ahead with the opening of these markets; yet it faces a number of domestic difficulties as both agriculture and coal mining are highly subsidized sectors in Germany with extremely influential interest groups that have thus far succeeded in preventing a reduction of subsidies. As a result of such pressures, Germany itself is of two minds when it comes to opening its markets to Eastern Europe.

In order to enhance Eastern European growth prospects, the CoCom (Coordinating Committee [for Export Controls]) list of goods embargoed for strategic reasons must also be scrapped. That list was shortened considerably in response to the revolutionary processes in Eastern Europe; the export of urgently needed products in numerous categories—notably microprocessors, personal computers, and wide-body aircraft—was allowed for the first time. Further liberalization, however, both in terms of goods and target countries, is still necessary.

For the time being, Eastern European countries are unlikely candidates for admission into the EC. Their economic, and possibly political, stability is still too tenuous, and the gap vis-à-vis Western Europe too wide. Even those countries that implemented reforms very quickly—Poland, Czechoslovakia, and Hungary—have a long way to go before they are in a position to apply for EC membership. At the same time, the new democracies in Eastern Europe need firm ground to stand on. As a consequence, the EC's primary mission in the near future must be to devise a strategy for expanding the Community without any negative side-effects on the "deepening" that is also necessary. In pursuit of such a strategy, it is conceivable that concentric circles of economic and political cooperation of varying intensity may develop around a hard core of Western European countries. The founder countries of the EC, together with Great Britain, Denmark, the Iberian Peninsula, and some of the EFTA countries, could combine, possibly as early as the end of the millennium, to form the nucleus of a "United States of Europe" by agreeing to renounce certain rights of sovereignty. The remaining EC and EFTA countries might form a second tier, in that they do not accept certain far-reaching Community regulations regarding, for instance, currency and security matters. A third circle could then be formed by associated countries, which would enjoy almost unrestricted access to the Common Market, but would have only limited influence on decision-making processes in Brussels. This circle could include the countries in Central Europe as well as the Baltic states.

Europe's Role in the World Economy

Increased Western European integration inevitably assigns the EC a more important role in the world economy. Once the single market is completed, the United States and Japan will find themselves in competition with an economic region of greater economic

clout than their own. Output of goods and services in the twelve
EC member states, with an overall population of just under 340
million, was around $6 trillion in 1990, compared with $5,465
billion in the United States. Germany accounted for about one-
fourth of the overall EC economy. By the year 2000, an expanded
European economic area—including the EFTA countries and the
successful economies in Eastern Europe—could encompass a population approaching 500 million.

Due to the EC 1992 program, European companies will be able
to make greater use of economies of scale in production, and thus
will be in a better position to amortize research and development
expenses. As a result, the single market will strengthen the competitiveness of European companies on world markets. For third-
country companies, of course, it also opens a range of interesting
possibilities. Such activities as investments, corporate takeovers,
and joint ventures on the part of companies with a home base
outside the EC—Japan in particular—have widened significantly
since the program was inaugurated.

The United States was slow in recognizing and realizing the
opportunities inherent in a single European market. "Fortress
Europe" was the buzzword dominating the American debate regarding Europe 1992. Fear was rife in America that the creation of
a single market would lead to a Europe cutting itself off from the
rest of the world. The fact that these fears have not materialized
must be credited in part to this debate, which helped to sensitize
public opinion around the world.

At the same time, America's preoccupation with this subject
caused it to underestimate the scope of European integration. Corporate America appears severely underinformed about the practical impact the single market will have. Two-thirds of companies
surveyed on "Market Access Europe" continue to take a largely
passive stance on the opportunities afforded by the single market;
nor has the other third necessarily already moved into Europe.
Some 57 percent of all companies polled, and a full 46 percent of
those already active in Europe, still see their best chances for
growth in the American domestic market. This restraint has cost
American companies a good deal of time, while competitors from
other countries were busily anchoring their European market posi-

tions in preparation for the single market. One must bear in mind, however, that close links have already been established through direct investments. EC countries accounted for 40 percent of U.S. investments abroad—a far higher percentage than that enjoyed by America's immediate neighbors (with Canada and Latin America each accounting for 16 percent). Conversely, direct investment by EC companies added up to nearly 60 percent of all foreign investments in the United States by the end of 1989.

Although the young democracies in Eastern Europe are primarily oriented toward Western Europe, they are also interested in establishing close trade relations with overseas countries, especially the United States. Not only are they in urgent need of financial aid, which all industrialized countries should provide, but they also seek to diversify their trade relations in order to avoid monolithic structures and dependencies. The United States thus stands to reap considerable economic benefits from the changes in Eastern Europe, too—assuming, of course, that it steps up its aid to Eastern Europe and agrees to further liberalize the CoCom provisions.

Up to now, Pacific Rim countries have been rather cautious in redefining their economic relations with Eastern Europe. Their share in Western aid to the region has lagged far behind their relative positions in the world economy. Nor have they displayed much enthusiasm for direct investments. In particular, relations between Japan and the now-moribund Soviet Union continue to be chilly. Japan has made the provison of extensive aid to the Soviet Union contingent on the return of the so-called Northern Territories. In fact, immense Soviet financial needs and the declining importance of the military establishment make the restitution of the Kuriles likely. In the medium term, therefore, Japan, followed by the newly industrializing countries in Southeast Asia, can be expected to increase its involvement and capitalize on new opportunities in Eastern Europe.

With a new beginning under way in both Eastern and Western Europe, the Community enjoys an enormous potential for growth in the 1990s. In the medium term, EC growth is likely to eclipse U.S. growth by a wide margin. In particular, Germany, the European economic locomotive, will continue to perform significantly better than the United States. While a variety of factors fosters growth in Germany over the medium term, the American economy is still plagued by structural problems. The crisis in the banking industry has not yet been overcome. Some portions of its labor force, especially numerous immigrants from the South, are poorly trained. In several areas public infrastructure needs a thorough overhaul. These difficulties limit the scope for significant productivity gains. An excessive budget deficit, estimated to reach more than $350 billion in 1992, all but precludes further borrowing and constrains the Federal Reserve's leeway to lower interest rates in order to stimulate the economy.

The relaxation of East-West tensions has also changed the nature of relations between the industrialized countries and the Third World. In the past, North-South economic relations were to a great extent a reflection of the East-West conflict. Western industrialized nations would mainly cooperate with Western oriented developing countries, while the Soviet Union and its allies provided aid for countries with Marxist leanings. This pattern has become largely obsolete as communism has faded away in Eastern Europe, which finds itself in need of development aid. Thus old traditions, which were submerged during the cold war, and important geographic factors will once again determine North-South trade patterns.

Many observers hold the view that the developing countries will suffer the most from the relaxation of East-West tensions, as international capital flows are being rerouted to Eastern Europe in order to meet that region's high capital requirements. This would indeed put a further damper on Third World development prospects. Capital shortfalls, however, have important—and frequently neglected—beneficial effects as well. The relaxation of international tensions has prompted many developing countries to cast off their narrow-minded ideological orientations. Developing countries are now offered an opportunity to curb their excessive military spending and to invest the resources that are freed up in more productive ways. Even more important is the fact that many countries are gradually remodeling their economic policies in a free market spirit, a shift that stems to no small extent from intensified competition for capital. The successes of newly industrializing countries in Asia and the more recent examples of such developing countries as Mexico, Malaysia, and Thailand illustrate that a successful process of development critically depends on liberal, growth oriented economic policies. Only they unleash forces for domestic growth, thus creating incentives for the inflow of foreign capital. Developing countries that resolutely pursue such policies will continue to receive foreign capital. Even so, the poorer countries in the Third World must still rely on significant transfer payments from the rich North.

Overcoming Protectionist Trends: An Important Task

The future development of North-South relations depends crucially on whether protectionist trends in the world economy can be held in check. The outcome of the Uruguay Round of the GATT talks is of crucial importance in this regard. Originally, this GATT round was supposed to wind up its business by December 1990. However, unresolved problems in critical areas, above all the dismantling of trade barriers in agriculture, led to a further extension of the negotiations. Prospects for a softening of the rather entrenched positions taken by the main protagonists are not without promise. Yet it remains to be seen whether the most profound effort to date to liberalize international trade, and to adapt GATT to the new global economic realities, will reach a successful conclusion.

An ultimate collapse of the GATT talks would mean that an important opportunity to provide the world economy with a tremendous growth stimulus will have come to naught. Following the recession of the early 1980s, world trade expanded, on the average, by 5.5 percent per year. Exports of commercial services rose even more, reaching 22 percent of trade in goods. In other words, the intensified division of labor was an important growth factor for the world economy, which expanded by 3.5 percent annually between 1983 and 1990. Substantial trade liberalization would therefore boost the prospects for significant gains in general economic welfare. According to official U.S. estimates, these gains could total $4 trillion worldwide over the next ten years, equal to nearly 75 percent of the U.S. gross national product of 1990.

The International Monetary Fund (IMF) estimates that the complete elimination of all agricultural subsidies alone would raise the export earnings of developing countries by about $50 billion,[2] an amount equal to the funds disbursed in the form of development aid in 1989. This comparison illustrates just how little financial transfer payments from the West alone can actually contribute to solving the problems facing the Third World. As long as those payments are not accompanied by improved opportunities to increase their export earnings, less developed countries will be hard put to reduce their foreign debt burden in the long run. They, as much as the countries of Eastern Europe, can only serve as markets for Western exports to the extent that they themselves are able to export their goods elsewhere.

The world's key economic regions, too, stand to suffer from a lack of international market liberalization. The list of potential trade conflicts is long, not only in the transatlantic area, but also in regard to trade relations with Japan.

In the 1980s Japan's industry launched a large-scale export offensive and conquered major areas of the American market. It made use of new technologies in the transport, communications, and machine tool sectors, which allow rapid product alterations as well as low-cost mass production. Moreover, competitors were forced on the defensive by aggressive pricing policies. When the European Community's single market program was announced, Japanese companies intensified their activities in Europe, particularly since the United States turned increasingly hostile to goods and direct investment from the Far East. Japanese enterprises registered significant gains in the areas of consumer electronics, automobiles, and microelectronics. In the field of memory chip production, frequently considered one of the key technologies of the information age, Japan has achieved a near monopoly. On both sides of the Atlantic Ocean, concerned observers fear that the Japanese could soon establish predominant positions in other key technologies as well, in which case the rest of the world is in danger of becoming ever more dependent on Japanese technology.

In marked contrast to Japan's economic success abroad, American and European companies have so far been unable to penetrate the Japanese market on a larger scale. Japan's export offensive is reflected in the large surpluses of its foreign trade balance, whereas the United States and Europe frequently report considerable deficits in their trade with Japan. These imbalances have been an important source of instabilities and conflicts.

Politicians in several European capitals as well as in Washington would like to see Japan slowed down by protectionist measures. They quite rightly point to the unreasonably high barriers obstructing efforts by foreign companies to enter—and successfully compete in—the Japanese market. Nonetheless, protectionism cannot be the answer to the Japanese challenge. Economic history has frequently shown that enterprises that are threatened by foreign competition will hardly make a sufficient effort to improve their competitiveness behind protective walls. (Japan's success in world markets is no counter-example as it is due to other factors, especially the Japanese mentality, the willingness to stick to a common goal, for example.) In addition, there is the danger of retaliatory measures, which could cause an erosion of the entire world trade. There is also the difficult question of which sectors to protect or promote by means of subsidies. In most cases governments are not in a position to decide which sectors and which technologies will actually play a leading role in the future. Nor is it necessary for every large industrialized country to rank among the leaders in all areas of technological development. Any attempt to do so would mean to question the entire system of the international division of labor. As a matter of fact, a national promotion of individual sectors has become virtually impossible in the age of multinational companies.

However, to argue against protectionist efforts does not imply that governments and enterprises on both sides of the Atlantic need not take action. Governmental intervention is required to offer and maintain attractive industrial locations. In the case of Germany it is a matter of boosting people's willingness to work by reducing the tax burden and increasing their confidence in the market economy, as well as providing companies with greater opportunities, not least in the financial area. In this context, the United States can serve as a model for a determined market oriented policy of deregulation and reduced corporate tax rates.

Companies must actively meet the Japanese challenge by facing up to the competition from the Far East. The best place to do this is on the spot, i.e., in Japan. The highly dynamic region of Southeast Asia, however, plays only a minor role in German corporate investment strategies. In 1990 a mere 2 percent of total German direct investment went into this region. Only if German industry commits itself more strongly to this region will it be able to maintain its leading position on the world markets in the long run. Increased cooperation between firms on both sides of the Atlantic should be another way to meet the Japanese challenge. European and American companies can regain lost ground by means of strategic alliances, particularly in the fields of research and development, and thus secure for themselves favorable starting positions in the ever-harder fight for market penetration within this triad.

The transatlantic relationship is deeply rooted in the minds of a broad majority of the German population. Even though the East-West conflict no longer exists, this relationship has important functions to fulfill. After all, the alliance was kept together not by this conflict, but rather by virtue of a common Western heritage with its commitment to freedom, self-determination, democracy, and liberal institutions. These values have lost nothing of their importance over the past forty years. On the contrary, in an ever more complex world their significance as the basis for the coexistence of different nations has, if anything, grown. This is true particularly of international economic relations.

It is only in the framework of a liberal economic system that the world's economic problems, such as the integration of the former COMECON countries and the modernization of their economies, the reduction of disparities between North and South, or the dismantling of current account disequilibria, can be solved. Germany, strongly committed to the international division of labor, attaches great importance to open markets. A generally liberal United States represents an important partner for Germany in this endeavor. Together, the United States and Germany should be in a strong position to master the economic challenges of the post-Wall world.

Notes

[1] See Deutsches Institut fuer Wirtschaftsforschung (Berlin), *Wochenbericht,* 32/1991, p. 454.
[2] IMF Survey, December 10, 1990, p. 381.

10

Conclusion

Problems and Prospects for
Partners in Leadership

GEBHARD SCHWEIGLER

The Post-Wall World

" **M**r. Gorbachev, tear down this wall!" the American president, standing in front of the Wall at Brandenburg Gate on June 12, 1987, pleaded with the Soviet leader. "If you seek peace, if you seek prosperity for the Soviet Union and Eastern Europe, if you seek liberalization, come here to this gate. Mr Gorbachev, open this gate!" For the Soviet news agency TASS, Ronald Reagan's speech at the Wall—masterfully organized for maximum television effect—was just another "openly propagandist speech couched in the spirit of the cold war era."

GEBHARD SCHWEIGLER is senior research associate at the Research Institute for International Affairs and Security of the Institute for Science and Politics in Ebenhausen, Germany. His previous professional experience includes posts at the Research Institute of the German Society for Foreign Affairs, the German Marshall Fund of the United States, and the Carnegie Endowment for International Peace. His publications include books on West German and U.S. foreign policy, and numerous articles published both in Germany and the United States.

Twenty-nine months later, the Wall was opened and soon thereafter torn down. And the cold war era was history.

From the perspective of events following that memorable night of November 9, 1989, President Reagan's exhortation to "tear down this wall" marked an interesting, if not perhaps defining, step on the road to ending the cold war. For many observers in Germany, that demand was yet another instance of a politically naive American president—a former actor at that, who admittedly read his lines well and put on a good show—proclaiming a policy that seemed neither realistic nor necessarily desirable. To be sure, the Wall was more than just an eyesore or a local inconvenience; and the Federal Republic's president himself had kept reminding the world that the German question remained open as long as the Brandenburg Gate was closed. But in reality, a political consensus had long emerged in West Germany that called for small, careful, and deliberate steps to bring about a state of detente in Europe where divisive borders might lose their importance, as individual countries—including two separate German states—opened up to each other and cooperated ever more closely. In the face of such a consensus, an outright call for tearing down the Wall appeared to lay down a challenge unacceptable to the Soviet leadership. Many Germans held such a challenge counterproductive.

But the American president, however inexperienced and ideologically rigid he may have been, apparently had the better political instincts. To what extent the hard line laid down by President Reagan contributed to the demise of the Soviet empire will, absent conclusive evidence, be a controversial question for some time to come. Germans, in particular, like to think that it was due to their detente approach—the *Genscherism* so often derided by Reaganite critics—that the Soviet empire finally crumbled. Nor is this controversy of merely historical interest, for there are potentially important lessons at stake, such as the value of "hard" versus "soft" lines in confrontations with dictatorial systems, or even the adequacy of mutual perceptions of leadership qualities.

The fact remains, however, that the American side pushed a policy that proved successful. The gate was opened and the Wall torn down much sooner than anyone in Germany expected. This was achieved mostly by the East Germans themselves, who finally rose up against their tottering Communist regime; but it was made possible by Mr. Gorbachev, who—for reasons of his own that might have included the rewards held out by the American president—decided not to intervene. After that momentous development, it was again an American administration that encouraged the Germans in East and West to pursue the reunification of their country at a rapid pace. In the end, American encouragement and support made possible what the hesitant Germans, inclined to disbelief, caution, and myriad concerns, at first hardly felt was within their reach. Gratitude, as well as a sense of embarrassment, marked the reactions of many Germans to the American role in the reunification of Germany—reactions that are now important elements in German-American relations.

The cold war was, of course, being fought not just in—or over—Germany. Still, the Berlin Wall, with all its terrifying ugliness, stood as a symbol of the cold war; its fall, therefore, rightly symbolized its end. To call the post–cold war world a post-Wall world seems justified for that reason alone. But the term carries another, more important meaning as well. Walls are important structural elements; they provide—for better or for worse—stability, solidity, and thus a sense of certainty. The Wall in Berlin, and its barbed wire extension throughout Europe, forming an "Iron Curtain" that was first lifted by courageous Hungary in the summer of 1989, constituted the main supportive structure of the cold war world. As such, it was never welcome. But it did make possible a "remarkably stable and predictable set of relations among the great powers," as U.S. Deputy Secretary of State Lawrence Eagleburger argued in September 1989—something that had rarely been the case throughout previous European history. "Let us not fool ourselves," Eagleburger had then admonished his listeners (some of whom felt he was already waxing nostalgic about the cold war), "both we and the Soviets are faced with a frankly diminished capacity to influence events and promote our respective interests throughout the world on the scale to which we have become accustomed." In that sense, too, it appears appropriate to refer to a post-Wall world—a world without the stability and predictability that the Wall seemingly afforded, and a world that is no longer subject to the nearly exclusive control of the superpowers.

President Bush, when asked in February 1990 who the new enemies might be after the Soviet Union had been defeated, replied: "The enemy is unpredictability. The enemy is instability." Viewed from this perspective, one of the main tasks for a post-Wall world is an architectural one: to design a stable system of international relations without taking recourse to such drastic measures as violently confining and otherwise insurmountable walls. European political leaders—Germans in the forefront—had long argued for such a new "European architecture," designed to create that "just and lasting order of peace in Europe" first outlined in NATO's 1967 Harmel Report. Soviet leaders had similarly begun to suggest the construction of a "common European house."

American leaders worried that a European house constructed without American participation might lack important elements of stability, if not comfort; they soon insisted, therefore, that the United States be part of any European architecture. Secretary of State James Baker called for the establishment of a "Euro-Atlantic community that extends east from Vancouver to Vladivostok," or for the "construction of the new Euro-Atlantic commonwealth of free nations."[1] More ambitiously yet, the Bush administration, no doubt reflecting perceptions of American global responsibilities, set its sights even higher: it wanted to create nothing less than a "new world order"—"to build a new international system in accordance with our own values and ideals, as old patterns and certainties crumble around us."[2]

The cold war was fought, in the main, over ideals and values. If it can be said that the West won the cold war, then precisely in the sense that Western ideals and values—of freedom, democracy, and the personal "pursuit of happiness"—ultimately prevailed. If the United States now seeks to install a new world order based on its own values and ideals, its sights are not necessarily set too high, for, as the Bush administration rightly emphasizes, the Western world—by definition—already shares many of those values and ideals, while newly liberated peoples appear eager to adopt them.

In principle, a constructive role on the part of the United States in the creation of a new European architecture is overwhelmingly supported on both sides of the Atlantic. Yet the uncertainties of the post-Wall world pertain to that American role as well. Proponents of the Euro-Atlantic community are confronted by a dilemma. If the nations of Europe do indeed emerge as democracies fully imbued with Western values, they would—because of these shared values—be able to live in peace and harmony with each other. Certainly the nations of Western Europe appear to have reached that nearly ideal state of affairs. No longer threatened by the Soviet Union, and its ability to live at peace no more in doubt, does Western Europe still need the United States as its pacifier, or even as its balancer of last resort? To admit that it does is either to question the Europeans' self-confidence, or the peaceful nature of individual nations (Germany still being a prime candidate). Consequently, since Western European nations will not readily admit that they cannot yet be trusted to live in peace with each other, arguments in favor of the need for a balancing or pacifying U.S. presence in Europe will meet with increasing disbelief.

Furthermore, to admit that rich, democratic, and peaceful Western Europe still requires American help in order to deal with potentially dangerous instabilities and uncertainties arising between Berlin and the Bug, or even between the Bug and Vladivostok, is to question not only its own capabilities, but also its willingness to bear the burden. Questions of this kind are, in fact, being raised, by Europeans (the French above all) who argue for more self-assertiveness, and by Americans who plead for burden relief. They tend to put in doubt, on both sides of the Atlantic, permanent American structural contributions to Europe's new architecture. The logic inherent in the idea of a Euro-Atlantic community may thus inhibit its creation, or, once created, lead to its early demise.

Much depends on future threat assessments. Certainly, as Karl Kaiser argues in his analysis of "classical" and newly arising threats, a U.S. role in Europe will be necessary as long as the maintenance of a nuclear balance is required, if only to provide a necessary element of reinsurance. Should the United States and the remnants of the Soviet Union eventually agree on a posture of minimal deterrence, however, and reduce their nuclear arsenals drastically—that is, to a level at or even below 1,000 strategic warheads and zero tactical systems—the (presumably) remaining British and French nuclear systems (amounting to around 600 warheads each) could then counterbalance a residual Russian threat. The logic of Western European efforts to establish a "security identity" of its own—pushed primarily by France—appears to portend such a development.

Other threats are more difficult to determine. Traditional international rivalries and intranational unrest as the result of ethnic conflicts are prime candidates; some observers, in fact, already see a return of tribalism to a Europe without walls. The violent breakup of Yugoslavia seems to prove the point. Yet how many such conflicts are there still? What are the chances that they can be contained peacefully? And—most important—what is the likelihood for outside intervention? Compared to prewar Europe, the conflict potential certainly seems reduced, if only because the Second World War and its aftermath led to a significant (though deplorably violent) rearrangement of the ethnic landscape in Europe. This is, of course, true especially in regard to Germany. Indeed, Germany's successful integration of more than 10 million refugees from formerly German territories and from German communities sprinkled throughout Eastern Europe, and its recognition of postwar Germany's borders as final, eliminated a major source of traditional unrest in the heart of Europe. Elsewhere in Europe, successful arrangements for the protection of minority rights hold out the hope that many countries may be able to cope with their ethnic conflicts peacefully.

Where violence does arise, intervention may turn out to be inadvisable. Yugoslavia is again a case in point. Here, as in other simmering ethnic confrontations (such as Northern Ireland), ancient ethnic rivalries are compounded by religious conflicts. The role of the churches, otherwise important sources of peace-inspiring moral authority, is thus compromised. Outside intervention appears inappropriate in such conflicts, in part precisely because religious issues are at stake (which are generally taboo to interference), but, more important, because the hatred built up in ethnic-religious conflicts hardly allows for effective intervention that might not cause more hardship than it is intended to prevent.

To permit such hatred to run its course (at best channeled through the imposition of some clearly defined limits) may well be a cynical approach in the face of the human suffering at stake, and one at odds (as Karl Kaiser points out) with the empathy that democratic nations feel for countries and peoples striving to exercise democratic self-determination. Yet as Yugoslavia has revealed, the incipient Euro-Atlantic community seems inclined to such cynicism born of realism. That realism is due not least to a determination that Serbia in 1991 would not excite a dreadful sequence of events similar to the one that began in Sarajevo in June 1914. Threats to the security of Europe arising from local ethnic conflicts could, in other words, be contained through careful neglect. The disturbing question remains, however, whether nonintervention is an adequate expression of those values that the Euro-Atlantic community would like to project and promote.

Partners in Leadership

The post-Wall order, whatever its eventual shape, will not come about simply because American—or, more generally, Western—ideals and values are universally accepted. Much architectural work must be done. For the time being—likely to last at least until the situation in the former Soviet empire has settled down to a stable and predictable state of affairs—an American involvement in designing and constructing a peaceful European architecture is considered indispensable on both sides of the Atlantic, as all contributions to this volume show. The United States, as the sole remaining superpower, has indeed claimed, and been accorded, a leadership role in that process. Germany, by virtue of its location, its economic power, and its proven political reliability, also is called upon to play a prominent role. The Bush administration, anticipating the end of the cold war, took cognizance of this fact when it invited the Federal Republic in May 1989 to become a "partner in leadership."

United Germany cannot decline that invitation. Historically, Germany is responsible for Yalta, that is, a situation where the victorious powers of the Second World War felt compelled, in the interest of maintaining peace, to divide Europe—and Germany itself—into spheres of interests controlled by the emerging superpowers. Yalta, as Christoph Bertram argues, was a historical aberration, in that an internally weak Soviet Union took over the burden of maintaining an empire. Eventually, that burden (the weight of which was increased by the West's containment policies) became too much, and the Soviet empire collapsed under it. It is now incumbent upon a Germany once again united to help make sure that the post-Yalta world will not witness a return to the pre-Yalta Europe of dictatorships, denied self-determination, political unrest, and international hostility. One of the ways it can do so is by anchoring the American commitment to the creation of a peaceful order in Europe. Yalta implied that commitment to half of Europe; post-Yalta—a "Europe whole and free"—still requires it; and Germany, as Lothar Ruehl argues, must provide its anchor.

Politically, Germany has a special role to play because it, like the United States, has become a role model of sorts for newly liberalized countries. After its defeat in 1945, Germany was more destroyed physically, more devastated politically, and more compromised morally than any Eastern European country after the end of the cold war. Germany's success in recovering from such devastation and destruction and in building up a democratic system should serve as a reminder that it can, in fact, be done—that losers can, in the end, emerge as winners. The experiences gained in that process, from external (Marshall Plan) help to internal adjustments (ranging from constitutional provisions to the build-up of a "social" market economy), should now be made available to countries facing similar problems. In addition, the German unification process itself offers further, more up-to-date instruction on the do's and don'ts of shifting from planned economies to market economies and of moving from single-party dictatorship to multiparty democracy. Germany not only has much practical experience to offer, it also has a moral obligation to make it available.

Germany, even after reabsorbing its decrepit Eastern part, is one of the richest, economically most powerful countries in Europe. As such, it has an obvious responsibility to help neighbors now in need. As Norbert Walter argues (supported by Robert Blackwill's plea for a "grand bargain" with the Soviet Union), such help is also in its national interest, for Germany is poised to reap substantial economic benefits over the long term, while over the short run its support may help prevent a potentially huge wave of refugees from sweeping into Germany and the rest of rich Western

Europe. The difficult process of East German rehabilitation raises serious questions as to whether it can be done quickly enough to satisfy pent-up demands and high expectations. But those difficulties present no argument against offering any help at all.

The special responsibility faced by united Germany and the United States in building a new European and world order is beyond question. Very much a matter of contention, however, is the question to what extent they will actually be able to effect a successful partnership in leadership—to devise both a proper division of labor as well as the necessary institutional arrangements. As Karl Kaiser points out, both countries may become beset with problems of "domesticism" that prevent them from properly exercising their international responsibilities. In addition, changing power relationships—mostly the result of the increased importance of economic factors in international relations—may make new burden-sharing arrangements—or responsibility sharing, as Robert Hormats describes it—difficult to design and achieve.

At first sight, the two countries would seem well positioned for effective cooperation. On the one side, Washington, while talking partnership, clearly places the emphasis on its own indispensable leadership role. On the other side, the Germans, while accepting some leadership demands, are still quite obviously uncomfortable with the idea of having to exercise much leadership at all. Thus Germany might continue to find some sort of junior partnership acceptable. In the end, though, it would probably prefer it the other way around: instead of being a (possibly subordinate) partner in *leadership*, to be a leader in genuine *partnership*, paving the way for a state of affairs where it does not have to expose itself either to the demands of leadership or to the denigrations of mere followership. German enthusiasm for the establishment of myriad multilateral institutions—from the European Community via NATO, the Western European Union (WEU), and the Conference on Security and Cooperation in Europe (CSCE) all the way to the Euro-Atlantic community—reflects this dislike of leadership and the desire for partnership, as its membership in such institutions allows Germany comfortably to hide the pursuit of its own interests behind common policies.

Yet how much room there is for such partnership in America's approach to international affairs remains as much open to doubt as does the finality of Germany's seeming renunciation of leadership claims. The post-Wall world presents both sides with new demands and temptations, where the United States may yield to its natural inclination to demand followership, while united Germany may shed its hesitancy to exercise leadership. Thus the two may indeed become partners in leadership; but whether they will also be true partners remains to be seen.

Broadly speaking, the United States and united Germany, if they are to play their roles as partners in leadership effectively, must be clear about where they would like to lead and how they think they might get there; they must also be fully aware of their own, as well as each other's, strengths and weaknesses along the way. Finally, if they are truly interested in partnership, they must also devise the institutional ways and means for securing that partnership. Definitive answers to these questions are, however, difficult, since a country's vision of a preferred future, once it reaches beyond the merely self-evident (such as peace, liberty, security, well-being), as well as its perception of internal and external limits along the way are, in the end, subject to democratic decision-making processes. What may be desirable and acceptable at a given time for one set of political leaders might be rejected at another time by a different leadership. In the post-Wall world, marked as it is by democratic processes that must contend with new temptations and frustrations, uncertainties pertaining to preferred policies will be compounded. The German-American partnership will not be able to escape those uncertainties.

In the face of uncertainties, but confronted with new architectural requirements, there is a strong inclination to hold on to known structures of proven quality, and to build on them. The contributions to this volume reflect this inclination. The successful institutions of the cold war world, from the United Nations to the General Agreement on Tariffs and Trade (GATT), NATO, CSCE and the European Community, are seen as mainstays of the post-Wall world. A world without walls will be more interdependent and thus more in need of cooperative efforts, ranging from the maintenance of peace (through appropriate arms control and disarmament measures) and the protection of the environment to the advancement of economic well-being. Institutions of international cooperation and integration must, therefore, perform an ever more important role. For Germany, as Christoph Bertram argues, there is almost no alternative to integration in the European Community, which, as he sees it, must be "deepened" to a true Political and Economic Union, if it is to be effective in dealing with the problems that now confront Germany and Europe. "Widening" the European Community by including Eastern European countries, which have not yet achieved the levels of political and economic development enjoyed by the EC's core countries, could dilute its effectiveness and thus be counterproductive. Robert Blackwill makes a similar point when he states flatly "no new NATO members, please!"

Yet as the very debate over the relative merits of "deepening" versus "widening" in regard to the European Community and NATO indicates, there is no real consensus on how to proceed. The post–cold war world, John Lewis Gaddis has argued, will witness a "contest between forces of integration and fragmentation."[3] That contest is currently in full swing, and unlikely to come to any conclusion soon. Given the Western world's own sense of uncertainty concerning the desirability of giving up national sovereignty in the interest of international cooperation (which might interfere with interests and values considered vital for one's own country), it seems doubtful that the West can offer much help or encouragement to Eastern Europe now caught in the conflict between integration and fragmentation.

The European Community's pitiful efforts to prevent the violent conflicts during the break-up of Yugoslavia clearly illustrated its own indecision regarding the validity of claims to national self-determination. It also revealed the ineffectiveness of its diplomatic machinery, based, as it is, on a cumbersome consensus procedure that does not allow speedy and determined reactions. Thus the European Community, even though it may well have followed a realistic course in this instance, demonstrated its lack of real and persuasive power. This demonstration of helplessness underlined, for some, the need for a stronger European Community; for others, it may, however, also have undermined support for a strengthening of the Community.

President Bush's call for "partners in leadership" reflects both the need for action as well as the dilemmas now faced. To deal with the challenges presented by a postwar world, leadership seems absolutely essential. The United States exercised such leadership after the Second World War, when it almost single-handedly designed the postwar world. But in the post-Wall world such leadership is not necessarily willingly accepted by countries looking for the presumed pleasures and privileges of national self-determination; nor can it always be convincingly offered by a United States that, as Charles Mathias points out, has itself emerged with deep scars from the forty-year effort of the cold war.

International requirements and domestic constraints argue for a partnership approach—for shared leadership responsibilities. Yet an attempt at collective action frequently results in efforts reflecting the lowest common denominator—or, all too often, in no action at all. As Operation Desert Storm showed, strong leadership is an almost essential requirement for successful action. It also revealed that—under a very specific set of circumstances that is unlikely to be present in many cases—the exercise of American leadership is still acceptable, both at home and abroad. The post-cold war contest between integration and fragmentation will thus be characterized by a simultaneous conflict between collective approaches and leadership claims. In each instance, outcomes will remain highly uncertain.

Sharing the Burden

There is little overt conflict between American and German visions for the post-Wall order. Because prospects for the future are marked by instability, both sides are intent on holding on to, and then enlarging, currently existing structures. At the same time, the acute awareness of how unpredictable, indeed how laden with dilemmas, the post-Wall situation is forces both sides to recognize the limits of any vision and to concentrate efforts on what seems practicable. Definitions of practicability, however, crucially depend on considerations of affordability—on questions of costs and sharing the burden. It is in this area where the German-American partnership will be subject to significant strains.

Especially in regard to developments in the Soviet Union and, to a lesser extent, in the rest of Eastern Europe, the vision of a preferred future is very much restricted. Both sides share a commitment to the protection of the world of democratic diversity now emerging, but both sides are equally aware that the potential for the creation of a "tinderbox of seething resentment and despair" (as Paul Nitze describes it) requires cautious approaches and the maintenance of security structures of last resort.

Even though the proposal, advanced by Robert Blackwill and others, for a "grand bargain" with the Soviet Union (trading Western help for specific reform measures) met with a good deal of skepticism because of its suggested scope, the underlying concept itself is not controversial. The West will offer a good deal of help, in part to alleviate shortages and to relieve immediate suffering, but mostly in the way of technical assistance to enable the remaining elements of what was once the Soviet Union to undertake commensurate reforms—all in the hope that such efforts will suffice to keep the fragments of the imploding Soviet empire from themselves exploding in a chain reaction fueled by frustration and resentment.

What is controversial is the division of labor. Germany is already loudly protesting that its more than DM 60 billion commitment to the Soviet Union (a good portion of which admittedly covers some of the costs of reunification) amounts to nearly 60 percent of overall Western help and thus does not reflect an adequate burden-sharing arrangement. Germany, concludes Norbert Walter, has clearly reached the limits of its resources. Whether other financially potent countries—above all Japan and the United States—will commit resources of this magnitude and thus provide for a more equitable sharing of the burden in regard to help for the Soviet Union and Eastern Europe remains very much in doubt. Japan may be holding out for its own reunification goals, though it has always insisted that it will not pay to acquire something—its Northern Territories—that it already owns, so that Japanese largess even after a return of the Kurile Islands could well be limited. In the United States, public opinion reveals a decided lack of willingness to commit massive resources for aid to the former Soviet Union. In the light of longstanding—and often haughtily rejected—complaints that its European alliance partners were not carrying enough of the common defense burden, German protestations concerning inadequate burden-sharing arrangements today may be more a source of quiet amusement than a spur to action in the United States.

Americans quite clearly feel that they have reached the limits of their resources as well. Whatever "peace dividend" the end of the cold war may yield, it should be spent on bringing its own house in order, and not be reinvested in a dubious effort to help the former enemy remain at peace with itself and the outside world. However shortsighted this refusal to provide massive help may turn out to be, it does reflect the fact that the United States is itself in serious need of domestic reforms. Now that the constraints imposed by the requirements of the cold war have disappeared, domestic concerns will rightly claim priority attention. It can even be argued that unless the Western world brings its own house in order, it will neither be able to offer itself as a role model for countries emerging from the ravages of totalitarian socialism nor be in a position to produce the resources required for significant help.

How much of a repair job the Western world requires is, in principle, also beyond dispute. National economies must be put on a solid basis through responsible fiscal and budgetary policies that reduce potentially dangerous deficits. Social problems at home—unemployment, crime, poverty, racial discrimination, functional illiteracy, etc.—should be solved speedily and with compassion. International trade must largely be free and not be skewed by protectionist barriers or massive state subsidies. Capital should be readily available and affordable. The environment must be protected, and other global challenges (such as drugs and terrorism) properly dealt with.

As for security policies, minimum efforts at both conventional and nuclear deterrence must be maintained and coordinated through existing alliance structures. Additional structures may be put up where necessary, in order, for instance, to allow the European Community its own defense identity as an independent pillar of the Atlantic alliance (perhaps by assigning new roles and responsibilities to the Western European Union), or in order to further cooperation with former Warsaw Pact countries that are now looking for Western help in protecting their security (through the establishment of a "North Atlantic Cooperation Council"). How meaningful such structural adjustments, designed to protect the central role of the Atlantic alliance in building the post-Wall world, may turn out to be can well be doubted (as does Robert Blackwill). They should, in any case, be made with caution (lest uncontrolled security guarantees emerge) and due regard for bureaucratic and financial parsimony.

Whether, or even how quickly, such an improved Western world can be brought about is subject to a good deal of skepticism. The end of the cold war and the concomitant decline of security concerns have removed many disciplining constraints on national decision making. Where the structures and processes of a "security state" have been particularly predominant, the disappearance of threat perceptions may lead to resurgent efforts to subject security policies (and their underlying institutions) to long neglected democratic control procedures. The incipient debate in the United States about the future role of its intelligence apparatus, for instance, is an early reflection of such a development, as is the renewed conflict in Germany over the stationing of nuclear weapons or the emerging controversy over the future shape and size of the *Bundeswehr*.

The lack of political discipline once imposed by security concerns carries over into other fields as well. Trade conflicts, previously constrained by the requirements of alliance cohesion, may now turn into full-fledged trade wars. Much effort will have to be expended to prevent such a development. The United States and Germany, who respectively produce 21 and 7 percent of the world's GNP, share both an interest in and responsibility for settling trade conflicts before they get out of hand, as Robert Hormats argues convincingly. Germany's influence must be brought to bear particularly in the context of the European Community (which absorbs more than half of Germany's total exports). As Norbert Walter points out (by quoting official U.S. estimates), the potential gains of trade liberalization through a new GATT regime could amount to $4 trillion worldwide over the next decade—an amount equal to almost three-quarters of U.S. GNP at the beginning of the nineties. The world can ill afford to forgo such vitally needed additions to its general economic welfare.

The capacity of the Western world to engage in successful cooperative efforts depends to a considerable degree on its success in defining mutually satisfying divisions of labor (which also imply an appropriate division of rewards). Some elements of the existing division of labor will remain beyond contention. The United States is bound to continue bearing the main burden of nuclear deterrence. It therefore also has to carry the main weight of efforts aimed at achieving a stable military balance, partly through arms control agreements, increasingly through unilateral disarmament steps. In that regard, Germany will be more than an interested bystander, but it cannot do much to lessen the American burden (nor is it likely that the United States would look for much outside help in this area of central importance to its status as a superpower).

Germany, whose public has always been torn between the presumed deterrent benefits of nuclear weapons and the much feared effects of their employment should deterrence fail, finds itself in a new position as the result of unification. Eastern Germany, in accordance with agreements reached between the two German states and the four allied powers in regard to the final settlement of German questions, is a nuclear-free zone. Why should the rest of Germany not enjoy the same status, especially since nuclear weapons stationed on German soil no longer can cover any meaningful targets? Not least as a result of consequent pressure from the German government, the Bush administration—on the basis of confirmed expectations that the Soviet Union would follow suit—decided on the total elimination of all land based short-range nuclear weapons. That unilateral step may have been taken in part with the hope that it could help preempt any more determined debate about the future of other, i.e., air launched, nuclear weapons in Germany, for Washington continues to insist that Germany share some of the risks of nuclear deterrence, while Bonn is fearful of public resistance. Whether such a debate can be prevented, and the German government will, in fact, be able to resist public pressures for a total elimination of nuclear weapons from German soil, appears increasingly in doubt. As far as this division of labor is concerned, the Germans may yet opt out.

Less doubtful, though not entirely beyond contention, is the continued stationing of foreign troops on German soil. For the time being, the Germans express a desire particularly for the presence of American troops; the American side, in turn, professes its willingness to stay—as long as American troops are welcome. But there are some new undercurrents to this issue. For one, East Germany, once remaining Soviet troops have left by the end of 1994, will not only be a nuclear-free zone, it will also be a foreign troop–free zone. Why, an increasing number of Germans may ask, should not all of Germany be free of foreign troops, especially now that Germany is no longer a front-line state and the threat has disappeared in any case? After all, countries in a similar position, such as France, do not allow foreign troops to be stationed on their soil either. Possibly in order to forestall a public debate along those lines, Bonn has quietly begun to sound out its allies over the possibility of stationing German troops on their soil and thus create at least the impression of an even division of labor in this regard— initially with little success (which tended to prove the point of Germany's singularity). One of the attractions of a common European defense effort is precisely that it would help mitigate this problem; the announcement of the establishment of a Franco-German corps points in this direction. Whether it would also help solve the issue of a continued American troop presence in Europe is, however, an entirely different question.

The German government, in an effort aimed partly at stressing German sovereignty and thus mollifying a restive public opinion, has entered into negotiations with its allies over new legal provisions for their troop stationing in Germany. It is, in particular, insisting that foreign troops behave no differently from German troops—that they observe, for instance, the same restrictions in regard to military exercises, low-level training flights, etc. Whether allied troops will readily agree to such restrictions remains to be seen. The Pentagon has let it be known that American troops, which might be called upon for duties outside NATO, must maintain a higher state of readiness than the *Bundeswehr*. In the end, therefore, the United States could feel compelled to conclude that the stationing of combat forces on German soil under such restrictive conditions no longer meets its interests and requirements; this may be particularly the case should Washington hold on to its dogma of "no nukes—no troops." It is at present hard to believe that Germany and the United States could work themselves into a situation where American troops might actually depart entirely from German soil. But both sides must take special care that such a situation does, in fact, not emerge.

One division-of-labor issue highly controversial in Germany pertains to the employment of German forces outside the NATO treaty area. Prevailing constitutional interpretations hold that the *Bundeswehr* may be used only for defensive purposes within the NATO context; that interpretation, however, as Lothar Ruehl argues, can be challenged as incorrect. The legalistic debate over the meaning of relevant constitutional provisions merely reflects an intense political conflict over this issue. Germany finds itself confronted with the question whether it can still afford—now that it is reunified, once again fully sovereign, and therefore endowed with new responsibilities—to hold on to its reticence concerning the use of its military forces. The Persian Gulf crisis highlighted this problem, when Germany abstained from military participation on constitutional grounds, but agreed instead to contribute a significant share of the overall cost of the operation to liberate Kuwait. It reemerged in less prominent, though possibly more embarrassing, form when the German government supported some form of European military intervention to keep peace in Yugoslavia, but stressed at the same time that, for historical as well as constitutional reasons, German combat forces could, of course, not participate.

Germany is clearly torn between its desire to remain a "civil power" (and thus enjoy not only the benefits of the moral high road, but also the potentially costly labors of others), and its realization that true partnership requires it to share some of the hardships of international politics as well. A consensus is gradually emerging that will allow at least the participation of *Bundeswehr* units in peacekeeping missions organized by the United Nations, or, at some future stage, the European Community.[4] But whether such a "blue helmet" role will be enough to satisfy demands for a stronger German share in doing the "hard work of freedom" (as President Bush once put it during the Gulf War) is doubtful.

Under the "blue helmet" formula, for instance, German forces could not have participated in Operation Desert Storm, nor could they be used to intervene in such civil wars as took place in Yugoslavia. The need for military force in the post-Wall world will likely go beyond "blue helmet" missions.

One of the new characteristics of international politics after the cold war is a redefinition of the obligations on the part of the international community regarding the protection of human rights in individual states. Germany, too, is among those nations that argue for the right of outside intervention in cases where democratic institutions are under siege and human rights under attack. If the call for putting democracy and human rights under the protection of the international community is to be meaningful at all, provisions must be made for enforcement measures. The repertoire of possible sanctions is fairly broad, but in the end it must include—as Saddam Hussein made all too clear—the possibility of using military force. International law enforcement—some kind of police action, in other words—cannot be ruled out. Where it is applied, it must not be the work of a lone—or possibly rogue—policeman, but rather rest on the open support of the world community (for which reason the United Nations was originally founded and will receive renewed importance in the post-Wall world). Police action, to be worthy of such support, must be commensurate to its provocation and be designed to ensure habitual compliance with the generally agreed norms of international behavior—it must, in other words, have a deterrent effect.

Still, police work is not highly attractive. The American public, as both Mathias and Nitze argue, is unlikely to support a U.S. role as global policeman, especially if the United States is seen as carrying a disproportionate share of the burden. But, as the American president has insisted, "We remain the country to whom others turn when in distress," and in cases where intervention met "our own interests and our own conscience," the United States has, in fact, played the role of global policeman—with massive support on the part of the American public, as public opinion polls showed after interventions in Libya, Grenada, Panama, and Iraq. Ever since Theodore Roosevelt first spelled out America's willingness to engage in international police action at the beginning of this century, the United States has, time and again, found it necessary and appropriate to act accordingly. The American involvement in Europe since its entry into the Second World War has been nothing but one continued police action to keep Europe at peace. In light of this historical evidence, American protestations concerning its reluctance to act as a global policeman should be taken with a grain of salt, for otherwise (as even Charles Mathias admits) the rest of the world will be forever surprised when it does act—as was Saddam Hussein. Nevertheless, complaints that the United States cannot do it all alone must be taken seriously. Where there is agreement on the need for international law enforcement, others must clearly share some of the burden.

There is little inclination in Germany to join the ranks of an international police force. German history, now internalized in German attitudes and politics as constraints on any forceful German role abroad, allegedly argues against it, though it may be increasingly difficult for Germans to convince others of the moral rectitude of such reticence in cases where forceful intervention could prevent much human suffering. Whether Germany will be able to convince itself, however, that under specific circumstances it must contribute its share to international law enforcement efforts remains very much in doubt. The German dilemma could be alleviated once a united Europe is in a position to take over international functions and responsibilities. In such a European framework, Germany should be able to shed its reluctance and contribute to international police efforts aimed at keeping peace and protecting democracies and human rights. But would a united Europe, with Germany in a position of leadership, actually accept such responsibilities? Americans may well continue to wonder. The issue of burden sharing, here as elsewhere, will remain troublesome.

Impediments to Partnership

Partnership is required for dealing with the tasks of the post-Wall world and for devising an adequate sharing of resulting burdens. Conversely, however, disagreements over the shape of a new international order and over the division of labor tend to threaten that partnership. It is, therefore, all the more important that the foundations of that partnership be constantly reinforced in order that they may better withstand the strains and stresses of such disagreements.

There are a number of good reasons to assume that the foundations of the German-American partnership remain solid enough in the post-Wall world, even though one of the major elements of their stability—the Wall itself—has disappeared. For one, the role played by the United States in the destruction of the Wall and the subsequent reunification of Germany has left both sides with good feelings toward each other—feelings of achievement, pride, gratitude, and commitment. The importance of such feelings should not be underestimated, even though they may be of a fleeting nature. Furthermore, the West's victory in the cold war has renewed confidence in the value of Western-style democracy. It has not been very long that—in the aftermath of the oil crises of the 1970s—the survivability of Western democracies was put in doubt by experts and publics alike. With the convincing demonstration of the superiority of Western values, many of those doubts have been dispelled, commitments to the maintenance of those values confirmed, and the mutual attraction and cohesiveness of Western democracies strengthened. German-American relations stand to benefit from these developments, as the Germans' commitment to Western values had on occasion been considered doubtful during the course of the cold war (when Germany was seen as being tempted to turn away from the West in pursuit of its national ambitions). Such doubts can now be laid to rest once and for all.

Yet while there is cause for optimism regarding the future of the German-American partnership, there are also reasons for concern. Most of these have to do with the evident temptation after the stressful effort of the cold war to turn inward, in part to focus on the solution of domestic problems, but in part also simply to enjoy the relaxation afforded by the end of the cold war. Giving in to this temptation would, in many instances, lead to a renationalization of foreign and security policies. Western policy makers—with the United States and Germany indeed playing the role of partners in leadership—are hard at work to preclude such a process of renationalization, as all the efforts to institutionalize a Euro-

Atlantic community clearly show. Yet the pressures of domestic developments may make it increasingly difficult to sustain such efforts.

Germany is caught up in the novel and extraordinarily complex task of reunifying a country that was not merely divided for more than forty years, but subjected to the imposition of two diametrically opposed political and social systems. To bring about true unity, the overwhelming majority of Germans early on determined that united Germany would, in essence, be the Federal Republic of Germany writ large—that East Germany, in other words, should be absorbed by West Germany. There is still some debate in Germany as to whether the Germany so united will—or should—in fact be a new, or different, Germany. But as the process of unification proceeds at its rapid pace, and the scope of the West German takeover of East Germany becomes ever more apparent, the likelihood of united Germany emerging as a new country is fast receding. In that sense, united Germany will not be a different partner for the United States: its system of democracy (and thus its decision-making processes), its commitment to common values (and thus the foundations for its decisions), and its international relations (and thus the importance it places on alliance relations) remain the same.

Yet the dangers of renationalization are also present in Germany, not in the sense that it would, in any way, return to the nationalistic excesses of its past, but in that it turns inward to accord priority attention to domestic—i.e., unification—concerns. The very fact of reunification points to such a possibility. After all, before the Wall came down, German political leaders consistently emphasized that Germany would not seek the reestablishment of a unified nation-state; when it did, it rightly acted opportunistically, but also against its earlier convictions.

Now Germany finds itself confronted with the task of truly making one out of two. This is an enormously expensive undertaking, literally and figuratively taxing Germans to the limits. There are the promises of unification (well described by Norbert Walter), in particular the prospect of a revitalized economy becoming stronger yet. But there are also its many immediate problems (analyzed by Lothar Ruehl), ranging from drastic increases in public deficits (with their considerable impact on capital markets) to an occasionally sour mood in the country due to still existing "walls in the head" (expressing itself at one very unfortunate extreme in indiscriminate attacks on foreign asylum seekers). Both the promises and the problems of unification concentrate the German mind on domestic affairs. Less attention is being given to foreign affairs, including relations with the United States. Even American business people are beginning to complain that German businesses are showing a noticeable drop in interest regarding commercial relations. A Germany thus preoccupied with itself will be a different, perhaps even more difficult, kind of partner.

In more than just a manner of speaking, the fall of the Wall has allowed Germany to "come home." The United States, now that the cold war has been won, similarly finds itself under pressure to "come home." This implies not only a dramatic reduction of military forces from positions around the world, but also a determined effort to deal with long-neglected and newly arisen problems at home. There is some reason to doubt that the United States will turn fully inward to tackle its domestic problems, if only because American presidents as of late—and President Bush in particular—generally seem to find it more attractive and politically more rewarding to pursue strong profiles in foreign affairs than to risk getting bogged down in difficult domestic problems (the solution of which, as former Senator Mathias describes it, is hampered by increasingly messy domestic politics). Still, even if the United States were to make only a half-hearted attempt to "come home," it too would no longer be the kind of partner it was throughout the duration of the cold war.

America's partners are themselves in a bind concerning developments in the United States. They would like to have a strong, self-confident, and internationally active United States as their partner in leadership; yet they realize that strength and self-confidence can be sapped by festering domestic problems. Any attempt to deal with those problems successfully, however, will tend to reduce America's international involvement. This dilemma is compounded by the fact that one of the strengths of the United States traditionally has been its almost unique appeal as a role model for others. President Bush sought to evoke that appeal when he claimed that the *Federalist Papers* are now being widely read throughout Eastern Europe. (Some European observers, in turn, acknowledge the European Community's lack of appeal when they bemoan the fact that the EC has produced reams of bureaucratic regulations, but, alas, no *Federalist Papers*.)

It is one of the sad ironies of the post-Wall world that America's claim to being a role model is put in doubt by its domestic problems at the very moment when, as the winner of the cold war, it could proudly point to its own proven superiority. Of even greater irony is the fact that many of its problems reflect efforts—stimulated by the cold war competition—to create a more just society and a more democratic political system. It is all too often forgotten that the presumably healthy—and therefore model-like—America at the onset of the cold war was marked by a vicious system of racial discrimination and social disparities, which was supported by a political system with less than a full commitment to democratic values and procedures. When the United States finally began to address these problems, it opened itself up not only to a whole range of new problems, but also to much closer scrutiny and criticism. Still, the America at the end of the cold war arguably is a more democratic and socially conscious country than it was at its beginning. The dilemma is that, confronted with today's problems, some nostalgic-minded Americans would like to turn the clock back, while reform-minded Americans must harp on today's inadequacies in order to gather support for necessary reform efforts. As a result, the United States' appeal as a role model has been denigrated at home, while it has suffered abroad.

"The United States is the world's top producer of garbage," writes Paul Nitze. He is, of course, referring to America's unfortunate role as one of the world's worst environmental offenders—a significant enough problem as it is. Yet in much of the rest of the world, and certainly in Europe, that statement is considered correct far beyond its literal meaning. This is evident as much in the low regard for American consumer goods[5] as in efforts to combat the predominance of American productions on European television screens. All too often, such a negative assessment extends to the quality of American politics—and leadership—itself (likely to be shared by many Americans as well).

Such a disparaging attitude toward things American is no minor matter. It need not necessarily amount to full-fledged anti-Americanism—though at its extremes it probably does—to become an impediment to partnership. This is a problem to which Germans may be particularly susceptible due to the complex historical background of German-American relations. Especially among Germany's intellectual elite, reports about the United States' allegedly imminent decline as a superpower probably meet as much with a certain degree of *Schadenfreude* (pleasure at bad news) as with concern over the difficulties faced by Germany's most important ally. That glee over America's decline rests on a rejection of the United States as a role model, which in turn tends to question the relevance of the United States as an ally and partner. While such feelings may be limited in scope, they nevertheless encompass significant elements of German society (including now East Germany, where attitudes toward democracy in general and the United States in particular are still deformed by forty years of hostile propaganda). This could eventually endanger the foundations for solid relations between united Germany and the United States of America.

The tasks at hand are clear, as are the dilemmas. The United States must indeed get its own house in order, not least in the interest of once again increasing the luster of its appeal. At the same time, it must not shrink away from international responsibilities and the requirements of genuine partnership. President Bush's attempt to create a new world order as a New World order—i.e., "in accordance with our own values and ideals"—will not make much progress unless the New World is itself in order, and significant others are convinced that American values and ideals do indeed form a solid foundation for a post-Wall international system.

Germany, too, is faced with the problems of getting its own, recently much enlarged, house in order. And as it does, it also cannot afford to turn its back on much of the rest of the world. It must, in particular, maintain and strengthen its ties with the United States. This requires not only significant efforts in the areas of politics and economics, but also in the field of fostering mutual understanding. There is still much that can be learned from the

United States (in regard to multicultural societies, for instance). There is also much that the United States can learn from Germany (such as the design of properly functioning social systems). In many ways, the two major Western winners of the cold war can—and should—depend on each other in working toward the post-Wall world.

The post-Wall world has seen the emergence of the United States as the sole remaining superpower, and the development of Germany into the preponderant European power. These positions of importance tie Germany and the United States together into a partnership of responsibility. The Wall has come down. Now is the time for reconstruction: of houses at home and of bridges abroad.

Notes

[1] See the secretary of state's address of June 18, 1991, to the Aspen Institute Berlin on "The Euro-Atlantic Architecture: From West to East," and the joint statement by Secretary Baker and Foreign Minister Genscher of October 3, 1991.

[2] This and the following quotes according to the president's 1991 Report on National Strategy.

[3] Gaddis (1991), p. 103.

[4] In May 1991, 54 percent of West German respondents expressed themselves in favor of German participation in U.N. peacekeeping missions; only 25 percent were opposed. *Sueddeutsche Zeitung,* August 23, 1991, p. 8.

[5] In Germany, according to a 1991 public opinion poll, the quality of U.S. goods is "admired" by only 26 percent; only 21 percent believe "American workers cared much about the quality of the goods they produced or the services they performed." *Washington Post,* October 1, 1991, p. D4.

Bibliography

Allison, Graham. 1971. *Essence of Decision: Explaining the Cuban Missile Crisis.* Boston: Little, Brown and Company.

Allison, Graham, and Robert D. Blackwill. 1991. "America's Stake in the Soviet Future." *Foreign Affairs,* Summer 1991.

————. 1992. "The Grand Bargain: The West and the Future of the Soviet Union." in Allison and Treverton 1992.

Allison, Graham, and Gregory F. Treverton. eds. 1992. *Rethinking America's Security.* New York: W.W. Norton.

Barnet, Richard J. 1983. *The Alliance.* New York: Simon and Schuster.

Blackwill, Robert D. 1991. "Conventional and Nuclear Theater Forces." in Kruzel 1991.

Brown, Lester. et al. 1991. *The State of the World 1991.* New York: W.W. Norton.

Chamberlain, Neville. 1939. *In Search of Peace.* New York: G.P. Putnam and Sons.

Council on Competitiveness. 1988. *Competitiveness Index.* Washington, D.C.

Dornbusch, Rudiger, and Steve Marcus. eds. 1991. *International Money and Debt.* San Francisco: ICS Press.

Gaddis, John Lewis. 1991. "Toward the Post–Cold War World." *Foreign Affairs,* Spring 1991.

Hammond, Allen L., Eric Rodenburg, and William Moomaw. 1991. "Calculating National Accountability for Climate Change." *Environment*, January/February 1991.

International Institute for Strategic Studies. 1990. *The Military Balance, 1990–1991*. London: IISS.

Kaiser, Karl, and Klaus Becher. 1991. "Germany and the Iraq Conflict." in Roper and Gnesotto 1991.

Kielinger, Thomas. 1991. "The Gulf War and the Consequences from a German Point of View." *Aussenpolitik*, March 1991.

Kirby, Ralph C., and Andrew S. Prokopovitsh. 1976. "Technological Insurance against Shortages in Minerals and Metals." *Science*, February 20, 1976.

Kissinger, Henry. 1979. *White House Years*. Boston: Little, Brown and Company.

Kruzel, Joseph. ed. 1991. *American Defense Annual, 1991–1992*. Lexington, Mass.: Lexington Books.

Mahncke, Dieter. ed. 1991. *Amerikaner in Deutschland. Grundlagen und Bedingungen der transatlantischen Sicherheit*. Bonn/Berlin: Bouvier.

Marer, Paul. 1991. "The Transition to a Market Economy in Central and Eastern Europe." *The OECD Observer*, April/May 1991.

Mathews, Jessica Tuchman. 1989. "Redefining Security." *Foreign Affairs*, Spring 1989.

Norris, Robert S., and William M. Arkin. 1991. "Nuclear Notebook." *Bulletin of the Atomic Scientists*, May 1991.

Rattinger, Hans. 1991. "Deutsche Einstellungen und ihre Auswirkungen auf die amerikanische Präsenz." in Mahncke 1991.

Roper, John, and Nicole Gnesotto. eds. 1991. *Western Europe and the Gulf*. Paris: Western European Union Institute for Security Studies.

Sked, Alan. 1991. "Cheap Excuses: Germany and the Gulf Crisis." *National Interest*, Summer 1991.

Spector, Leonard S. 1990. *Nuclear Ambitions*. New York: Westview Press.

Stigliani, William M. et al. 1991. "Chemical Time Bombs: Predicting the Unpredictable." *Environment*, May 1991.

Stockholm International Peace Research Institute. 1990. *SIPRI Yearbook 1990*. New York: Oxford University Press.

Wilson, E.O. ed. 1988. *Biodiversity*. Washington, D.C.: National Academy Press.

Final Report
of the Eightieth
American Assembly

At the close of their discussions, the participants in the Eighti-
eth American Assembly, on *The United States of America and
United Germany: Pillars of a Post-Wall World*, at Arden House, Harriman, New York, November 14–17, 1991, reviewed as a group the
following statement. This statement represents general agreement;
however, no one was asked to sign it. Furthermore, it should be
understood that not everyone agreed with all of it.

Preamble

Humanity achieved a rare triumph when the cold war ended.
The people of Eastern Europe liberated themselves from decades
of relentless repression. The triumph had a special sweetness for
two of the democracies. Germany achieved unification. The
United States attained victory earned by arduous and costly leadership. But freedom has a price.

The disintegration of the Soviet empire has plunged the world
into uncertainty. The cold war froze Europe into stability, however repugnant in Eastern Europe. Now waters once frozen are
arush in uncharted torrents. Triumph may be twinned by tragedy.

Yugoslavia is a sad case in point. New dangers, however, are matched by new opportunities.

At such a time assessments and recommendations are an act of faith and courage. Such faith and courage are rooted in the ability of the democratic world, despite all naysayers, to put the challenge of communism to rest, and in the confidence that the great democracies will prove equally able to achieve a new and satisfactory stability.

Germany and the United States, the two Western nations that gained the most from the end of the cold war, cannot escape major responsibilities for the preservation and promotion of freedom, prosperity, and security. The United States now bears the unavoidable burdens of being the world's sole superpower. Germany remains on the border of that part of Europe now struggling to master its new unity and liberty. The Iron Curtain has lifted, but Europe is not yet united. Where that Iron Curtain stood, East and West are still divided. The East will not long accept freedom marred by poverty, insecurity, and the unchecked clash of nationalistic, ethnic, and religious tensions. If many in the East seek relief across the line, their passage in large numbers will create serious problems not only for Germany, but for the whole of Europe.

The German-American partnership, forged in the cold war, remains indispensable, but it must now be recast. As two of the world's largest and most successful democracies, the United States and Germany, already endowed with a legacy of partnership in their mutual defense, must now build on that foundation to achieve a new partnership based on common values, joint purpose, and shared responsibility so as to attain a peaceful and stable world.

Political Issues

United and sovereign Germany now seeks to integrate its future within an evolving European Community (EC). The United States should welcome and encourage this German quest and recognize it as the culmination of policies championed for decades by successive American administrations, even though the United States will have to deal from time to time with European positions that differ from American policies.

For its part, the United States finds itself beset with burdensome worldwide commitments, drastically reduced resources to meet those commitments, and growing popular pressure for solutions to domestic social, economic, and infrastructural problems too long neglected. Germany and its European partners must understand and respect this American predicament. It is, after all, in part the price America has had to pay for victory in the cold war. A viable American posture in the world demands greater attention to domestic needs in the United States.

As they restructure their relationship, both Americans and Germans should recognize that they will now have to interact on four different levels. The first is bilateral and, compared with the past, it will tend to decrease in importance.

The second is the Euro-lateral level of relations between the United States and the European Community. This level will attain ever greater significance as the Community assumes powers previously vested in its individual member states and becomes the principal decision-making institution both for Europe itself and for Europe's role in global politics. In this context, it must be recognized that Germany's acceptance within Europe throughout the entire postwar period has been critically dependent on a close and enduring link with France. Franco-German cooperation remains an indispensable basis for the further evolution of the European Community. The United States will have to recognize this European fact of life, exasperating as occasionally it may be, and seek accommodations that are not contrary to either U.S. or alliance interests. Germany, for its part, has to pursue the line of European progress without undermining the transatlantic partnership.

The third level involves the Atlantic community area. This is an area of great vitality that currently embraces a wide range of existing organizations, including the North Atlantic Council. It serves as the vital center for the world's democracies and will increasingly take on issues particularly designed to strengthen and expand the democratic process beyond its geographic confines. Democratic institution-building in East/Central Europe is a case in point. This community of democracies has the potential to work with a unique sense of common purpose and coherence of action.

The fourth level is multilateral. It encompasses participation in Western and global institutions such as G-7, the Organization for

Economic Cooperation and Development (OECD), the World Bank, International Monetary Fund (IMF), and the United Nations. The significance of this level is bound to be enhanced.

Such multiple roles and multiple challenges require new definitions of the German-American partnership. Priorities previously accorded to military security will recede. The agenda of high politics will change. Politics will be preoccupied and probably even dominated by new global concerns: preservation of the environment; proliferation of technologies capable of mass destruction; underdevelopment; and overpopulation.

These issues penetrate even more deeply into all aspects of social life than do military and security affairs. Accordingly, as they grow in importance, government-to-government interactions increasingly will need to be complemented by direct contacts and interactions between societies. Relations between the United States and Germany already display solid underpinning for such involvement of nongovernmental actors.

The German-American partnership has long been assisted by an exceptional degree of mutual acquaintance, resulting significantly from the fact that much of a whole generation of German scholars and scientists received part of their education in the United States, and that millions of young Americans have been long-term residents of Germany during their military service.

The future partnership of the United States and Germany needs a determined commitment by both countries to preserve and strengthen this exceptional degree of mutual acquaintance and understanding, by finding and funding new ways of contact and exchange at many levels, especially among the youth of both countries. For forty years, 16 million East Germans were deprived of the opportunity to participate in the close interaction between the American and German societies. Consequently, a special effort is required to achieve a comparable degree of familiarity between the American people and the East German population.

The norms of democracies are diverse, and therein lies their strength. But such diversity also offers difficult choices, indeed dilemmas. One such dilemma, for instance, is to be found in the question of national self-determination. Whereas established Western democracies are seeking to overcome the predominance of the nation-state—and thus the evils of nationalism—through supranational integration, peoples newly liberated from outside oppression are looking toward the establishment of their own nation-states. Those countries that have overcome the dangerous aspects of nationalism now face a special responsibility to help others avoid them.

The Yugoslav tragedy runs its course at the very doorstep of the European Community—and there is a risk that it could be repeated elsewhere in Eastern Europe. Not enough agreement now exists, either within Europe or between Europe and the United States, as to how to react. Germany and the United States should give first priority to devising a strategy for early crisis prevention and reactions to threats of armed nationalist clashes. The integrity of democracy, respect for human lives and minority rights, and the maintenance of peace simply demand more than helpless indecision. Minority rights will have to be respected so as to reconcile self-determination with democracy. The West should stretch out a helping hand to integrate the emerging nations into existing structures for conflict resolution and peaceful change.

Security Issues

The very success of the Atlantic alliance now requires redefinition of its purpose. Europe has launched a renewed drive toward a more perfect union, including a defense identity of its own. It will be necessary to shape a defense structure of the European Community that also conforms to existing North Atlantic Treaty Organization (NATO) mechanisms. NATO's Rome Summit restated the requirement for the "complementarity" and "compatibility" of a future European military identity with the existing institutions of the alliance.

NATO is far from obsolete. In the period ahead, its primary purpose is to provide a continuing tie between North America and Western Europe, to furnish the essential forum for consultations with regard to global security, and to provide a safeguard against residual and new risks confronting the alliance.

Such risks arise from the troubled transition of Eastern Europe, from the danger of dictatorship in Moscow, from the presence of large numbers of nuclear weapons in the former Soviet Union, and from the possibility that these weapons might come into the possession of secessionist successor republics. In the face of these perils, NATO is still needed to provide reassurance and to protect peace.

In addition to these traditional tasks of the alliance, NATO must be prepared to deal with new threats looming on the horizon: the proliferation of nuclear, biological, and chemical weapons as well as long-range delivery systems among ambitious and aggressive countries around the world; international terrorism; and drug traffic. The alliance can and must devise common strategies to counter these new perils.

The new situation also requires a redefinition of and rationale for the continued military presence of the United States in Europe. This is not primarily a question of numbers. Europeans, especially Germans, welcome the presence of a sizable U.S. force as a stabilizing factor for the indefinite future. Such an American commitment will anchor the United States as a "European power," in the words of President Bush, and also serve to assuage fears of other Europeans about potential dominance or hegemony of a single country.

Beyond such political considerations, American forces in Europe continue to play an indispensable military role. They provide the link to the American nuclear deterrent; they are pivotal to NATO's integrated command structure; and their deployment in Europe, including Germany, facilitates operations outside the NATO area when the alliance deems these necessary. Negotiations toward a new legal basis for American troop stationing in Germany are already under way. Their terms will have to balance American requirements for freedom of action against the demands of German national sovereignty.

NATO has already evidenced concern with the security of the newly free states of Central and Eastern Europe. The question of extending the security umbrella of the Atlantic alliance over these countries has been raised; an answer cannot long be delayed. Even their full membership in the alliance could be envisaged, taking into consideration also the interests of the successors of the Soviet Union.

Care must be taken to assure that the shape of new security structures in and for Europe does not compromise America's role in European defense. However, American concerns cannot be allowed to impede the European defense endeavor. The complementary nature of various institutions—EC, Western European Union (WEU), Conference on Security and Cooperation in Europe (CSCE), and NATO—will make some overlap tolerable, provided that the further strengthening of the European pillar within the alliance will reinforce the integrity and effectiveness of NATO. Some "double-hatting" may be inevitable, but will then require full agreement on mechanisms for consultation and resource allocation. The creation of workable European arrangements should be primarily the responsibility of the Europeans.

For Germany, it is necessary to clarify the future role it will play in out-of-area contingencies, commensurate with the resources and responsibilities as one of the West's major democracies. Speedy clarification with respect to legal, constitutional, and political issues must remove doubts within the international community concerning Germany's participation in future peacekeeping and peacemaking missions. The example of the Gulf War illustrates the importance of Germany as a reliable and predictable partner with a clear public posture.

The civil war in Yugoslavia can be seen as a warning of potential future conflicts, that is, out-of-area in traditional NATO terms, yet European in nature. Both the United States and its European partners need to develop criteria and mechanisms for dealing with such a situation. As yet, neither NATO nor existing regional security organizations have an explicit mandate to undertake this task. Here there is room for a WEU role as well as for a CSCE and/or U.N. involvement, and even NATO action should not be entirely excluded from consideration. What is called for is not primarily or exclusively direct military intervention, but rather early agreement on preventive measures: mediation, an over-the-horizon presence in the theater, a timely show of force, and a clear manifestation of the will to institute economic and/or military action if necessary.

Defined rules of international law, and adherence thereto, are essential to establish acceptable norms of international community behavior.

In summary, then, a revised NATO will retain important missions. The alliance must evolve, but it cannot be allowed to disappear. The United States must recognize that a European defense identity is an inevitable attribute of the emerging United States of Europe. Europeans for their part need to understand that the evolution of a separate defense identity must be structured to strengthen rather than weaken the Atlantic alliance.

Economic Issues

Increasingly, economic strength has been gaining in importance as a factor in international affairs. As a result, the relative power positions of the United States and Germany have changed.

While the economies of both the United States and Germany are huge and, despite some significant weaknesses, fundamentally strong, there are two handicaps that limit the abilities of both countries to perform on the international stage: the requirements of successful reunification in Germany and the need for domestic improvement in the United States. Both countries should recognize the urgent need to get their houses in order: in Germany, to bring the five new states up to the standard of living in the rest of the Federal Republic; in the United States, to rectify its deficit problems and to correct its deficiencies in education as well as in the economic and social infrastructure.

The United States must recognize that Germany has to formulate its economic policies within the European Community. Germany, on the other hand, must bear significant responsibilities for shaping the character of the Community, particularly so as to ensure that it observes standards of competitiveness, free trade, and nonprotectionism.

The United States and Germany must accept special responsibility for maintaining the health of the world economic system, including the world monetary system. Both countries should use their influence to guarantee openness for investment, market access, and reduction of subsidies. They need to promote compromises to make certain that regional trading blocs do not go protectionist; to ensure a successful conclusion of the Uruguay Round of the General Agreement on Tariffs and Trade (GATT); and to impress on Japan and other major trading partners in Asia and elsewhere the need to accelerate market-opening measures and to intensify efforts to dismantle structural barriers to market access.

The world agricultural system is in urgent need of reform. Germany has a special responsibility within the European Community to push for acceleration and completion of reform of its Common Agricultural Policy. The United States also has a responsibility to reform its own farm policies. Both countries should promote market access for agricultural products of the Third World and Central and Eastern Europe.

The countries of Central and Eastern Europe and the successor states of the Soviet Union are currently undergoing two fundamental transformations: from dictatorship to political democracy, and from command economies to market economies. These two transformations are closely related. Success in economic reform is vital to the substance of political democracy. Economic shortages might cause political destabilization, domestic chaos, and mass emigration. The United States and Germany must assign importance to measures designed to address the economic crises of the new democracies. These measures should include provisions for general market access in order to allow these new democracies to compete more effectively and thereby build up their own economies.

It is necessary for the United States and Germany to coordinate their strategies concerning the desirable sequence of such actions. There should be a balance between insisting on political and economic reforms and the observance of human rights, and aid given to achieve those objectives. Experiences collected by both countries during recent decades involving the change from dictatorship to democracy should be considered.

With regard to the successor states of the Soviet Union, conditions must be attached to a) diplomatic recognition; b) economic aid (except humanitarian aid, which should be nonconditional); and c) membership in international financial organizations such as the IMF, World Bank, European Bank for Reconstruction and Development, and, in the case of Soviet Central Asia, the Asian Development Bank. Therefore, the United States and Germany should insist that Soviet successor states that expect Western aid meet such conditions as adherence to a responsible nuclear weapons regime, including adherence to the Non-Proliferation Treaty (NPT), civilian control of the military, observance of the Strategic Arms Reduction Talks (START) and Conventional Forces in Europe (CFE) treaties as well as other commitments to arms control and the CSCE agreements.

Economic aid takes different forms. In granting aid, the United States and Germany should carefully distinguish between emergency humanitarian and economic aid; transfer of know-how through training, the presence of Western experts on site, infrastructural projects, and joint ventures in key areas; and long-term financial assistance. A threat exists of an imminent Soviet default on its international debt. Germany and the United States should agree that this debt not be written off but rather rescheduled under appropriate conditions.

Arrangements to furnish aid to successor republics of the Soviet Union can no longer be made effectively by dealing exclusively through central authorities. A parallel approach should deal both with the Union institutions and pursue a "bottom-up" strategy that, to the extent feasible, works with regions and republics while also insisting on comprehensive economic reforms and the creation of an open trading system among them. Moreover, the two countries should work together to promote a healthy climate for private investment, which is crucial to long-term development.

Controls imposed by the Coordinating Committee for Export Control (COCOM) as now constituted represent an impediment to the economic development of Eastern Europe and the Soviet Union. The United States and Germany therefore should seek to accelerate appropriate revisions of the COCOM list. However, there remains a crucial need for controls on exports to geopolitical crisis areas. This pertains especially to nuclear, biological, and chemical weapons technologies, missile technologies, conventional weapons, and dual-use items. Accordingly, Germany and the United States should work together to define the threat and to institute appropriate and realistic controls on a multilateral basis. At the same time, the two countries should intensify efforts to redress the problems that feed the demand for destabilizing goods and technologies in the first place.

The opening of borders, coupled with economic and political instabilities, is likely to lead to increased migration into Western Europe. This would particularly affect Germany because of its territorial proximity to Eastern Europe, its liberal laws, and its attractive economic situation.

As the European Community grows into a political union, it will have to carry the responsibility for forging a common answer to the problems of migration. For this purpose, the experience of the United States in accepting and integrating newcomers may be of value to European policy makers, but American immigration policy must be understood as a special case that therefore cannot on the whole serve as a model.

A further increase in mass migration would call for multilateral responses with a need for the United States to participate.

Conclusion

For forty years the "special relationship" between the United States and Germany was based on the American guarantee of German security and on Germany's front-line location in the cold war. Now the cold war has ended. One successful outcome was German unity, brought about with consistent and wholehearted American support.

A new and different German-American relationship is evolving, rooted partly in the past, but primarily based on the necessities of the future. Beyond its present preoccupation with implementing its unification, Germany is moving steadily to ever greater integration within the European Community. At the same time, it faces unprecedented challenges and opportunities in Central and Eastern Europe. The United States has been freed from much of the burden it shouldered for the defense of Western Europe. It is now adjusting to its role as the world's sole remaining superpower while also facing the need to address long neglected domestic priorities.

In essence, the bond that still most closely links Germany and the United States is their shared commitment to human rights, democracy, political liberty, and open markets. This shared commitment will further stimulate the growth of a true international community of democracies, which remains an ultimate German-

American goal. As successful democracies and global economic powers they carry a special responsibility for continuing their partnership, in order to preserve Western values and promote an international political agenda conducive to those values. The international system will benefit from future German-American cooperation based on the firm foundation of mutual trust and understanding.

Participants
The Eightieth American Assembly

RUDOLF G. ADAM
Policy Planning Staff
Foreign Office
Bonn

+ RONALD D. ASMUS
The RAND Corporation
Santa Monica, California

†KURT H. BIEDENKOPF,
MdL
Minister President
Free State of Saxony
Dresden

JAMES D. BINDENAGEL
Director, International
Government-Business
Programs
Rockwell International
Corporation
Arlington, Virginia

ROBERT D. BLACKWILL
Lecturer in Public Policy
John F. Kennedy School of
Government
Harvard University
Cambridge, Massachusetts

CARROLL BROWN
President
American Council on
Germany
New York

‡RICHARD R. BURT
Former U.S. Ambassador to
the Federal Republic of
Germany
Special Consultant
McKinsey & Company
Washington, DC

W. BRUCE COOK
Vice President, Financial &
Corporate Affairs
Exxon Company, International
Florham Park, New Jersey

HANS W. DECKER
Vice Chairman
Siemens Corporation
New York

JOHN DESPRES
Select Committee on
Intelligence
United States Senate
Washington, DC

BRIAN DICKINSON
Editorial Columnist
Providence Journal
Providence, Rhode Island

KLAUS VON DOHNANYI
Former First Mayor of the City
of Hamburg
Hamburg

FREIMUT DUVE
Member of the *Deutscher
Bundestag*
Chairman
Working Group USA in the
SPD Parliamentary Group
Bonn

STEPHAN EISEL
Head of Department
Section for Political Analysis
Federal Chancellor's Office
Bonn

*THOMAS L. HUGHES
President Emeritus
Carnegie Endowment for
    International Peace
Washington, DC

REIMUT JOCHIMSEN
President
Landeszentralbank in
    Northrhine-Westphalia,
Member of Central Bank
    Council of the Deutsche
    Bundesbank
Duesseldorf

*KARL KAISER
Professor of Political Science
Rheinische Friedrich-
Wilhelms-Universität
    of Bonn;
Director, Research Institute of
    the German Council on
    Foreign Relations
Bonn

CATHERINE McARDLE
    KELLEHER
Visiting Fellow
The Brookings Institution
Washington, DC

**THOMAS KIELINGER
Editor-in-Chief
Rheinischer Merkur
Bonn

HORST LANGER
Member of the Managing
    Board
Siemens AG
Erlangen, Germany

BEATE LINDEMANN
Executive Vice Chairman and
    Program Director
Atlantik-Brücke e.V.
Bonn

ROBERT GERALD
    LIVINGSTON
Director
The American Institute for
    Contemporary German
    Studies
Washington, DC

REIMAR LÜST
President
Alexander von
    Humboldt-Stiftung
Bonn

‡PHILLIP MARTIN
Department of Agricultural
    Economics
University of California at
    Davis
Davis, California

GEORGE McGHEE
Former U.S. Ambassador to
    the Federal Republic of
    Germany
Washington, DC

ELIZABETH MIDGLEY
President
Working English
Washington, DC

ADONIA MOSCOVICI
Consul
Consulate General of the
    Federal Republic of
    Germany
New York

STEVEN MULLER
Chairman
The 21st Century Foundation
Washington, DC

PAUL H. NITZE
Diplomat in Residence
The Paul H. Nitze School of
Advanced International
Studies
The Johns Hopkins University
Washington, DC

GÜNTHER
NONNENMACHER
Senior Foreign Editor
Frankfurter Allgemeine Zeitung
Frankfurt am Main

RICHARD M. ORNITZ
Partner
Stroock & Stroock & Lavan
New York

‡KARL OTTO PÖHL
President (ret.)
Deutsche Bundesbank
Frankfurt am Main

ELIZABETH POND
John D. & Catherine T.
MacArthur Fellow
Bonn

JOST PRESCHER
President
Wemex Machine Tool Trade
Berlin

LIESEL QUAMBUSCH
Head, Foreign Trade
Department
Deutscher Industrie- und
Handelstag
Bonn

WALTER RAYMOND, JR.
Assistant Director
Senior Coordinator
President's Eastern European
Initiative
United States Information
Agency
Washington, DC

JOHN E. RIELLY
President
The Chicago Council on
Foreign Relations
Chicago

LOTHAR RUEHL
State Secretary (ret.) formerly
of the Ministry of Defense
Secretary General
Forum für Deutschland
Bonn

VOLKER SCHLEGEL
Head of Division
Parliamentary and Cabinet
Affairs
Foreign Office
Bonn

ENID C.B. SCHOETTLE
Senior Fellow
Director, Project on
International Organizations
& Law
Council on Foreign Relations
New York

GEBHARD L.
SCHWEIGLER
Senior Research Associate
Stiftung Wissenschaft und
Politik
Ebenhausen, Germany

BRIGITTE
   SEEBACHER-BRANDT
Freelance Journalist
Unkel, Germany

*THEO SOMMER
Editor-in-Chief
Die Zeit
Hamburg

HELMUT SONNENFELDT
Guest Scholar
The Brookings Institution
Washington, DC

JOAN E. SPERO
Executive Vice President
American Express Company
New York

ANGELA STENT
Associate Professor
Department of Government
Georgetown University
Washington, DC

‡FRITZ STERN
Seth Low Professor of History
Columbia University
New York

JOSEPH R.L. STERNE
Editor, Editorial Pages
The Baltimore Sun
Baltimore, Maryland

KURT STEVES
Member of the Managing
   Board
Federation of German
   Industries
Cologne

EDWIN M. TRUMAN
Staff Director
Division of International
   Finance
Board of Governors of the
   Federal Reserve System
Washington, DC

KARSTEN D. VOIGT
Member of the *Deutscher
   Bundestag*
SPD Parliamentary Group
Spokesman for Foreign Policy
Bonn

‡PAUL A. VOLCKER
Chairman
James D. Wolfensohn, Inc.
New York

NORBERT WALTER
Chief Economist
Deutsche Bank AG
Frankfurt am Main

JÜRGEN WARNKE
Member of the *Deutscher
   Bundestag*
CDU/CSU Parliamentary
   Group
Deputy Chairman
Christlich Soziale Union
   (CSU)
Bonn

HENNING WEGENER
Deputy Secretary
Press and Information Office
German Federal Government
Bonn

PETER R. WEITZ
Director of Programs
The German Marshall Fund of
    the United States
Washington, DC

HEINZ WIEZOREK
President
Coca-Cola Germany
Max-Keith-Strasse 66
Essen, Germany

* Discussion Leader
** Rapporteur
† Delivered formal address
‡ Panelist

MEMBERS OF STEERING COMMITTEE

On U.S./Germany Program

Robert D. Blackwill
Kenneth W. Dam
Richard W. Fisher
Guido Goldman
Josef Joffe
Karl Kaiser
Peter J. Katzenstein
Walther Leisler Kiep,
  Co-Chairman
Mathias Kleinert
Horst Langer
Beate Lindemann

Elizabeth Midgley
Herbert S. Okun
Christian-Peter Prinz
  Wittgenstein
Ronaldo Schmitz
Daniel A. Sharp
Theo Sommer
Helmut Sonnenfeldt
Fritz Stern
Dietrich Stobbe
Horst Teitschik
Paul A. Volcker, Co-Chairman

About the American Assembly

The American Assembly was established by Dwight D. Eisenhower at Columbia University in 1950. It holds nonpartisan meetings and publishes authoritative books to illuminate issues of United States policy.

An affiliate of Columbia, with offices in the Helen Goodhart Altschul Hall on the Barnard College campus, the Assembly is a national, educational institution incorporated in the State of New York.

The Assembly seeks to provide information, stimulate discussion, and evoke independent conclusions on matters of vital public interest.

American Assembly Sessions

At least two national programs are initiated each year. Authorities are retained to write background papers presenting essential data and defining the main issues of each subject.

A group of men and women representing a broad range of experience, competence, and American leadership meet for several days to discuss the Assembly topic and consider alternatives for national policy.

All Assemblies follow the same procedure. The background papers are sent to participants in advance of the Assembly. The Assembly meets in small groups for four or five lengthy periods. All groups use the same agenda. At the close of these informal sessions participants adopt in plenary session a final report of findings and recommendations.

Regional, state, and local Assemblies are held following the national session at Arden House. Assemblies have also been held in England, Switzerland, Malaysia, Canada, the Caribbean, South America, Central America, the Philippines, and Japan. Over one hundred sixty institutions have cosponsored one or more Assemblies.

About the Atlantik-Brücke

The Atlantik-Brücke (Atlantic Bridge), organized and incorporated as a private, independent, nonpartisan, and nonprofit association, was founded in Hamburg in 1952. Members and sponsors come from business, politics, the sciences, the media, and trade unions.

The Atlantik-Brücke seeks to strengthen both the understanding of Germany in the United States and Canada and of the United States and Canada in Germany. In particular, it conducts meetings between Germans and Americans in the economic, political, and cultural centers of both countries. The Atlantik-Brücke Study Group on the United States brings together important figures from public life in Germany for nonpartisan and confidential dialogue, covering such topics as foreign, security, economic, and domestic policy issues. Every other year the Atlantik-Brücke awards the Eric M. Warburg Prize to a public figure in Germany or the United States who has made an outstanding contribution to the German-American partnership.

THE AMERICAN ASSEMBLY

Columbia University

Horst Elfe
Dr. Dieter Feddersen
Prof. Dr. Wilhelm G. Grewe
Prof. Dr. Rudolf Haas
Prof. Dr. Helga Haftendorn
Prof. Dr. Manfred Meier-Preschany
Dr. Alexander Menne
Wolfgang Oehme
Dr. Rolf Pauls
Dr. Peter Pechel
Berndt von Staden
Rüdiger Freiherr von Wechmar, MdEP
Casimir Prinz Wittgenstein

Index